D1118620

THE EVOLUTION OF A

JUDICIAL

PHILOSOPHY

SELECTED OPINIONS

AND PAPERS OF

JUSTICE

John M. Harlan

Edited by David L. Shapiro

HARVARD UNIVERSITY PRESS

CAMBRIDGE, MASSACHUSETTS

1969

© Copyright 1969 by the
President and Fellows of Harvard College

All rights reserved

Distributed in Great Britain by Oxford University Press, London

Library of Congress Catalog Card Number 70–89971

SBN 674–27125–4

Frontispiece by Nina Leen, LIFE magazine © Time Inc.

Printed in the United States of America

LIBRARY

JAN 29 1970

UNIVERSITY OF THE PACIFIC

211430

TRUSTEES OF THE

WILLIAM NELSON CROMWELL

FOUNDATION

Joseph M. Proskauer
David W. Peck
Bruce Bromley
J. Edward Lumbard
John F. Brosnan
Whitney North Seymour
Lawrence Edward Walsh
Bethuel M. Webster
Bernard Botein
Eli Whitney Debevoise
Henry N. Ess, III
Orison S. Marden
Dudley B. Bonsal

Editor's Preface

The year of publication of this book is the year of John Marshall Harlan's seventieth birthday. His career has been and continues to be one of extraordinary personal achievement and public service; it is hoped that this volume will help to bring that career into clearer focus for both the bar and the general public. If it adds to the understanding of the Justice's philosophy, of his integrity, and of his craftsmanship, it will have served its purpose.

The Justice came to the Supreme Court after some thirty years at the trial bar, with only a year on the bench of a United States Court of Appeals, to find himself confronted from the outset with constitutional issues that would have strained the mind and heart of one who had spent his life immersed in such problems. The story of this book—told principally through the Justice's opinions during the first fourteen terms of his service on the Court[1]—is the story of his response to that challenge. It is the story of the evolution of a judicial philosophy undoubtedly molded in part by the views of those he most respects—Justices Cardozo, Jackson, and Frankfurter, to mention a few—yet very much his own.

Selection from among almost five hundred opinions and dozens of addresses given by the Justice during this period was difficult, as was the effort to organize and present them in a meaningful way. But there still remained the necessity of editing them to bring the volume within readable dimensions. In some cases, this editing required eliminating the discussion of collateral issues; in others, condensing arguments or historical

---

[1] The terms covered run from the October 1954 Term through the October 1967 Term, which ended in June 1968. Some references to opinions written early in the 1968 Term are included in the notes, but publication deadlines did not permit selection among them for presentation in text.

materials. Discursive footnotes have been drastically curtailed, and most citations have been deleted except for those cases and other materials that are discussed in text or that are the source of quotations.[2] All omissions other than citations and footnotes are indicated by ellipses. Introductory notes to the cases, bracketed materials in the opinions, and footnotes followed by [Ed.] are my own. Although I have made every effort in this editing to preserve the integrity of the original, I recognize the pitfalls of any such attempt and urge the student to consult the full opinion, as well as other opinions in the case, for a more complete picture.

There are many to whom I am indebted for their help on this project, most especially to the William Nelson Cromwell Foundation for its sponsorship, to Judge Henry Friendly, Leo Gottlieb, Judge J. Edward Lumbard, and Bethuel M. Webster for giving so graciously of their time, and to Ethel McCall and Paul Burke for their invaluable assistance. In selecting the materials for inclusion, I was fortunate in having been a clerk to the Justice in the 1962 Term and in having the counsel of those others who served as his law clerks during the Terms covered by this volume: Wayne G. Barnett (1955), Paul M. Bator (1956), Michael Boudin (1965), Louis R. Cohen (1967), Norman Dorsen (1957), Jay A. Erens (1959), Charles Fried (1960), Kent Greenwalt (1963), Phillip B. Heymann (1960), Richard J. Hiegel (1962), Leonard M. Leiman (1955), Howard Lesnick (1959), Nathan Lewin (1961), William T. Lifland (1954), Charles E. Lister (1966, 1967), Michael M. Maney (1964), Charles R. Nesson (1964), Matthew Nimetz (1965, 1966), E. Barrett Prettyman, Jr. (1954), Bert W. Rein (1966), John B. Rhinelander (1961), Henry P. Sailer (1958), Norbert A. Schlei (1956), Stephen N. Shulman (1958), Henry J. Steiner (1957), Thomas B. Stoel, Jr. (1967), Lloyd L. Weinreb (1963). To all these people, my sincerest thanks.

Cambridge, Massachusetts   D.L.S.
April 1969

---

[2] Footnotes of particular significance have been retained and have been renumbered consecutively in each opinion. The specific sources of quotations have been identified, with the exception of quotations from other opinions in the same case and of quotations from the record in the case.

Contents

I

ORDERED LIBERTY
IN A FEDERAL SYSTEM

CONTENTS

II

THE FIRST AMENDMENT AND THE FOURTEENTH: THE DELICATE BALANCE

CONTENTS

III

THE INDIVIDUAL AND THE
ADMINISTRATION OF
FEDERAL JUSTICE   191

IV

FURTHER ASPECTS OF THE
ROLE OF THE COURT   223

xi

CONTENTS

V

THE ART OF JUDGING AND THE
EXERCISE OF JUDICIAL RESPONSIBILITY

VI

CODA

Foreword by Paul A. Freund

Good wine needs no bush, and the pressings collected here are of the choicest vintage. Nevertheless a few words may not be superfluous if they help to savor the offerings that Professor Shapiro has placed before us from the vineyard of Mr. Justice Harlan as he completes fifteen years of service on the Supreme Court.

Justice Harlan's judicial opinions have furnished the contents of this collection almost in spite of himself, for he is not an anthologist's judge but a lawyer's and a judge's judge. His basic responsibility, as he conceives it, is to decide the case before him, with that respect for its particulars, its special features, that marks alike the honest artist and the just judge. One can imagine Justice Harlan, like Justice Brandeis before him, painstakingly combing a complex record in order to set down the essential facts of the case before trusting himself to launch into a disquisition on the applicable principles of law and justice.

Like the true artist, however, the great judge—and especially a Justice of the Supreme Court, called on to draw the frontiers of legal doctrine— is not content with reproduction or recapitulation; bound by fidelity to his subject, he also succeeds in enhancing it by bringing to bear on it his experience, insights, and judgment, by persuading and even moving us to see that the ultimate composition is right.

Justice Harlan's special quality is precisely this gift of conjoining the particular with the general, or rather of finding the general implanted within the particular. Thus one reads his opinions with the secure feeling that they will convey an understanding of the exact controversy to be resolved and will disclose the philosophical wellsprings of the Justice's position. One or the other effect alone is not difficult for a judge to achieve;

xiii

together, if they do not quite warrant a combination patent for their designer, they are at least rare enough to be remarkable.

This accomplishment, I believe, is what principally attracts law school students to Justice Harlan's opinions. The positions he takes on constitutional issues, stressing continuity and tradition more strongly than is fashionable with many students, do not cloud their appreciation of the opinions themselves. Indeed, the very students who more often than not regret the Justice's position freely acknowledge that when he has written a concurring or dissenting opinion they turn to it first, for a full and candid exposition of the case and an intellectually rewarding analysis of the issues. They sometimes regret that their heart's desire has not been supported with equal cogency in the Court's prevailing opinion, sharing as they do an aversion to what a certain English judge called well-meaning sloppiness of thought.

It is appropriate that this volume should begin with the issues of federalism, for they profoundly implicate a judge's constitutional outlook. The objectives of federalism are not difficult to describe: to safeguard against tyranny by diffusion of power; to augment political participation by dispersal of the centers of decision-making; to foster innovation, experimentation, and self-determination. Straightforward as these objectives may appear, they are not free from paradox and inner tension. When, for example, a judge is called on to consider the validity of a poll tax as a condition of voting under state law, he sees that the central authority of the Court is invoked to promote access to local decision-making, overriding in the process the self-determination of the local law-making body. There is no single pathway through the maze; each judge will find his own Ariadne's thread.

For Justice Harlan, in all of this, the role of the judge is a cardinal tenet and guide. Recognizing that Congress itself enjoys wide powers to shape and reshape our federal system, Justice Harlan has been circumspect about the judicial function in this area. Moreover, he has read the guarantees of liberty and property in the Fourteenth Amendment as allowing a greater latitude to the states than is to be found in the more pointed mandates of the Bill of Rights addressed to the national government. In dealing with obscenity, for example, he would accept greater controls at the level of state law than on a nation-wide basis. This view of differentiated limits on federal and state power reflects earlier suggestions made by Justice Holmes and Justice Jackson. Indeed, in many respects Justice Harlan is the intellectual inheritor no less than the formal successor of his fellow New Yorker, Robert H. Jackson.

Not only the complex issues of federalism, but the whole range of legal-philosophical questions that pass under the title of constitutional law, are explored in these opinions. Through the expert and discerning guidance of Professor Shapiro, we are able to see these issues illuminated in the handiwork of a judge whose craftsmanship is his inner daemon.

Harvard Law School
May 15, 1969

Biographical Note

The first member of the Harlan family to come to the United States arrived in 1687 and eight years later became governor of Delaware. His distinguished career was more than matched by those of his descendants. [1] The present Justice's great-grandfather was a congressman from Kentucky and attorney general of his state. His grandfather, the first Justice John Marshall Harlan, served on the United States Supreme Court for almost thirty-four years after his appointment by President Hayes in 1877. His father, born in Kentucky in 1864, moved to Chicago to practice law and later served as an alderman in that city and a member of the Interstate Commerce Commission. Twice he ran for mayor of Chicago on the Republican ticket and once as an independent for governor of Illinois.

The Justice's grandfather was one of the most important figures in American judicial history. Though a former slaveowner himself, he dissented sharply from the Court's refusal to apply civil rights legislation to a broad area of racial discrimination, [2] and protested against the inadequacy of the "separate but equal" doctrine declared in *Plessy* v. *Ferguson*. "Our Constitution," he insisted, "is color-blind." [3] He is also remembered, however, for his adherence on some occasions to notions of freedom of contract that led the Court to strike down so many legislative efforts at social reform. [4] Perhaps both aspects of his judicial personality were con-

[1] Biographical data relating to the Justice, in addition to the materials cited in the notes that follow, may be found in Ballantine, "John M. Harlan for the Supreme Court," 40 *Iowa L. Rev.* 391 (1955); Friedman, "Mr. Justice Harlan," 30 *Notre Dame Lawyer* 349 (1955); Seymour, "John Marshall Harlan," 1 *New York Law Forum* 1 (1955).

[2] Civil Rights Cases, 109 U.S. 3, 26 (dissenting opinion).

[3] 163 U.S. 537, 552, 559 (dissenting opinion).

[4] See, e.g., his opinion for the Court in Adair v. United States, 208 U.S. 161. Compare, however, his dissent in Lochner v. New York, 198 U.S. 45, 65.

sistent with the ruggedness and strong sense of righteousness that shine through in contemporary photographs. Described by Justice Holmes as "the last of the tobacco-spitting judges," he was immortalized by another colleague, who said that he "goes to bed every night with one hand on the Constitution and the other on the Bible, and so sleeps the sweet sleep of justice and righteousness."[5]

The present Justice Harlan was born in Chicago on May 20, 1899. After receiving his elementary and secondary education at schools in the United States and Canada, he entered Princeton in 1916 and received his A.B. degree in 1920. In the words of the *Daily Princetonian* in 1954, he "was perhaps the most distinguished undergraduate here in his Senior year,"[6] serving on several committees, as president of the Ivy Club, chairman of the Senior Council, president of his class, and chairman of the *Princetonian.*

Four years at Princeton were followed by three at Balliol College, Oxford, where the Justice went as a Rhodes scholar and stayed to study law and to receive both B.A. and M.A. degrees. Returning to the United States, he went to work as an apprentice in the growing firm of Root, Clark, Buckner & Howland[7] and completed his legal education as a part-time student at New York Law School. At Root, Clark, Justice Harlan began his association with Emory Buckner, one of the nation's ablest and most respected trial lawyers. The closeness of the relationship between the two men is well documented in Martin Mayer's admirable biography, *Emory Buckner,* in which Buckner is quoted as writing to Felix Frankfurter of the "really precocious maturity of a man like John."[8] Buckner could not resist a gentle dig at the quality of legal education in England—or perhaps in the United States—when he wrote to then Harvard Law professor Felix Frankfurter that: "He [Harlan] worked very hard at Oxford for three years on everything except law, as we understand it, and is an extremely valuable man. How much is due to innate ability and how much more or less capacity he would have if he had taken the Harvard Law course, instead of the Oxford course, it is impossible to know."[9]

In 1925, Buckner was named to replace Colonel William Hayward as United States Attorney for the Southern District of New York. Buckner's

---

[5] The colleague was Justice David Brewer. See P. Freund, A. Sutherland, M. Howe, & E. Brown, *Constitutional Law* xxxii–xxxiii (3d. ed. 1967).

[6] *The Daily Princetonian,* Nov. 9, 1954, p. 1.

[7] When the Justice was named to the Court of Appeals in 1954, the firm was Root, Ballantine, Harlan, Bushby and Palmer. Later it became Dewey, Ballantine, Bushby, Palmer & Wood.

[8] Buckner to Frankfurter, February 7, 1941, quoted in M. Mayer, *Emory Buckner* 144 (1968).

[9] Buckner to Frankfurter, January 22, 1925, quoted in Mayer, *Buckner* 143.

desire to undertake this assignment was tempered somewhat by his distaste for the prohibition laws, but when he did accept, it was with the determination to make prohibition effective so long as it remained the law. Unwilling to work with the political appointees he found in the office when he arrived, Buckner took on some fifty young lawyers as members of his staff, and the roster of "Buckner's Boy Scouts" includes many who today stand at the top of their profession.[10] At twenty-six, John Harlan was appointed by Buckner to the thankless but pivotal job of head of the Prohibition Division.

The work of the U.S. Attorney's office was not limited to prohibition cases. It ranged over a broad field and, during Buckner's tenure, included the Miller-Daugherty prosecution, in which a former U.S. Attorney General and a former Alien Property Custodian were tried on charges arising out of alleged bribes to release seized enemy property.[11] The Justice was responsible for implementation of the policy of padlocking of speakeasies, a policy that appeared briefly to pose a real threat that prohibition might work. In addition, he assisted Buckner in the Miller-Daugherty proceedings and a number of other cases, perhaps the most celebrated of which was the prosecution and conviction of the theatrical producer, Earl Carroll. In grand jury investigations, Carroll had denied the reports that at a theater party he had given a chorus girl had bathed in an unidentified liquid from which guests had been served. At Carroll's trial on several counts of perjury, two of which arose out of these denials, his lawyer argued that if Carroll had lied on this point to protect the lady in the tub, after all, "he lied like a gentleman."[12] The Justice conducted a good deal of the examination of witnesses at the trial and worked on the appellate brief. A contemporary publication compared the "able young assistant" who did much of the questioning to his distinguished father and grandfather: "The grandson is not so tall, leaner, faintly stooped; the pointed jaw gives his face a cast of ascetic scholarship, emphasized by the domed Harlan cranium which came down to him modified but still recognizable from the intermediate Harlan, his lawyer-father, John Maynard Harlan, in whom it is magnificently preserved today . . . The grandson's voice is bass, but soft, slightly nasal and with a humorous catch—a voice for shrewd argument instead of old-time oratory."[13] Carroll's conviction was affirmed on appeal, the appellate court rejecting

---

[10] See *id.* at 180–181.

[11] See Mayer, *Buckner* 209–236. At the first trial of Miller and Daugherty, the jury was unable to agree on a verdict as to either defendant. At the second trial, Miller was convicted but there was still no agreement as to Daugherty. The indictment against Daugherty was later dismissed.

[12] Mayer, *Buckner* 201.

[13] *Time*, May 31, 1926, p. 30.

the argument that the presence or absence of a woman in the tub was not material to the grand jury's investigation of possible prohibition law violations: "The spectacular immersion of Miss Hawley in the tub, standing alone, was inconsistent with the story of the plaintiff in error [Carroll] before the grand jury. Her stepping into the tub with 15 or 20 men passing by drinking from it to her health became a material matter in the investigation whether there was a violation of the Volstead Law."[14]

In 1927, Buckner returned to practice at Root, Clark, and the Justice was one of three lawyers at the U.S. Attorney's office who went with him. From then until 1942, the Justice was actively engaged in private practice, with special emphasis on litigation, serving as Buckner's executive officer, becoming a partner in the firm in 1931, and moving increasingly into a position of ultimate responsibility as Buckner's health continued to fail. In November 1928, shortly after his return to the firm, the Justice married Ethel Andrews.

In 1928, Buckner was appointed special counsel for the state in the investigation and prosecution of Maurice E. Connolly, Borough President of Queens, for alleged graft in the construction of storm sewers. The Justice was head of the staff conducting the investigation and preparing for trial, and Judge Lumbard, one of the members of the staff and formerly a co-worker of the Justice's at the United States Attorney's office, recalls the enormous difficulty of the case and the thoroughness of the Justice's work.[15]

Other cases on which the Justice worked during this period included the defense of Gene Tunney against an action by Tim Mara for breach of a contract to arrange the Dempsey-Tunney fight; defense of the American Optical Company against antitrust charges; an unsuccessful defense in *Randall* v. *Bailey*,[16] a case which involved the propriety of certain dividend payments and which has served as the nucleus of law school courses in dividend policy and practice; and an unsuccessful effort on behalf of members of the New York City Board of Higher Education to appeal from a lower court order requiring the Board to cancel Bertrand Russell's contract to teach at City College. In this last case, perhaps one of the dark-

---

[14] Carroll v. United States, 16 F.2d 951, 954 (2d Cir.).

[15] The Justice has attributed Connolly's conviction in significant part to Buckner's forensic talents. Mayer, *Buckner* 262. In an interview with Mayer, the Justice referred with particular admiration to a 4′ by 30′ chart erected by the prosecution on which comparative prices for sewer pipe were chalked as the witnesses testified.

[16] 288 N.Y. 280, 43 N.E.2d 43. Commissioner v. Hirshon Trust, 213 F.2d 523 (2d Cir.), was an opinion written by the Justice during his service on the Court of Appeals for the Second Circuit. That opinion referred to the rule of Randall v. Bailey and then stated, 213 F.2d at 527: "Other states, perhaps more in keeping with sound accounting and business practice, do not permit unrealized appreciation to be counted in computing corporate surplus."

est moments in American jurisprudence, the trial court had issued its much criticized order on the merits of the case in response to the defendant's motion to dismiss the action. The city's corporation counsel decided not to appeal, giving the flimsiest of reasons,[17] and efforts by members of the Board to appeal by retaining private counsel were rejected by the appellate court.[18] Louis Lusky, once an attorney in the Justice's firm, has said that he saw him really angry only once—at the action of the courts in this case.[19]

Perhaps the most celebrated case in the firm during this period—described in one newspaper as "the Mystery of the Century"[20]—was the contest over the will of Miss Ella Wendel, an eccentric recluse who had left most of her $40 million estate to various charities. In 1931, the charities retained Root, Clark to defend the will against relatives and alleged relatives who were challenging Miss Wendel's capacity to make a will and who at one time were turning up by the dozens every week. When Buckner suffered a stroke soon after the case came into the office, principal responsibility fell on the Justice and his chief assistant, Henry Friendly, now a judge of the United States Court of Appeals for the Second Circuit. After the number of claimants had been reduced from about 2,300 to fewer than 40, the two lawyers set to work on the remaining claims, including that of Thomas Patrick Morris, who purported to be Miss Wendel's nephew and closest surviving relative. Judge Friendly recalls that when the Justice left for Scotland to investigate certain aspects of Morris' story, a list was prepared of some twenty-three points to be checked out on this side of the Atlantic. To his great satisfaction, Judge Friendly was able to establish that Morris was lying on twenty-one of these points, but when he happily reported his success to the Justice on his return from Scotland, the Justice simply asked about the remaining two. Judge Friendly, somewhat miffed, suggested that it should be adequate to establish that Morris had lied twenty-one times, but the Justice responded with quiet forcefulness: "I really think we ought to pursue those other two points." The results of this thoroughness were revealed to the public in November 1932, when, in the words of one report, "John Marshall Harlan, shrewd young attorney for the Wendel estate, went to work on the Morris claim" and "tore it to shreds."[21] Morris was later convicted of perjury and the three persons who alleged a fourth-degree relationship to Miss Wendel failed to establish their claims at trial. After Buckner's

[17] See Cohen, "A Scandalous Denial of Justice," in *The Bertrand Russell Case* 131, 143–147 (J. Dewey & H. Kallen ed. 1941).

[18] Kay v. Board of Higher Education, 260 App. Div. 849, 23 N.Y.S.2d 479 (1st Dep't).

[19] See *Louisville Courier-Journal*, Nov. 10, 1954, section 2, p. 1.

[20] *New York Daily Mirror*, June 8, 1934, p. 16.

[21] *Time*, Nov. 28, 1932, p. 15.

health permitted him to return to the case, a settlement was arrived at under which a number of accepted fifth-degree claimants received about $2 million and the rest went to the charities.

During World War II, the Justice served in England as lieutenant colonel, and later as colonel, in charge of the Operational Analysis Section of the Eighth Air Force. This section consisted of a group of civilian experts in various fields brought together to advise the commander of the force that was charged with our share of European bombing operations about ways of improving its methods. In the course of his work, the Justice sought leave to go on a bombing mission and manned a gun in a raid on Gelsenkirchen. A number of combat operational changes were made as a result of the section's recommendations, and the Justice himself was awarded the Legion of Merit by the United States and the Croix de Guerre by Belgium and France. His wartime service also included participation in the Post-War Planning Section of the Air Force under Major General Robert Harper.

After the war, the Justice returned to private practice and was recognized as one of the nation's outstanding trial and appellate advocates. His work included representation of the Du Pont family interests in complex and protracted antitrust litigation; the successful argument of several well-known Supreme Court cases, including *De Beers Mines* v. *United States* in 1945[22] and *Cohen* v. *Beneficial Industrial Loan Corp.* in 1949;[23] and service as Director of the Legal Aid Society and as chairman of the Professional Ethics and Judiciary Committees of the Association of the Bar of the City of New York.

From 1951 to 1953, Justice Harlan served as General Counsel of the New York State Crime Commission. This commission, created by executive order of the governor and headed by Joseph M. Proskauer, was instructed to examine "the relationship between the government of the State and local criminal law enforcement."[24] The Justice's work involved active participation in many commission hearings, which probed deeply into the impact of organized crime on the operation of government, and successful resistance to a judicial challenge to the commission's authority.[25] The recommendations of the commission, embodied in a series of reports issued in 1953 and 1954, led to many reforms, notably the establishment of a Waterfront Commission of New York Harbor.

In January 1954, the Justice was nominated by President Eisenhower to succeed Augustus Hand as a judge of the United States Court of Appeals

[22] 325 U.S. 210.
[23] 337 U.S. 541.
[24] Executive Order of the Governor of New York, March 29, 1951, Article III.
[25] In re Di Brizzi, 303 N.Y. 206, 101 N.E.2d 464.

for the Second Circuit. Confirmation by the Senate was prompt, and the Justice took his seat on March 6, 1954. During his year of service, the Justice's output was substantial: over twenty opinions for the court and two dissents. Among these opinions were several intricate tax cases and a decision affirming the convictions of a number of "second-string" officials of the Communist Party of the United States.[26] Although the opinions displayed the careful attention to detail, thoughtfulness, and craftsmanship that had been so characteristic of the Justice in his practice, they afforded little opportunity for the articulation of a broader philosophy of the role of the courts in our system of government, and even those who knew him well might have been hard-pressed to anticipate at this stage how that philosophy would develop.

On November 8, 1954, President Eisenhower nominated the Justice to fill the Supreme Court seat left vacant by the death of Justice Jackson. The nomination was acclaimed by the press and the bar. The *New York Times* noted on November 9 that the President had obliged those who had sought the appointment of a man "aloof from the political arena"[27] and stated on November 10 that the appointment "deserves the enthusiastic approval it has so widely received."[28] "His character, ability and legal experience," the *Times* added, "amply justify his rapid advance."[29] The *New Yorker*, in a delightful report of an interview with the nominee, described the Justice as "tall, spare, and gray haired—dark brows slanting down over wary blue eyes, and—well, let's say that we've never seen a man fitter to be on the Supreme Court in our life."[30] The Justice was quoted in the interview as reflecting somewhat apprehensively on the life of a judge: "To some extent, a judge is, and ought to be, a man apart. Not that I have any intention of turning into a solemn old hermit. No, by heaven, I won't have that!"

After talking about his career in that same interview, the Justice asked: "It does sound awfully tame and correct, doesn't it?" Whether tame or not, it certainly seemed to be above reproach. But the mid-fifties were troubled times, and the Supreme Court was under particularly heavy attack from southern congressmen for its decision in the school segregation cases.[31] Opposition formed on several fronts, particularly from southern senators who may have been concerned about the first Justice Harlan's

---

[26] United States v. Flynn, 216 F.2d 354 (2d Cir.).

[27] *New York Times*, Nov. 9, 1954, p. 18, col. 3.

[28] *Id.*, Nov. 10, 1954, p. 32, col. 3.

[29] *Ibid.*

[30] *New Yorker*, Dec. 4, 1954, pp. 40–41.

[31] Brown v. Board of Education, 347 U.S. 483, decided in June 1954. The Court's opinion dealing with the manner of relief was not rendered until 1955, after Justice Harlan had taken his seat. Brown v. Board of Education, 349 U.S. 294.

dissent in *Plessy* v. *Ferguson*, and who in any event believed that delay might prevent the Court from acting to implement its decision in the school cases. One announced basis for opposition was fear that the Justice was a "one worlder," who would sacrifice the sovereignty of the United States. The evidence was that the Justice had been a Rhodes scholar—Congressman Burdick observed that such men are generally world federalists[32]—and that he was an inactive member of the Council of the Atlantic Union Committee. That body, consisting of many distinguished citizens of varied backgrounds and political affiliations, including, for example, Gardner Cowles, Colgate Darden, Oveta Culp Hobby, Clare Booth Luce, and Telford Taylor, had supported legislative and executive exploration of the possibility of closer union with other NATO countries.[33] Such were the grounds on which Senator Eastland announced that "world government is really the issue in this case."[34]

Despite widespread criticism of both the reasoning and the motives of the Justice's opponents, those opponents managed to block any action by the Senate during the special session in 1954, and the President resubmitted the nomination early in 1955. Hearings were finally held in February, and a large portion of the 182 pages of printed transcript were taken up with accusations of internationalism, with charges by a New York politician who claimed his career had been ruined by the activities of the New York State Crime Commission,[35] and with charges by such critics as the Maryland State Society of the Daughters of the American Revolution, which attacked the Justice's work on behalf of the "well-known leftist" "Bertram" Russell.[36] In early March, after the *Times* had complained that the Eastlands and Langers must have "their little fling at the expense of the people and the Government of the United States,"[37] the committee reported the nomination favorably by a 10–4 vote, and the Senate confirmed, 71–11. On March 28, 1955, the Justice was sworn in and took his seat on the Supreme Court.

The remainder of the narrative, up to the date of this volume, is perhaps best told in the selection of opinions and other papers that make up the present book. But a few observations on the Justice's work while

[32] 101 *Cong. Rec.* 2185 (1955).

[33] See *Hearings before the Senate Committee on the Judiciary on the Nomination of John Marshall Harlan, of New York, to be Associate Justice of the Supreme Court of the United States*, 84th Cong., 1st Sess. 129–137 (1955). The Justice had accepted the invitation of retired Supreme Court Justice Owen Roberts to join the Council. *Id.* at 136–137.

[34] 101 *Cong. Rec.* 3013 (1955).

[35] See, e.g., *Hearings, supra* note 33, at 4–31, 55–60.

[36] *Id.* at 3.

[37] *New York Times*, Feb. 3, 1955, p. 22, col. 2. Senator Langer, said the Times, appeared to be opposed to the nomination because the Justice "was not a North Dakotan and is not even from one of the small states."

serving on the Court may be appropriate here. One of the most notable aspects of that work is its sheer magnitude: a total of 484 opinions through June 1968.[38] Studies of the work of individual justices by the *Harvard Law Review* show that during the ten-year period beginning with the 1958 Term, the Justice had the highest output of opinions per Term of any member of the Court.[39] During the five years beginning with the 1963 Term, the comparison with other justices is particularly striking:

1963–1967 Terms

Justice	Average number of opinions per Term
Harlan	43.0
Douglas	30.4
Black	29.8
Goldberg	28.5
Stewart	25.4
White	24.8
Fortas	24.3
Clark	19.5
Brennan	16.2
Warren	13.0
Marshall	12.0

This extraordinary productivity is in part attributable to the many occasions on which the Justice has reached the same result as the majority but by a very different route. Thus in the 1967 Term, for example, he wrote twenty concurring opinions while some members of the Court wrote only one and no other justice wrote more than eleven.[40] But to a greater extent, his output is a result of the frequency with which the Justice finds himself in dissent. Less than a year after he took his seat, the Justice said in a speech to the New York Patent Law Association: "I am inclined to think that dissenting opinions are sometimes due as much to inadequate advocacy of opposing views within the court as they are to basic differences of opinion among the judges. And when that is so, dissenting opinions are often apt to be little more than vehicles for express-

[38] This figure is derived from statistics published each November in the *Harvard Law Review* on the work of the Supreme Court. The total does not include unsigned per curiam opinions prepared by the Justice, of which there are several every year, nor does it include his opinions on applications to a single justice for interlocutory or other relief.

[39] "The Supreme Court, 1962 Term," 77 *Harv. L. Rev.* 62, 92 (1963); "The Supreme Court, 1967 Term," 82 *Harv. L. Rev.* 63, 312 (1968).

[40] *Id.* at 306.

ing ideas that should have been threshed out within the conference. For my part, such opinions are better left unwritten."[41] But the Justice, it seems clear, has come to believe that the dissenting opinion has an important place and that the judge as advocate of his own convictions must speak to future courts, to the bar, and to the public, as well as to his colleagues. Thus the Justice went from twenty-three dissenting votes and eight dissenting opinions during his first full Term to ninety-seven dissenting votes and twenty-four dissenting opinions in the 1963 Term.[42] Again a comparison with other justices during the five years beginning with the 1963 Term is instructive:[43]

1963–1967 Terms

Justice	Average dissenting votes per Term
Harlan	62.6
Stewart	38.6
Black	37.6
Douglas	32.4
Clark	26.0
White	24.6
Goldberg	18.5
Fortas	16.7
Warren	12.2
Brennan	6.0
Marshall	1.0

Many of our most important judicial statements, of course, have been made in dissent, when a judge may speak with far fewer constraints than he may when he speaks for a majority of the court. It has been said of Justice Brandeis that he worked even harder on his dissents than on his majority opinions, and indeed the pressures that attend upon isolation and dissent may have contributed greatly to the development of the philosophy embodied in this book. As a practitioner, Justice Harlan was able to sharpen the skills of his craft to a fine point, but he had little occasion to dwell upon the issues that confront one who sits at the top of our judicial system. It came as little surprise to his friends and associates that throughout his service on the Court the Justice's legal talents and

[41] "Some Impressions and Observations of a Newcomer to the Federal Bench," address delivered before the New York Patent Law Association, New York City, March 14, 1956.
[42] "The Supreme Court, 1955 Term," 70 *Harv. L. Rev.* 83, 101 (1956); "The Supreme Court, 1963 Term," 78 *Harv. L. Rev.* 143, 182 (1964).
[43] "The Supreme Court, 1967 Term," 82 *Harv. L. Rev.* 63, 312 (1968).

fairmindedness have been consistently evident in his work. But there must be few who foresaw the larger evolution that is the essential theme of this volume.

That evolution cannot be captured in a phrase, or a paragraph, or perhaps even a chapter, and it is certainly a mistake to categorize his philosophy simply as "conservative," or to look for it solely in his dissents. Though he has often resisted what he regards as improper use of judicial power, he has not hesitated to strike out in new directions when he believed that circumstances warranted. A full appreciation of the many facets of his judicial personality can come only with careful study of his work.

It is at least as difficult to capture for the reader the spirit of the man, his warmth and humanity, or the affection and respect of his friends and co-workers. But some of his qualities and his contributions to the Court were simply and eloquently summarized by John Frank in his recent study of the Warren Court: "John Harlan stands high with his colleagues. He deserves to. He has character beyond reproach, workmanship hard to equal, and a gift for turning a good sentence . . . Whether he agrees with his fellow Justices or not, Harlan achieves better performance for them all by his insistent probing for a true base of decision."[44]

[44] J. Frank, *The Warren Court* 112 (1964).

THE EVOLUTION OF A
JUDICIAL PHILOSOPHY

I

Ordered Liberty

in a

Federal System

The tension between the rights of the individual and the interests of society is one of the principal themes of constitutional litigation in the United States. But when the Supreme Court is asked to determine the constitutionality of action by a unit of state or local government, there is a third element in the balance: the need to preserve the vitality of the federal system. For Justice Harlan this element, inherent in our constitutional structure, is an essential aspect of the division of governmental authority that serves to safeguard the individual from the dangers of monolithic rule.

At the same time, the Justice is sensitive to the importance of protecting the fundamental freedoms of the individual from impairment by any governmental body, state or federal. Indeed this sensitivity may not be fully appreciated by those who consider the Justice a bastion of conservatism in an activist age. It is true, as the opinions in Part I indicate, that the Justice has fought hard against what he regards as the erosion of the federal system, that he has resisted the notion that the Fourteenth Amendment "incorporates" in whole or in part the provisions of the Bill of Rights, and that he has been unable to accept the equal protection clause as the fount of the Court's power to compel the states to meet the majority's notions of social justice. But it is also true, as shown by opinions in this Part such as *Estes* v. *Texas, In re Gault, Poe* v. *Ullman,* and *Griswold* v. *Connecticut,* that he does not view the guarantees of fundamental freedom as in any sense static, that he has always been aware of the need continually to appraise those guarantees in the light of present-day conditions, and that he opposes "incorporation" not only because it may serve to impose wholly inappropriate limitations on the states but also because it "may be used to *restrict* the reach of Fourteenth Amendment Due Process."[1] The Justice may be conservative in that he sees much in our system that needs to be preserved; he has never been a champion of the status quo for its own sake.

Although it was not planned that way, it is noteworthy that none of the opinions in Part I is an opinion for the Court. This underscores the basic philosophical differences between the Justice and other members of the Court. But those differences can be exaggerated. In some of these cases virtually every member of the Court was moved to write; in several of them the Justice reached the same result as the majority but by a different route; and in the controversy over the Connecticut birth-control laws with which Part I ends, the Justice took the lead in articulating a constitutional ground for invalidating those laws.

[1] Griswold v. Connecticut, 381 U.S. 479, 500 (1965).

Fair Trial in
State Courts

Estes v. Texas

381 U.S. 532, 587 (1965)

Among the several trials of Billie Sol Estes was one in a Texas state court on an indictment for swindling. Prior to the trial a hearing, which was carried live on television and radio, was held on Estes' motion to prevent telecasting, radio broadcasting, and news photography of the trial itself. The motion was denied, and although live telecasting was prohibited during most of the trial, certain portions were carried live and film clips of other portions were shown, largely on regularly scheduled news programs. Estes was convicted, and the state trial and appellate courts rejected his contention that televising and broadcasting of the courtroom proceedings violated his Fourteenth Amendment right to due process of law.

On review by the Supreme Court, the judgment was reversed in a 5–4 decision. The case was the first in which the Supreme Court had considered the impact of television on a criminal defendant's right to a fair trial, and it stirred almost as much public interest as the machinations of Mr. Estes. Six opinions were written: one for the Court by Justice Clark (in which Justice Harlan joined with reservations), concurrences by the Chief Justice and Justice Harlan, and dissents by Justices Stewart, White, and Brennan. Justice Harlan's opinion reveals his concern for the conflicting interests at

3

stake—procedural due process, freedom of the press, and the health of the federal system—and for limiting the decision to the facts presented in this as yet uncharted area.

Mr. Justice Harlan, concurring . . .

The constitutional issue presented by this case is far-reaching in its implications for the administration of justice in this country. The precise question is whether the Fourteenth Amendment prohibits a State, over the objection of a defendant, from employing television in the courtroom to televise contemporaneously, or subsequently by means of videotape, the courtroom proceedings of a criminal trial of widespread public interest. The issue is no narrower than this because petitioner has not asserted any isolatable prejudice resulting from the presence of television apparatus within the courtroom or from the contemporaneous or subsequent broadcasting of the trial proceedings. On the other hand, the issue is no broader, for we are concerned here only with a criminal trial of great notoriety, and not with criminal proceedings of a more or less routine nature.

The question is fraught with unusual difficulties. Permitting television in the courtroom undeniably has mischievous potentialities for intruding upon the detached atmosphere which should always surround the judicial process. Forbidding this innovation, however, would doubtless impinge upon one of the valued attributes of our federalism by preventing the States from pursuing a novel course of procedural experimentation. My conclusion is that there is no constitutional requirement that television be allowed in the courtroom, and, at least as to a notorious criminal trial such as this one, the considerations against allowing television in the courtroom so far outweigh the countervailing factors advanced in its support as to require a holding that what was done in this case infringed the fundamental right to a fair trial assured by the Due Process Clause of the Fourteenth Amendment.

Some preliminary observations are in order: All would agree, I am sure, that at its worst, television is capable of distorting the trial process so as to deprive it of fundamental fairness. Cables, kleig lights, interviews with the principal participants, commentary on their performances, "commercials" at frequent intervals, special

4

wearing apparel and makeup for the trial participants—certainly such things would not conduce to the sound administration of justice by any acceptable standard. But that is not the case before us. We must judge television as we find it in this trial—relatively unobtrusive, with the cameras contained in a booth at the back of the courtroom.

I

No constitutional provision guarantees a right to televise trials. The "public trial" guarantee of the Sixth Amendment, which reflects a concept fundamental to the administration of justice in this Country, certainly does not require that television be admitted to the courtroom. Essentially, the public-trial guarantee embodies a view of human nature, true as a general rule, that judges, lawyers, witnesses, and jurors will perform their respective functions more responsibly in an open court than in secret proceedings. A fair trial is the objective, and "public trial" is an institutional safeguard for attaining it.

Thus the right of "public trial" is not one belonging to the public, but one belonging to the accused, and inhering in the institutional process by which justice is administered. Obviously, the public-trial guarantee is not violated if an individual member of the public cannot gain admittance to a courtroom because there are no available seats. The guarantee will already have been met, for the "public" will be present in the form of those persons who did gain admission. Even the actual presence of the public is not guaranteed. A public trial implies only that the court must be open to those who wish to come, sit in the available seats, conduct themselves with decorum, and observe the trial process. It does not give anyone a concomitant right to photograph, record, broadcast, or otherwise transmit the trial proceedings to those members of the public not present, although to be sure, the guarantee of public trial does not of itself prohibit such activity.

The free speech and press guarantees of the First and Fourteenth Amendments are also asserted as embodying a positive right to televise trials, but the argument is greatly overdrawn. Unquestionably, television has become a very effective medium for transmitting news. Many trials are newsworthy, and televising them might well provide the most accurate and comprehensive means of conveying their content to the public. Furthermore, television is capable of performing an educational function by acquainting the public with the judicial process in action. Albeit these are credible policy arguments in favor of television, they are not arguments of constitutional proportions. The rights to print and speak, over television as elsewhere, do not embody an independent right to bring the mechanical facilities of the broadcasting and printing industries into the courtroom. Once beyond the confines of the courthouse, a news-gathering agency may publicize, within wide limits, what its representatives have heard and seen in the courtroom. But the line is drawn at the courthouse door; and within, a reporter's constitutional rights are no greater than those of any other member of the public. Within the courthouse the only relevant constitutional consideration is that the accused be accorded a fair trial. If the presence of television substantially detracts from that goal, due process requires that its use be forbidden.

I see no force in the argument that to exclude television apparatus from the courtroom, while at the same time permitting newspaper reporters to bring in their pencils and notebooks, would discriminate in favor of the press as against the broadcasting services. The distinctions to be drawn between the accouterments of the press and the television media turn not on differences of size and shape but of function and effect. The presence of the press at trials may have a distorting effect, but it is not caused by their pencils and notebooks. If it were, I would not hesitate to say that such physical paraphernalia should be barred.

II

The probable impact of courtroom television on the fairness of a trial may vary according to the particular kind of case involved. The impact of television on a trial exciting wide popular interest may be one thing; the impact on a run-of-the-mill case may be quite another. Furthermore, the propriety of closed circuit television for the purpose of making a court recording or for limited use in educational institutions obviously presents markedly different considerations. The Estes trial was a heavily publicized and highly sensational affair. I therefore put aside all other types of cases; in so doing, however, I wish to make it perfectly clear that I am by no means prepared to say that the constitutional issue should ulti-

6

mately turn upon the nature of the particular case involved. When the issue of television in a non-notorious trial is presented it may appear that no workable distinction can be drawn based on the type of case involved, or that the possibilities for prejudice, though less severe, are nonetheless of constitutional proportions. The resolution of those further questions should await an appropriate case; the Court should proceed only step by step in this unplowed field. The opinion of the Court necessarily goes no farther, for only the four members of the majority who unreservedly join the Court's opinion would resolve those questions now.

I do not deem the constitutional inquiry in this case ended by the finding, in effect conceded by petitioner's counsel, that no isolatable prejudice was occasioned by the manner in which television was employed in this case. Courtroom television introduces into the conduct of a criminal trial the element of professional "showmanship," an extraneous influence whose subtle capacities for serious mischief in a case of this sort will not be underestimated by any lawyer experienced in the elusive imponderables of the trial arena. In the context of a trial of intense public interest, there is certainly a strong possibility that the timid or reluctant witness, for whom a court appearance even at its traditional best is a harrowing affair, will become more timid or reluctant when he finds that he will also be appearing before a "hidden audience" of unknown but large dimensions. There is certainly a strong possibility that the "cocky" witness having a thirst for the limelight will become more "cocky" under the influence of television. And who can say that the juror who is gratified by having been chosen for a front-line case, an ambitious prosecutor, a publicity-minded defense counsel, and even a conscientious judge will not stray, albeit unconsciously, from doing what "comes naturally" into pluming themselves for a satisfactory television "performance"?

Surely possibilities of this kind carry grave potentialities for distorting the integrity of the judicial process bearing on the determination of the guilt or innocence of the accused, and, more particularly, for casting doubt on the reliability of the fact-finding process carried on under such conditions. To be sure, such distortions may produce no telltale signs, but in a highly publicized trial the danger of their presence is substantial, and their effects may be far more pervasive and deleterious than the physical disruptions which all concede would vitiate a conviction. A lively public interest could increase the size of the viewing audience immensely, and the masses of spectators to whom the trial is telecast would have become emotionally involved with the case through the dissemination of pretrial publicity, the usual concomitant of such a case. The presence of television would certainly emphasize to the trial participants that the case is something "special." Particularly treacherous situations are presented in cases where pretrial publicity has been massive even when jurors positively state they will not be influenced by it. To increase the possibility of influence and the danger of a "popular verdict" by subjecting the jurors to the view of a mass audience whose approach to the case has been conditioned by pretrial publicity can only make a bad situation worse. The entire thrust of rules of evidence and the other protections attendant upon the modern trial is to keep extraneous influences out of the courtroom . . . The knowledge on the part of the jury and other trial participants that they are being televised to an emotionally involved audience can only aggravate the atmosphere created by pretrial publicity.

The State argues that specific prejudice must be shown for the Due Process Clause to apply. I do not believe that the Fourteenth Amendment is so impotent when the trial practices in question are instinct with dangers to constitutional guarantees. I am at a loss to understand how the Fourteenth Amendment can be thought not to encompass protection of a state criminal trial from the dangers created by the intrusion of collateral and wholly irrelevant influences into the courtroom. The Court has not hesitated in the past to condemn such practices, even without any positive showing of isolatable prejudice . . .

The arguments advanced against the constitutional banning of televised trials seem to me peculiarly unpersuasive. It is said that the pictorial broadcasting of trials will serve to educate the public as to the nature of the judicial process. Whatever force such arguments might have in run-of-the-mill cases, they carry little weight in cases of the sort before us, where the public's interest in viewing the trial is likely to be engendered more by curiosity about the personality of the well-known figure who is the defendant (as here), or about famous witnesses or lawyers who will appear on the television screen, or about the details of the particular crime involved, than by innate curiosity to learn about the workings of the judicial process itself. Indeed it would be naïve not to suppose that it would be largely such factors that would qualify a trial for commercial television "billing," and it is precisely that kind of case where the risks of permitting television coverage of the proceedings are at their greatest.

It is also asserted that televised trials will cause witnesses to be more truthful, and jurors, judges, and lawyers more diligent. To say the least this argument is sophistic, for it is impossible to believe that the reliability of a trial as a method of finding facts and determining guilt or innocence increases in relation to the size of the crowd which is watching it. Attendance by interested spectators in the courtroom will fully satisfy the safeguards of "public trial." Once openness is thus assured, the addition of masses of spectators would, I venture to say, detract rather than add to the reliability of the process. A trial in Yankee Stadium, even if the crowd sat in stony silence, would be a substantially different affair from a trial in a traditional courtroom under traditional conditions, and the difference would not, I think, be that the witnesses, lawyers, judges, and jurors in the stadium would be more truthful, diligent, and capable of reliably finding facts and determining guilt or innocence.[1] There will be no disagreement, I am sure, among those competent to judge that precisely the opposite would likely be the case.

Finally, we should not be deterred from making the constitutional judgment which this case demands by the prospect that the day may come when television will have become so commonplace an affair in the daily life of the average person as to dissipate all reasonable likelihood that its use in courtrooms may disparage the judicial process. If and when that day arrives the constitutional judgment called for now would of course be subject to re-examination in accordance with the traditional workings of the Due Process Clause. At the present juncture I can only conclude that televised trials, at least in cases like this one, possess such capabilities for

[1] There may, of course, be a difference in impact upon the atmosphere and trial participants between the physical presence of masses of people and the presence of a camera lens which permits masses of people to observe the process remotely. However, the critical element is the knowledge of the trial participants that they are subject to such visual observation, an element which is, of course, present in this case.

interfering with the even course of the judicial process that they are constitutionally banned. On these premises I concur in the opinion of the Court.

Gideon v. Wainwright

372 U.S. 335, 349 (1963)

Clarence Earl Gideon, since immortalized in this case and in Anthony Lewis' *Gideon's Trumpet*, was charged in a Florida state court with the felony of having broken and entered a poolroom with intent to commit a misdemeanor. He was unable to afford private counsel, and his request for appointed counsel was denied. Following a verdict of guilty and the imposition of a five-year sentence, Gideon filed a petition for habeas corpus in the Florida Supreme Court, attacking his conviction on the ground that the refusal to appoint counsel was a denial of his constitutional rights. The state court rejected the petition, and the Supreme Court agreed to hear the case. Abe Fortas, then in private practice, was appointed to represent Gideon, and both sides were requested to discuss the question: "Should this Court's holding in *Betts* v. *Brady*[1] be reconsidered?" The *Betts* decision, in rejecting a claim of the right to appointed counsel in a noncapital case, had held that the refusal to appoint counsel under the particular facts and circumstances there presented was not so "offensive to the common and fundamental ideas of fairness"[2] as to amount to a denial of due process.

A unanimous Court decided for Gideon. The Court's opinion overruling *Betts* v. *Brady* was written by Justice Black, who had dissented in the *Betts* case itself over twenty years earlier. Justice Harlan, concurring, focused on the developments that led him to agree with the rejection of the *Betts* "case-by-case" approach.

Mr. Justice Harlan, concurring.

I agree that *Betts* v. *Brady* should be overruled, but consider it entitled to a more respectful burial than has been accorded, at least on the part of those of us who were not on the Court when that case was decided.

I cannot subscribe to the view [expressed in the opinion of the Court by Justice Black] that *Betts* v. *Brady* represented "an abrupt

[1] 316 U.S. 455.
[2] *Id.* at 473

break with its own well-considered precedents." In 1932, in *Powell* v. *Alabama*, 287 U.S. 45, a capital case, this Court declared that under the particular facts there presented—"the ignorance and illiteracy of the defendants, their youth, the circumstances of public hostility . . . and above all that they stood in deadly peril of their lives" (287 U.S. at 71)—the state court had a duty to assign counsel for the trial as a necessary requisite of due process of law. It is evident that these limiting facts were not added to the opinion as an afterthought; they were repeatedly emphasized, and were clearly regarded as important to the result.

Thus when this Court, a decade later, decided *Betts* v. *Brady*, it did no more than to admit of the possible existence of special circumstances in noncapital as well as capital trials, while at the same time insisting that such circumstances be shown in order to establish a denial of due process. The right to appointed counsel had been recognized as being considerably broader in federal prosecutions, but to have imposed these requirements on the States would indeed have been "an abrupt break" with the almost immediate past. The declaration that the right to appointed counsel in state prosecutions, as established in *Powell* v. *Alabama*, was not limited to capital cases was in truth not a departure from, but an extension of, existing precedent.

The principles declared in *Powell* and in *Betts*, however, have had a troubled journey throughout the years that have followed first the one case and then the other. Even by the time of the *Betts* decision, dictum in at least one of the Court's opinions had indicated that there was an absolute right to the services of counsel in the trial of state capital cases. Such dicta continued to appear in subsequent decisions, and any lingering doubts were finally eliminated by the holding of *Hamilton* v. *Alabama*, 368 U.S. 52.

In noncapital cases, the "special circumstances" rule has continued to exist in form while its substance has been substantially and steadily eroded. In the first decade after *Betts*, there were cases in which the Court found special circumstances to be lacking, but usually by a sharply divided vote. However, no such decision has been cited to us, and I have found none, after *Quicksall* v. *Michigan*, 339 U.S. 660, decided in 1950. At the same time, there have been not a few cases in which special circumstances were found in little or nothing more than the "complexity" of the legal questions presented, although those questions were often of only routine difficulty. The Court has come to recognize, in other words, that the mere existence of a serious criminal charge constituted in itself special circumstances requiring the services of counsel at trial. In truth the *Betts* v. *Brady* rule is no longer a reality.

This evolution, however, appears not to have been fully recognized by many state courts, in this instance charged with the front-line responsibility for the enforcement of constitutional rights. To continue a rule which is honored by this Court only with lip service is not a healthy thing and in the long run will do disservice to the federal system.

The special circumstances rule has been formally abandoned in capital cases, and the time has now come when it should be similarly abandoned in noncapital cases, at least as to offenses which, as the one involved here, carry the possibility of a substantial prison sentence. (Whether the rule should extend to *all* criminal cases need not now be decided.) This indeed does no more than to make explicit something that has long since been foreshadowed in our decisions.

In agreeing with the Court that the right to counsel in a case such as this should now be expressly recognized as a fundamental right embraced in the Fourteenth Amendment, I wish to make a further observation. When we hold a right or immunity, valid against the Federal Government, to be "implicit in the concept of ordered liberty" [*Palko* v. *Connecticut,* 302 U.S. 319, 325] and thus valid against the States, I do not read our past decisions to suggest that by so holding, we automatically carry over an entire body of federal law and apply it in full sweep to the States. Any such concept would disregard the frequently wide disparity between the legitimate interests of the States and of the Federal Government, the divergent problems that they face, and the significantly different consequences of their actions. In what is done today I do not understand the Court to depart from the principles laid down in *Palko* v. *Connecticut,* 302 U.S. 319, or to embrace the concept that the Fourteenth Amendment "incorporates" the Sixth Amendment as such.

On these premises I join in the judgment of the Court.[3]

---

[3] In the retrial that followed the decision in this case, Gideon was acquitted. Anthony Lewis, *Gideon's Trumpet* 237 (1964). [Ed.]

Douglas v. *California*

372 U.S. 353, 360 (1963)

William Douglas and Bennie Meyes were jointly tried and convicted of thirteen felonies in a California state court. Being indigent, they applied to a state appellate court for the appointment of counsel to assist them on appeal. Following the applicable state rule of procedure, that court independently examined the record, concluded that appointment of counsel would not be of any value to the defendants or to the court, and denied the application. The appeal was then heard without the assistance of counsel, the convictions were affirmed, and the state's highest court denied further review.

On review by the Supreme Court, the judgment was reversed in a 6–3 decision handed down on the same day as *Gideon* v. *Wainwright* (see above). Justice Douglas, writing for the Court, stated that "where the merits of *the one and only appeal* an indigent has as of right are decided without benefit of counsel, we think an unconstitutional line has been drawn between rich and poor . . . There is lacking [in such a result] that equality demanded by the Fourteenth Amendment." Justice Harlan, dissenting, objected to an analysis of the case in terms of state "discrimination" between rich and poor, pointed out the inconsistency between the Court's approach in this case and that taken in *Gideon,* and argued that California had scrupulously fulfilled its obligation to afford fair procedure for the indigent.

Mr. Justice Harlan, whom Mr. Justice Stewart joins, dissenting.

In holding that an indigent has an absolute right to appointed counsel on appeal of a state criminal conviction, the Court appears to rely both on the Equal Protection Clause and on the guarantees of fair procedure inherent in the Due Process Clause of the Fourteenth Amendment, with obvious emphasis on "equal protection." In my view the Equal Protection Clause is not apposite, and its application to cases like the present one can lead only to mischievous results. This case should be judged solely under the Due Process Clause, and I do not believe that the California procedure violates that provision.

13

Equal Protection

To approach the present problem in terms of the Equal Protection Clause is, I submit, but to substitute resounding phrases for analysis. I dissented from this approach in *Griffin* v. *Illinois,* 351 U.S. 12, 29, 34–36,[1] and I am constrained to dissent from the implicit extension of the equal protection approach here—to a case in which the State denies no one an appeal, but seeks only to keep within reasonable bounds the instances in which appellate counsel will be assigned to indigents.

The States, of course, are prohibited by the Equal Protection Clause from discriminating between "rich" and "poor" *as such* in the formulation and application of their laws. But it is a far different thing to suggest that this provision prevents the State from adopting a law of general applicability that may affect the poor more harshly than it does the rich, or, on the other hand, from making some effort to redress economic imbalances while not eliminating them entirely.

Every financial exaction which the State imposes on a uniform basis is more easily satisfied by the well-to-do than by the indigent. Yet I take it that no one would dispute the constitutional power of the State to levy a uniform sales tax, to charge tuition at a state university, to fix rates for the purchase of water from a municipal corporation, to impose a standard fine for criminal violations, or to establish minimum bail for various categories of offenses. Nor could it be contended that the State may not classify as crimes acts which the poor are more likely to commit than are the rich. And surely, there would be no basis for attacking a state law which provided benefits for the needy simply because those benefits fell short of the goods or services that others could purchase for themselves.

Laws such as these do not deny equal protection to the less fortunate for one essential reason: the Equal Protection Clause does not impose on the States "an affirmative duty to lift the handicaps

---

[1] The majority in *Griffin* [in holding that an indigent defendant had a right to have the state furnish him with a transcript for purposes of appeal] appeared to rely, as here, on a blend of the Equal Protection and Due Process Clauses in arriving at the result. So far as the result in that case rested on due process grounds, I fully accept the authority of *Griffin.*

14

flowing from differences in economic circumstances."[2] To so construe it would be to read into the Constitution a philosophy of leveling that would be foreign to many of our basic concepts of the proper relations between government and society. The State may have a moral obligation to eliminate the evils of poverty, but it is not required by the Equal Protection Clause to give to some whatever others can afford.

Thus it should be apparent that the present case is not one properly regarded as arising under this clause. California does not discriminate between rich and poor in having a uniform policy permitting everyone to appeal and to retain counsel, and in having a separate rule dealing *only* with the standards for the appointment of counsel for those unable to retain their own attorneys. The sole classification established by this rule is between those cases that are believed to have merit and those regarded as frivolous. And, of course, no matter how far the state rule might go in providing counsel for indigents, it could never be expected to satisfy an affirmative duty—if one existed—to place the poor on the same level as those who can afford the best legal talent available.

Parenthetically, it should be noted that if the present problem may be viewed as one of equal protection, so may the question of the right to appointed counsel at trial, and the Court's analysis of that right in *Gideon* v. *Wainwright* [372 U.S. 335], decided today, is wholly unnecessary. The short way to dispose of *Gideon* v. *Wainwright,* in other words, would be simply to say that the State deprives the indigent of equal protection whenever it fails to furnish him with legal services, and perhaps with other services as well, equivalent to those that the affluent defendant can obtain.

The real question in this case, I submit, and the only one that permits of satisfactory analysis, is whether or not the state rule, as applied in this case, is consistent with the requirements of fair procedure guaranteed by the Due Process Clause. Of course, in considering this question, it must not be lost sight of that the State's responsibility under the Due Process Clause is to provide justice for all. Refusal to furnish criminal indigents with some things that others can afford may fall short of constitutional standards of fairness. The problem before us is whether this is such a case.

[2]Griffin v. Illinois, *supra* at 34 (dissenting opinion of this writer).

Due Process

It bears reiteration that California's procedure of screening its criminal appeals to determine whether or not counsel ought to be appointed denies to no one the right to appeal. This is not a case in which a court rule or statute bars all consideration of the merits of an appeal unless docketing fees are prepaid. Nor is it like *Griffin* v. *Illinois, supra,* in which the State conceded that "petitioners needed a transcript in order to get adequate appellate review of their alleged trial errors." 351 U.S. at 16. Here it is *this* Court which finds, notwithstanding California's assertions to the contrary, that as a matter of constitutional law "adequate appellate review" is impossible unless counsel has been appointed. And while *Griffin* left it open to the States to devise "other means of affording adequate and effective appellate review to indigent defendants," 351 U.S. at 20, the present decision establishes what is seemingly an absolute rule under which the State may be left without any means of protecting itself against the employment of counsel in frivolous appeals.[3]

It was precisely toward providing adequate appellate review—as part of what the Court concedes to be "California's forward treatment of indigents"—that the State formulated the system which the Court today strikes down. That system requires the state appellate courts to appoint counsel on appeal for any indigent defendant except "if in their judgment such appointment would be of no value to either the defendant or the court." *People* v. *Hyde*, 51 Cal. 2d 152, 154, 331 P. 2d 42, 43. This judgment can be reached only after an independent investigation of the trial record by the reviewing court. And even if counsel is denied, a full appeal on the merits is accorded to the indigent appellant, together with a statement of the reasons why counsel was not assigned. There is nothing in the present case, or in any other case that has been cited to us, to indicate that the system has resulted in injustice. Quite the contrary, there is every reason to believe that California appellate courts have made a painstaking effort to apply the rule fairly and to live up to the State Supreme Court's mandate.

---

[3] California law provides that if counsel is appointed on appeal, the court shall fix a reasonable fee to be paid by the State. It is of course clear that this Court may not require the State to compel its attorneys to donate their services.

We have today held that in a case such as the one before us, there is an absolute right to the services of counsel at trial. *Gideon* v. *Wainwright.* But the appellate procedures involved here stand on an entirely different constitutional footing. *First,* appellate review is in itself not required by the Fourteenth Amendment, and thus the question presented is the narrow one whether the State's rules with respect to the appointment of counsel are so arbitrary or unreasonable, *in the context of the particular appellate procedure that it has established,* as to require their invalidation. *Second,* the kinds of questions that may arise on appeal are circumscribed by the record of the proceedings that led to the conviction; they do not encompass the large variety of tactical and strategic problems that must be resolved at the trial. *Third,* as California applies its rule, the indigent appellant receives the benefit of expert and conscientious legal appraisal of the merits of his case on the basis of the trial record, and whether or not he is assigned counsel, is guaranteed full consideration of his appeal. It would be painting with too broad a brush to conclude that under these circumstances an appeal is just like a trial.

What the Court finds constitutionally offensive in California's procedure bears a striking resemblance to the rules of this Court and many state courts of last resort on petitions for certiorari or for leave to appeal filed by indigent defendants *pro se.* Under the practice of this Court, only if it appears from the petition for certiorari that a case merits review is leave to proceed *in forma pauperis* granted, the case transferred to the Appellate Docket, and counsel appointed. Since our review is generally discretionary, and since we are often not even given the benefit of a record in the proceedings below, the disadvantages to the indigent petitioner might be regarded as more substantial than in California. But as conscientiously committed as this Court is to the great principle of "Equal Justice Under Law," it has never deemed itself constitutionally required to appoint counsel to assist in the preparation of each of the more than 1,000 *pro se* petitions for certiorari currently being filed each Term. We should know from our own experience that appellate courts generally go out of their way to give fair consideration to those who are unrepresented.

The Court distinguishes our review from the present case on the grounds that the California rule relates to "the *first appeal,* granted as a matter of right." But I fail to see the significance of this difference. Surely, it cannot be contended that the requirements of fair procedure are exhausted once an indigent has been given one appellate review. Nor can it well be suggested that having appointed counsel is more necessary to the fair administration of justice in an initial appeal taken as a matter of right, which the reviewing court on the full record has already determined to be frivolous, than in a petition asking a higher appellate court to exercise its discretion to consider what may be a substantial constitutional claim.

Further, there is no indication in this record, or in the state cases cited to us, that the California procedure differs in any material respect from the screening of appeals in federal criminal cases that is prescribed by 28 U.S.C. § 1915 . . . Indeed in some respects, California has outdone the federal system, since it provides a transcript and an appeal on the merits in *all* cases, no matter how frivolous.

I cannot agree that the Constitution prohibits a State, in seeking to redress economic imbalances at its bar of justice and to provide indigents with full review, from taking reasonable steps to guard against needless expense. This is all that California has done. Accordingly, I would affirm the state judgment.

In Re Gault

387 U.S. 1, 65 (1967)

This case brought before the Court the question of the scope of constitutional protections applicable in a state juvenile court proceeding. Gerald Gault, aged fifteen, was taken into custody by Arizona authorities as a result of a complaint that he had made a lewd telephone call. Hearings were held before a state juvenile court judge, and the judge committed Gault as a juvenile delinquent to the State Industrial School "for the period of his minority, unless sooner discharged by due process of law."

A habeas corpus action was brought on Gault's behalf, in which it was alleged that various constitutional rights had been denied in the juvenile proceeding. The dismissal of the action by the Arizona state courts was reversed by the Supreme Court, 8–1, Justice Stewart dissenting. In a fifty-six-page opinion for the Court, Justice Fortas held that in such proceedings due process includes (1) the right to timely and adequate notice, (2) the right to be represented by counsel (to be appointed in the event of indigency), (3) the right of confrontation, (4) the right of cross-examination, and (5) recognition of the privilege against self-incrimination. Reversal was based on the failure of the state to fulfill these requirements, and the majority did not reach certain other claims made on Gault's behalf, including the claim of a right to appeal and to an adequate record of the proceedings.

Justice Harlan, concurring in part and dissenting in part, emphasized the unique aspects of juvenile proceedings and the need for caution in the early stages of the Court's consideration of the juvenile process.

Mr. Justice Harlan, concurring in part and dissenting in part.

Each of the 50 States has created a system of juvenile or family courts, in which distinctive rules are employed and special consequences imposed. The jurisdiction of these courts commonly extends both to cases which the States have withdrawn from the ordinary processes of criminal justice, and to cases which involve acts that, if performed by an adult, would not be penalized as criminal. Such courts are denominated civil, not criminal, and are characteristically said not to administer criminal penalties. One consequence of these systems, at least as Arizona construes its own, is that certain of the rights guaranteed to criminal defendants by the Constitution are withheld from juveniles. This case brings before this Court for the first time the question of what limitations the Constitution places upon the operation of such tribunals. For reasons which follow, I have concluded that the Court has gone too far in some respects, and fallen short in others, in assessing the procedural requirements demanded by the Fourteenth Amendment.

I

I must first acknowledge that I am unable to determine with any certainty by what standards the Court decides that Arizona's juvenile courts do not satisfy the obligations of due process. The Court's premise, itself the product of reasoning which is not described, is that the "constitutional and theoretical basis" of state systems of juvenile and family courts is "debatable"; it buttresses these doubts by marshaling a body of opinion which suggests that the accomplishments of these courts have often fallen short of expectations. The Court does not indicate at what points or for what purposes such views, held either by it or by other observers, might be pertinent to the present issues. Its failure to provide any discernible standard for the measurement of due process in relation to juvenile proceedings unfortunately might be understood to mean that the Court is concerned principally with the wisdom of having such courts at all.

If this is the source of the Court's dissatisfaction, I cannot share it. I should have supposed that the constitutionality of juvenile courts was beyond proper question under the standards now employed to assess the substantive validity of state legislation under the Due Process Clause of the Fourteenth Amendment. It can scarcely be doubted that it is within the State's competence to adopt measures reasonably calculated to meet more effectively the persistent problems of juvenile delinquency; as the opinion for the Court makes abundantly plain, these are among the most vexing and ominous of the concerns which now face communities throughout the country.

The proper issue here is, however, not whether the State may constitutionally treat juvenile offenders through a system of specialized courts, but whether the proceedings in Arizona's juvenile courts include procedural guarantees which satisfy the requirements of the Fourteenth Amendment . . . Nothing before us suggests that juvenile courts were intended as a device to escape constitutional constraints, but I entirely agree with the Court that we are nonetheless obliged to examine with circumspection the procedural guarantees the State has provided.

The central issue here, and the principal one upon which I am divided from the Court, is the method by which the procedural requirements of due process should be measured. It must at the outset by emphasized that the protections necessary here cannot be determined by resort to any classification of juvenile proceedings either as criminal or as civil, whether made by the State or by this Court. Both formulae are simply too imprecise to permit reasoned analysis of these difficult constitutional issues. The Court should instead measure the requirements of due process by reference both to the problems which confront the State and to the actual character of the procedural system which the State has created . . .

The Court has repeatedly emphasized that determination of the constitutionally required procedural safeguards in any situation requires recognition both of the "interests affected" and of the "circumstances involved" [*FCC* v. *WJR*, 337 U.S. 265, 277] . . .

No more evidence of the importance of the public interests at stake here is required than that furnished by the opinion of the Court; it indicates that "some 601,000 children under 18, or 2% of all children between 10 and 17, came before juvenile courts" in 1965, and that "about one-fifth of all arrests for serious crimes" in 1965 were of juveniles. The Court adds that the rate of juvenile crime is steadily rising. All this, as the Court suggests, indicates the importance of these due process issues, but it mirrors no less vividly that state authorities are confronted by formidable and immediate problems involving the most fundamental social values. The state legislatures have determined that the most hopeful solution for these problems is to be found in specialized courts, organized under their own rules and imposing distinctive consequences. The terms and limitations of these systems are not identical, nor are the procedural arrangements which they include, but the States are uniform in their insistence that the ordinary processes of criminal justice are inappropriate, and that relatively informal proceedings, dedicated to premises and purposes only imperfectly reflected in the criminal law, are instead necessary.

It is well settled that the Court must give the widest deference to legislative judgments that concern the character and urgency of the problems with which the State is confronted. Legislatures are, as this Court has often acknowledged, the "main guardian" of the public interest, and, within their constitutional competence, their understanding of that interest must be accepted as "well-nigh" conclusive. *Berman* v. *Parker*, 348 U.S. 26, 32. This principle does not, however, reach all the questions essential to the resolution of this case. The legislative judgments at issue here embrace assessments of the necessity and wisdom of procedural guarantees; these are questions which the Constitution has entrusted at least in part to courts, and upon which courts have been understood to possess particular competence. The fundamental issue here is, therefore, in what measure and fashion the Court must defer to legislative determinations which encompass constitutional issues of procedural protection.

It suffices for present purposes to summarize the factors which

I believe to be pertinent. It must first be emphasized that the deference given to legislators upon substantive issues must realistically extend in part to ancillary procedural questions. Procedure at once reflects and creates substantive rights, and every effort of courts since the beginnings of the common law to separate the two has proved essentially futile. The distinction between them is particularly inadequate here, where the legislature's substantive preferences directly and unavoidably require judgments about procedural issues. The procedural framework is here a principal element of the substantive legislative system; meaningful deference to the latter must include a portion of deference to the former. The substantive-procedural dichotomy is, nonetheless, an indispensable tool of analysis, for it stems from fundamental limitations upon judicial authority under the Constitution. Its premise is ultimately that courts may not substitute for the judgments of legislators their own understanding of the public welfare, but must instead concern themselves with the validity under the Constitution of the methods which the legislature has selected. The Constitution has in this manner created for courts and legislators areas of primary responsibility which are essentially congruent to their areas of special competence. Courts are thus obliged both by constitutional command and by their distinctive functions to bear particular responsibility for the measurement of procedural due process. These factors in combination suggest that legislatures may properly expect only a cautious deference for their procedural judgments, but that, conversely, courts must exercise their special responsibility for procedural guarantees with care to permit ample scope for achieving the purposes of legislative programs. Plainly, courts can exercise such care only if they have in each case first studied thoroughly the objectives and implementation of the program at stake; if, upon completion of those studies, the effect of extensive procedural restrictions upon valid legislative purposes cannot be assessed with reasonable certainty, the court should necessarily proceed with restraint.

The foregoing considerations, which I believe to be fair distillations of relevant judicial history, suggest three criteria by which the procedural requirements of due process should be measured here: first, no more restrictions should be imposed than are imperative to assure the proceedings' fundamental fairness; second, the restrictions which are imposed should be those which preserve, so far as possible, the essential elements of the State's purpose; and finally, restrictions should be chosen which will later permit the orderly selection of any additional protections which may ultimately prove necessary. In this way, the Court may guarantee the fundamental fairness of the proceeding, and yet permit the State to continue development of an effective response to the problems of juvenile crime.

II

Measured by these criteria, only three procedural requirements should, in my opinion, now be deemed required of state juvenile courts by the Due Process Clause of the Fourteenth Amendment: first, timely notice must be provided to parents and children of the nature and terms of any juvenile court proceeding in which a determination affecting their rights or interests may be made; second, unequivocal and timely notice must be given that counsel may appear in any such proceeding in behalf of the child and its parents, and that in cases in which the child may be confined in an institution, counsel may, in circumstances of indigency, be appointed for them; and third, the court must maintain a written record, or its equivalent, adequate to permit effective review on appeal or in collateral proceedings. These requirements would guarantee to juveniles the tools with which their rights could be fully vindicated, and yet permit the States to pursue without unnecessary hindrance the purposes which they believe imperative in this field. Further, their imposition now would later permit more intelligent assessment of the necessity under the Fourteenth Amendment of additional requirements, by creating suitable records from which the character and deficiencies of juvenile proceedings could be accurately judged . . .

Provision of counsel and of a record, like adequate notice, would permit the juvenile to assert very much more effectively his rights and defenses, both in the juvenile proceedings and upon direct or collateral review. The Court has frequently emphasized their importance in proceedings in which an individual may be deprived of his liberty; this reasoning must include with special force those who are commonly inexperienced and immature. The facts of this case illustrate poignantly the difficulties of review without either an adequate record or the participation of counsel in the proceeding's initial stages. At the same time, these requirements should not cause any substantial modification in the character of juvenile court proceedings: counsel, although now present in only a small percentage of juvenile cases, have apparently already appeared without incident in virtually all juvenile courts; and the maintenance of a record should not appreciably alter the conduct of these proceedings.

The question remains whether certain additional requirements, among them the privilege against self-incrimination, confrontation, and cross-examination, must now, as the Court holds, also be imposed. I share in part the views expressed in my Brother White's concurring opinion, but believe that there are other, and more deep-seated, reasons to defer, at least for the present, the imposition of such requirements . . .

In my view, the Court should approach this question in terms of the criteria, described above, which emerge from the history of due process adjudication. Measured by them, there are compelling reasons at least to defer imposition of these additional requirements. First, quite unlike notice, counsel, and a record, these requirements might radically alter the character of juvenile court proceedings. The evidence from which the Court reasons that they would not is inconclusive, and other available evidence suggests that they very likely would. At the least, it is plain that these additional requirements would contribute materially to the creation in these proceedings of the atmosphere of an ordinary criminal trial, and would, even if they do no more, thereby largely frustrate a central purpose of these specialized courts. Further, these are restrictions intended to conform to the demands of an intensely adversary system of criminal justice; the broad purposes which they represent might be served in juvenile courts with equal effectiveness by procedural devices more consistent with the premises of proceedings in those courts. As the Court apparently acknowledges, the hazards of self-accusation, for example, might be avoided in juvenile proceedings without the imposition of all the requirements and limitations which surround the privilege against self-incrimination. The guarantee of adequate notice, counsel, and a record would create conditions in which suitable alternative procedures could be devised; but, unfortunately, the Court's haste to impose restrictions taken intact from criminal procedure may well seriously hamper the development of such alternatives. Surely this illustrates that prudence and the principles of the Fourteenth Amendment alike require that the Court should now impose no more procedural restrictions than are imperative to assure fundamental fairness, and that the States should instead be permitted additional opportunities to develop without unnecessary hindrance their systems of juvenile courts.

I find confirmation for these views in two ancillary considerations. First, it is clear that an uncertain, but very substantial number of the cases brought to juvenile courts involve children who are not in any sense guilty of criminal misconduct. Many of these children have simply the misfortune to be in some manner distressed; others have engaged in conduct, such as truancy, which is plainly not criminal. Efforts are now being made to develop effective, and entirely noncriminal, methods of treatment for these children. In such cases, the state authorities are in the most literal sense acting *in loco parentis;* they are, by any standard, concerned with the child's protection, and not with his punishment. I do not question that the methods employed in such cases must be consistent with the constitutional obligation to act in accordance with due process, but certainly the Fourteenth Amendment does not demand that they be constricted by the procedural guarantees devised for ordinary criminal prosecutions . . .

Second, it should not be forgotten that juvenile crime and juvenile courts are both now under earnest study throughout the country. I very much fear that this Court, by imposing these rigid procedural requirements, may inadvertently have served to discourage these efforts to find more satisfactory solutions for the problems of juvenile crime, and may thus now hamper enlightened development of the systems of juvenile courts. It is appropriate to recall that the Fourteenth Amendment does not compel the law to remain passive in the midst of change; to demand otherwise denies "every quality of the law but its age." *Hurtado v. California,* 110 U.S. 516, 529.

III

Finally, I turn to assess the validity of this juvenile court proceeding under the criteria discussed in this opinion. Measured by them, the judgment below must, in my opinion, fall. Gerald Gault and his parents were not provided adequate notice of the terms and purposes of the proceedings in which he was adjudged delinquent; they were not advised of their rights to be represented by counsel;

and no record in any form was maintained of the proceedings. It follows, for the reasons given in this opinion, that Gerald Gault was deprived of his liberty without due process of law, and I therefore concur in the judgment of the Court.[1]

Duncan v. Louisiana

391 U.S. 145, 171 (1968)

This case is another landmark in the ongoing process of "selective incorporation," by which the Court has made many, but not yet all, of the provisions of the Bill of Rights applicable to the states.[1] Gary Duncan was convicted in a Louisiana state court of simple battery. The offense was punishable by two years' imprisonment and a $300 fine, though Duncan received only a sixty-day term and a $150 fine. His timely request for jury trial had been denied, and when the state supreme court found "no error of law in the ruling," he appealed to the United States Supreme Court. In a 7–2 decision, that Court reversed, in an opinion by Justice White, holding that "the Fourteenth Amendment guarantees a right of jury trial in all criminal cases which—were they to be tried in a federal court—would come within the Sixth Amendment's guarantee." Justice Harlan's dissent contains perhaps the fullest and most forceful statement of his opposition to selective incorporation, as well as a careful analysis of why, in his view, Duncan was not denied any element of fundamental procedural fairness.

Mr. Justice Harlan, whom Mr. Justice Stewart joins, dissenting.

Every American jurisdiction provides for trial by jury in criminal cases. The question before us is not whether jury trial is an ancient institution, which it is; nor whether it plays a significant role in the administration of criminal justice, which it does; nor whether

[1] This opinion should be contrasted with the concurring opinion of Justice Black, who said: "[My Brother Harlan] is here claiming for the Court a supreme power to fashion new Bill of Rights safeguards according to the Court's notions of what fits tradition and conscience. I do not believe that the Constitution vests any such power in judges, either in the Due Process clause or anywhere else. Consequently, I do not vote to invalidate this Arizona law on the ground that it is 'unfair' but solely on the ground that it violates the Fifth and Sixth Amendments made obligatory on the States by the Fourteenth." [Ed.]

[1] While the phrase "selective incorporation" has been used by dissenters and commentators to describe this process, the phrase has not appeared in any opinion for the Court. Indeed, the doctrine itself does not command a majority. See "The Supreme Court, 1967 Term," 82 *Harv. L. Rev.* 63, 149 n.7 (1968).

it will endure, which it shall. The question in this case is whether the State of Louisiana, which provides trial by jury for all felonies, is prohibited by the Constitution from trying charges of simple battery to the court alone. In my view, the answer to that question, mandated alike by our constitutional history and by the longer history of trial by jury, is clearly "no."

The States have always borne primary responsibility for operating the machinery of criminal justice within their borders, and adapting it to their particular circumstances. In exercising this responsibility, each State is compelled to conform its procedures to the requirements of the Federal Constitution. The Due Process Clause of the Fourteenth Amendment requires that those procedures be fundamentally fair in all respects. It does not, in my view, impose or encourage nationwide uniformity for its own sake; it does not command adherence to forms that happen to be old; and it does not impose on the States the rules that may be in force in the federal courts except where such rules are also found to be essential to basic fairness.

The Court's approach to this case is an uneasy and illogical compromise among the views of various Justices on how the Due Process Clause should be interpreted. The Court does not say that those who framed the Fourteenth Amendment intended to make the Sixth Amendment applicable to the States. And the Court concedes that it finds nothing unfair about the procedure by which the present appellant was tried. Nevertheless, the Court reverses his conviction: it holds, for some reason not apparent to me, that the Due Process Clause incorporates the particular clause of the Sixth Amendment that requires trial by jury in federal criminal cases—including, as I read its opinion, the sometimes trivial accompanying baggage of judicial interpretation in federal contexts. I have raised my voice many times before against the Court's continuing undiscriminating insistence upon fastening on the States federal notions of criminal justice, and I must do so again in this instance. With all respect, the Court's approach and its reading of history are altogether topsy-turvy.

I

I believe I am correct in saying that every member of the Court for at least the last 135 years has agreed that our Founders did not

27

consider the requirements of the Bill of Rights so fundamental that they should operate directly against the States. They were wont to believe rather that the security of liberty in America rested primarily upon the dispersion of governmental power across a federal system. The Bill of Rights was considered unnecessary by some but insisted upon by others in order to curb the possibility of abuse of power by the strong central government they were creating.

The Civil War Amendments dramatically altered the relation of the Federal Government to the States. The first section of the Fourteenth Amendment imposes highly significant restrictions on state action. But the restrictions are couched in very broad and general terms: citizenship, privileges and immunities; due process of law; equal protection of the laws. Consequently, for 100 years this Court has been engaged in the difficult process Professor Jaffe has well called "the search for intermediate premises."[2] The question has been, "Where does the Court properly look to find the specific rules that define and give content to such terms as 'life, liberty, or property' and 'due process of law'?"

A few members of the Court have taken the position that the intention of those who drafted the first section of the Fourteenth Amendment was simply, and exclusively, to make the provisions of the first eight amendments applicable to state action. This view has never been accepted by this Court. In my view, often expressed elsewhere, the first section of the Fourteenth Amendment was meant neither to incorporate, nor to be limited to, the specific guarantees of the first eight amendments. The overwhelming historical evidence marshalled by Professor Fairman demonstrates, to me conclusively, that the Congressmen and state legislators who wrote, debated, and ratified the Fourteenth Amendment did not think they were "incorporating" the Bill of Rights[3] and the very breadth and generality

[2] Jaffe, "Was Brandeis an Activist? The Search for Intermediate Premises," 80 *Harv. L. Rev.* 986 (1967).

[3] Fairman, "Does the Fourteenth Amendment Incorporate the Bill of Rights? The Original Understanding," 2 *Stan. L. Rev.* 5 (1949). Professor Fairman was not content to rest upon the overwhelming fact that the great words of the four clauses of the first section of the Fourteenth Amendment would have been an exceedingly peculiar way to say that "The rights heretofore guaranteed against federal intrusion by the first eight Amendments are henceforth guaranteed against state intrusion as well." He therefore sifted the mountain of material comprising the debates and committee reports relating to the Amendment in both Houses of Congress and in the state legislatures that passed upon it. He found that in the immense corpus of comments on the purpose and effects of the proposed amendment, and on its virtues and defects, there is almost no evidence whatever for "incorporation" . . .

of the Amendment's provisions suggest that its authors did not suppose that the Nation would always be limited to mid-19th century conceptions of "liberty" and "due process of law" but that the increasing experience and evolving conscience of the American people would add new "intermediate premises." In short, neither history, nor sense, supports using the Fourteenth Amendment to put the States in a constitutional straitjacket with respect to their own development in the administration of criminal or civil law.

Although I therefore fundamentally disagree with the total incorporation view of the Fourteenth Amendment, it seems to me that such a position does at least have the virtue, lacking in the Court's selective incorporation approach, of internal consistency: we look to the Bill of Rights, word for word, clause for clause, precedent for precedent because, it is said, the men who wrote the Amendment wanted it that way. For those who do not accept this "history," a different source of "intermediate premises" must be found. The Bill of Rights is not necessarily irrelevant to the search for guidance in interpreting the Fourteenth Amendment, but the reason for and the nature of its relevance must be articulated.

Apart from the approach taken by the absolute incorporationists, I can see only one method of analysis that has any internal logic. That is to start with the words "liberty" and "due process of law" and attempt to define them in a way that accords with American traditions and our system of government. This approach, involving a much more discriminating process of adjudication than does "incorporation," is, albeit difficult, the one that was followed throughout the 19th and most of the present century. It entails a "gradual process of judicial inclusion and exclusion,"[4] seeking, with due recognition of constitutional tolerance for state experimentation and disparity, to ascertain those "immutable principles . . . of free government which no member of the Union may disregard."[5] Due process was not restricted to rules fixed in the past, for that "would be to deny every quality of the law but its age, and to render it incapable of progress or improvement."[6] Nor did it impose nationwide uniformity in details, for

the Fourteenth Amendment does not profess to secure to all persons in the United States the benefit of the same laws and the

[4] Davidson v. New Orleans, 96 U.S. 97, 104.
[5] Holden v. Hardy, 169 U.S. 366, 389.
[6] Hurtado v. California, 110 U.S. 516, 529.

same remedies. Great diversities in these respects may exist in two states separated only by an imaginary line. On one side of this line there may be a right of trial by jury, and on the other side no such right. Each State prescribes its own modes of judicial proceeding.[7]

Through this gradual process, this Court sought to define "liberty" by isolating freedoms that Americans of the past and of the present considered more important than any suggested countervailing public objective. The Court also, by interpretation of the phrase "due process of law," enforced the Constitution's guarantee that no State may imprison an individual except by fair and impartial procedures.

The relationship of the Bill of Rights to this "gradual process" seems to me to be twofold. In the first place it has long been clear that the Due Process Clause imposes some restrictions on state action that parallel Bill of Rights restrictions on federal action. Second, and more important than this accidental overlap, is the fact that the Bill of Rights is evidence, at various points, of the content Americans find in the term "liberty" and of American standards of fundamental fairness . . .

In all of these instances, the right guaranteed against the States by the Fourteenth Amendment was one that had also been guaranteed against the Federal Government by one of the first eight amendments. The logically critical thing, however, was not that the rights had been found in the Bill of Rights, but that they were deemed, in the context of American legal history, to be fundamental. This was perhaps best explained by Mr. Justice Cardozo, speaking for a Court that included Chief Justice Hughes and Justices Brandeis and Stone, in *Palko* v. *Connecticut*, 302 U.S. 319 . . . [In that opinion he explained] that the Fourteenth Amendment did not impose on each State every rule of procedure that some other State, or the federal Courts, thought desirable, but only those rules critical to liberty:

> The line of division may seem to be wavering and broken if there is a hasty catalogue of the cases on the one side and the other. Reflection and analysis will induce a different view. There emerges the perception of a rationalizing principle which gives

[7] Missouri v. Lewis, 101 U.S. 22, 31.

to discrete instances a proper order and coherence. The right to trial by jury and the immunity from prosecution except as the result of an indictment may have value and importance. Even so, they are not of the very essence of a scheme of ordered liberty. To abolish them is not to violate a "principle of justice so rooted in the traditions and conscience of *our people* as to be ranked as fundamental." . . . Few would be so narrow or provincial as to maintain that a fair and enlightened system of justice would be impossible without them. *Id.* at 325. (Emphasis added.)

Today's Court still remains unwilling to accept the total incorporationists' view of the history of the Fourteenth Amendment. This, if accepted, would afford a cogent reason for applying the Sixth Amendment to the States. The Court is also, apparently, unwilling to face the task of determining whether denial of trial by jury in the situation before us, or in other situations, is fundamentally unfair. Consequently, the Court has compromised on the ease of the incorporationist position, without its internal logic. It has simply assumed that the question before us is whether the Jury Trial Clause of the Sixth Amendment should be incorporated into the Fourteenth, jot-for-jot and case-for-case, or ignored. Then the Court merely declares that the clause in question is "in" rather than "out."

The Court has justified neither its starting place nor its conclusion. If the problem is to discover and articulate the rules of fundamental fairness in criminal proceedings, there is no reason to assume that the whole body of rules developed in this Court constituting Sixth Amendment jury trial must be regarded as a unit. The requirement of trial by jury in federal criminal cases has given rise to numerous subsidiary questions respecting the exact scope and content of the right. It surely cannot be that every answer the Court has given, or will give, to such a question is attributable to the Founders; or even that every rule announced carries equal conviction of this Court; still less can it be that every such subprinciple is equally fundamental to ordered liberty . . .

One . . . example is directly relevant here. The co-existence of a requirement of jury trial in federal criminal cases and a historic and universally recognized exception for "petty crimes" has compelled this Court, on occasion, to decide whether a particular crime is petty, or is included within the guarantee. Individual cases have been decided without great conviction and without reference to a guiding principle. The Court today holds, for no discernible reason, that if and when the line is drawn its exact location will be a matter of such fundamental importance that it will be uniformly imposed on the States. This Court is compelled to decide such obscure borderline questions in the course of administering federal law. This does not mean that its decisions are demonstrably sounder than those that would be reached by state courts and legislatures, let alone that they are of such importance that fairness demands their imposition throughout the Nation.

Even if I could agree that the question before us is whether Sixth Amendment jury trial is totally "in" or totally "out," I can find in the Court's opinion no real reasons for concluding that it should be "in." The basis for differentiating among clauses in the Bill of Rights cannot be that only some clauses are in the Bill of Rights, or that only some are old and much praised, or that only some have played an important role in the development of federal law. These things are true of all. The Court says that some clauses are more "fundamental" than others, but it turns out to be using this word in a sense that would have astonished Mr. Justice Cardozo and which, in addition, is of no help. The word does not mean "analytically critical to procedural fairness" for no real analysis of the role of the jury in making procedures fair is even attempted. Instead, the word turns out to mean "old," "much praised," and "found in the Bill of Rights." The definition of "fundamental" thus turns out to be circular.

II

Since, as I see it, the Court has not even come to grips with the issues in this case, it is necessary to start from the beginning. When a criminal defendant contends that his state conviction lacked "due process of law," the question before this Court, in my view, is whether he was denied any element of fundamental procedural fairness. Believing, as I do, that due process is an evolving concept and that old principles are subject to re-evaluation in light of later experience, I think it appropriate to deal on its merits with the question whether Louisiana denied appellant due process of law when it tried him for simple assault without a jury.

32

The obvious starting place is the fact that this Court has, in the past, *held* that trial by jury is not a requisite of criminal due process . . . [*Discussion of prior cases is omitted.*]

Although it is of course open to this Court to reexamine these decisions, I can see no reason why they should now be overturned. It can hardly be said that time has altered the question, or brought significant new evidence to bear upon it. The virtues and defects of the jury system have been hotly debated for a long time, and are hotly debated today, without significant change in the lines of argument.

The argument that jury trial is not a requisite of due process is quite simple. The central proposition of *Palko, supra,* a proposition to which I would adhere, is that "due process of law" requires only that criminal trials be fundamentally fair. As stated above, apart from the theory that it was historically intended as a mere shorthand for the Bill of Rights, I do not see what else "due process of law" can intelligibly be thought to mean. If due process of law requires only fundamental fairness, then the inquiry in each case must be whether a state trial process was a fair one. The Court has held, properly I think, that in an adversary process it is a requisite of fairness, for which there is no adequate substitute, that a criminal defendant be afforded a right to counsel and to cross-examine opposing witnesses. But it simply has not been demonstrated, nor, I think, can it be demonstrated, that trial by jury is the only fair means of resolving issues of fact.

The jury is of course not without virtues. It affords ordinary citizens a valuable opportunity to participate in a process of government, an experience fostering, one hopes, a respect for law. It eases the burden on judges by enabling them to share a part of their sometimes awesome responsibility. A jury may, at times, afford a higher justice by refusing to enforce harsh laws (although it necessarily does so haphazardly, raising the questions whether arbitrary enforcement of harsh laws is better than total enforcement, and whether the jury system is to be defended on the ground that jurors sometimes disobey their oaths). And the jury may, or may not, contribute desirably to the willingness of the general public to accept criminal judgments as just.

It can hardly be gainsaid, however, that the principal original virtue of the jury trial—the limitations a jury imposes on a tyrannous judiciary—has largely disappeared. We no longer live in a medieval or colonial society. Judges enforce laws enacted by democratic decision, not by regal fiat. They are elected by the people or appointed by the people's elected officials, and are responsible not to a distant monarch alone but to reviewing courts, including this one.

The jury system can also be said to have some inherent defects, which are multiplied by the emergence of the criminal law from the relative simplicity that existed when the jury system was devised. It is a cumbersome process, not only imposing great cost in time and money on both the State and the jurors themselves, but also contributing to delay in the machinery of justice. Untrained jurors are presumably less adept at reaching accurate conclusions of fact than judges, particularly if the issues are many or complex. And it is argued by some that trial by jury, far from increasing public respect for law, impairs it: the average man, it is said, reacts favorably neither to the notion that matters he knows to be complex are being decided by other average men, nor to the way the jury system distorts the process of adjudication.

That trial by jury is not the only fair way of adjudicating criminal guilt is well attested by the fact that it is not the prevailing way, either in England or in this country . . . [*The opinion here discusses jury trial statistics in the two countries.*]

The Court recognizes the force of these statistics in stating,

> We would not assert, however, that every criminal trial—or any particular trial—held before a judge alone is unfair or that a defendant may never be as fairly treated by a judge as he would be by a jury.

I agree. I therefore see no reason why this Court should reverse the conviction of appellant, absent any suggestion that his particular trial was in fact unfair, or compel the State of Louisiana to afford jury trial in an as yet unbounded category of cases that can, without unfairness, be tried to a court.

Indeed, even if I were persuaded that trial by jury is a fundamental right in some criminal cases, I could see nothing fundamental in the rule, not yet formulated by the Court, that places the prosecution of appellant for simple battery within the category of "jury crimes" rather than "petty crimes." Trial by jury is ancient, it is true. Almost equally ancient, however, is the discovery that, because of it,

> the King's most loving Subjects are much travailed and otherwise encumbered in coming and keeping of the said six Weeks Sessions, to their Costs, Charges, Unquietness.[8]

As a result, through the long course of British and American history, summary procedures have been used in a varying category of lesser crimes as a flexible response to the burden jury trial would otherwise impose . . .

The point is not that many offenses that English-speaking communities have, at one time or another, regarded as triable without a jury are more serious, and carry more serious penalties, than the one involved here. The point is rather that until today few people would have thought the exact location of the line mattered very much. There is no obvious reason why a jury trial is a requisite of fundamental fairness when the charge is robbery, and not a requisite of fairness when the same defendant, for the same actions, is charged with assault and petit theft. The reason for the historic exception of relatively minor crimes is the obvious one: the burden of jury trial was thought to outweigh its marginal advantages. Exactly why the States should not be allowed to make continuing adjustments, based on the state of their criminal dockets and the difficulty of summoning jurors, simply escapes me.

In sum, there is a wide range of views on the desirability of trial by jury, and on the ways to make it most effective when it is used; there is also considerable variation from State to State in local conditions such as the size of the criminal caseload, the ease or difficulty of summoning jurors, and other trial conditions bearing on fairness. We have before us, therefore, an almost perfect example of a situation in which the celebrated dictum of Mr. Justice Brandeis should be invoked. It is, he said,

> one of the happy incidents of the federal system that a single courageous State may, if its citizens choose, serve as a laboratory . . . *New State Ice Co.* v. *Liebmann*, 285 U.S. 262, 280, 311 (dissenting opinion).

[8] 37 Hen. 8, c. 7.

35

This Court, other courts, and the political process are available to correct any experiments in criminal procedure that prove fundamentally unfair to defendants. That is not what is being done today: instead, and quite without reason, the Court has chosen to impose upon every State one means of trying criminal cases; it is a good means, but it is not the only fair means, and it is not demonstrably better than the alternatives States might devise.

I would affirm the judgment of the Supreme Court of Louisiana.[9]

[9] Here, as in *Gault* (see above) Justice Black took special pains to articulate his disagreement with the approach taken in Justice Harlan's opinion. Concurring for himself and Justice Douglas, Justice Black stated his reasons for rejecting the Fairman thesis of "nonincorporation" and noted: "The 'fundamental fairness' test is one on a par with that of shocking the conscience of the Court. Each of such tests depends entirely on the particular judge's idea of ethics and morals instead of requiring him to depend on the boundaries fixed by the written words of the Constitution. Nothing in the history of the phrase 'due process of law' suggests that constitutional controls are to depend on any particular judge's sense of values . . . I have never believed that under the guise of federalism the States should be able to experiment with the protections afforded our citizens through the Bill of Rights." [Ed.]

B

The Law Enforcement
Process in the States

Miranda v. Arizona

384 U.S. 436, 504 (1966)

In 1936, in *Brown* v. *Mississippi*,[1] the Court for the first time held that an involuntary confession of guilt was inadmissible in a state criminal proceeding. For the next three decades, the Court grappled with the troublesome concept of "voluntariness," extending it almost to the breaking point, or perhaps beyond, in such decisions as *Haynes* v. *Washington*.[2] *Escobedo* v. *Illinois*,[3] decided in 1964, marked a new starting point, the emphasis shifting away from voluntariness and toward the right to adequate warnings and to the services of counsel during interrogation. The uncertainty engendered by this decision was one of the factors that led the majority in *Miranda* to expand and elaborate the precise conditions under which a defendant's statement would be admissible in evidence.

Miranda was actually one of four cases—three state and one federal—which were decided together. In each of these cases, in a criminal proceeding, the defendant contended that the introduction in evidence of a statement obtained from him while he was in custody violated his constitutional rights.

[1] 297 U.S. 278.
[2] 373 U.S. 503, decided in 1963.
[3] 378 U.S. 478.

37

The majority, speaking through the Chief Justice, conceded that "we might not find the defendants' statements to have been involuntary in traditional terms." But those terms, in the Court's view, were not adequate to protect the accused from all the evils of the interrogation atmosphere. After extensive quotation from manuals written for the police and other discussion of police methods, the Court held that the privilege against self-incrimination was applicable during a period of custodial interrogation and that in order to protect that privilege, certain safeguards—most notably the giving of adequate warnings and the affording of the right to counsel—must be observed.[4] Since these requirements had not been fulfilled in any of the four cases, judgment for the defendant was rendered in each.[5]

Three dissenting opinions were filed. In his dissent, Justice Harlan attacked the Court's express reliance on the Fifth and implicit reliance on the Sixth Amendments, insisted that the test of voluntariness remained the appropriate one, and argued that the Court's new rules seriously threatened effective law enforcement.

Mr. Justice Harlan, whom Mr. Justice Stewart and Mr. Justice White join, dissenting.

I believe the decision of the Court represents poor constitutional law and entails harmful consequences for the country at large. How serious these consequences may prove to be only time can tell. But the basic flaws in the Court's justification seem to me readily apparent now once all sides of the problem are considered.

[4] Congress in 1968 provided that in any prosecution brought by the United States or by the District of Columbia, a confession shall be admissible "if it is voluntarily given," and that such matters as adequate warning and the affording of counsel shall simply be taken into consideration in determining the issue of voluntariness. 18 U.S.C. § 3501(a), (b). Although the majority in *Miranda* suggested that its decision did not preclude legislative efforts to deal with the problem, there is grave doubt of the constitutionality of this provision. See S. Rep. No. 1097, 90th Cong., 2d Sess. 147–53 (minority views) (1968).

The *Miranda* majority's evident dissatisfaction with the case-by-case approach which the voluntariness test requires is reminiscent of the Court's rejection of the "special circumstances" rule in Gideon v. Wainwright (see above). At the same time, it is far from clear that the rules declared in this case mark the terminal point of development. If the Court concludes that it is too difficult to determine whether notification was adequate and whether an effective waiver of rights was made, or too easy to circumvent these requirements, it may insist on an even more expansive exclusionary rule. Recent studies indicate that the police are in fact violating "both the letter and the spirit" of the *Miranda* decision. See *Time*, Nov. 1, 1968, p. 70; see also Medalie, Zeitz, and Alexander, "Custodial Police Interrogation in the Nation's Capital: The Attempt to Implement Miranda," 66 *Mich. L. Rev.* 1347 (1968).

[5] But in Johnson v. New Jersey, 384 U.S. 719, a case decided in the same Term of Court, it was held that the *Escobedo* and *Miranda* decisions were applicable only to those cases in which trial began after the decisions were announced.

I. Introduction

At the outset, it is well to note exactly what is required by the Court's new constitutional code of rules for confessions. The foremost requirement, upon which later admissibility of a confession depends, is that a fourfold warning be given to a person in custody before he is questioned, namely, that he has a right to remain silent, that anything he says may be used against him, that he has a right to have present an attorney during the questioning, and that if indigent he has a right to a lawyer without charge. To forgo these rights, some affirmative statement of rejection is seemingly required, and threats, tricks, or cajolings to obtain this waiver are forbidden. If before or during questioning the suspect seeks to invoke his right to remain silent, interrogation must be forgone or cease; a request for counsel brings about the same result until a lawyer is procured. Finally, there are a miscellany of minor directives, for example, the burden of proof of waiver is on the State, admissions and exculpatory statements are treated just like confessions, withdrawal of a waiver is always permitted, and so forth.

While the fine points of this scheme are far less clear than the Court admits, the tenor is quite apparent. The new rules are not designed to guard against police brutality or other unmistakably banned forms of coercion. Those who use third-degree tactics and deny them in court are equally able and destined to lie as skillfully about warnings and waivers. Rather, the thrust of the new rules is to negate all pressures, to reinforce the nervous or ignorant suspect, and ultimately to discourage any confession at all. The aim in short is toward "voluntariness" in a utopian sense, or to view it from a different angle, voluntariness with a vengeance . . .

II. Constitutional Premises

It is most fitting to begin an inquiry into the constitutional precedents by surveying the limits on confessions the Court has evolved under the Due Process Clause of the Fourteenth Amendment. This is so because these cases show that there exists a workable and effective means of dealing with confessions in a judicial manner; because the cases are the baseline from which the Court now departs and so serve to measure the actual as opposed to the professed distance it travels; and because examination of them helps reveal how the Court has coasted into its present position.

The earliest confession cases in this Court emerged from federal prosecutions and were settled on a nonconstitutional basis, the Court adopting the common-law rule that the absence of inducements, promises, and threats made a confession voluntary and admissible. While a later case said the Fifth Amendment privilege controlled admissibility, this proposition was not itself developed in subsequent decisions. The Court did, however, heighten the test of admissibility in federal trials to one of voluntariness "in fact," and then by and large left federal judges to apply the same standards the Court began to derive in a string of state court cases.

This new line of decisions, testing admissibility by the Due Process Clause, began in 1936 with *Brown* v. *Mississippi*, 297 U.S. 278, and must now embrace somewhat more than 30 full opinions of the Court. While the voluntariness rubric was repeated in many instances, the Court never pinned it down to a single meaning but on the contrary infused it with a number of different values. To travel quickly over the main themes, there was an initial emphasis on reliability, supplemented by concern over the legality and fairness of the police practices in an "accusatorial" system of law enforcement, and eventually by close attention to the individual's state of mind and capacity for effective choice. The outcome was a continuing re-evaluation on the facts of each case of *how much* pressure on the suspect was permissible . . .

There are several relevant lessons to be drawn from this constitutional history. The first is that with over 25 years of precedent the Court has developed an elaborate, sophisticated, and sensitive approach to admissibility of confessions. It is "judicial" in its treatment of one case at a time, flexible in its ability to respond to the endless mutations of fact presented, and ever more familiar to the lower courts. Of course, strict certainty is not obtained in this developing process, but this is often so with constitutional principles, and disagreement is usually confined to that borderland of close cases where it matters least.

The second point is that in practice and from time to time in principle, the Court has given ample recognition to society's interest in suspect questioning as an instrument of law enforcement. Cases countenancing quite significant pressures can be cited without difficulty, and the lower courts may often have been yet more tolerant. Of course the limitations imposed today were rejected by necessary implication in case after case, the right to warnings having been explicitly rebuffed in this Court many years ago . . .

Finally, the cases disclose that the language in many of the opinions overstates the actual course of decision . . . The tendency to overstate may be laid in part to the flagrant facts often before the Court; but in any event one must recognize how it has tempered attitudes and lent some color of authority to the approach now taken by the Court.

I turn now to the Court's asserted reliance on the Fifth Amendment, an approach which I frankly regard as a *trompe l'oeil.* The Court's opinion in my view reveals no adequate basis for extending the Fifth Amendment's privilege against self-incrimination to the police station. Far more important, it fails to show that the Court's new rules are well supported, let alone compelled, by Fifth Amendment precedents. Instead, the new rules actually derive from quotation and analogy drawn from precedents under the Sixth Amendment, which should properly have no bearing on police interrogation.

The Court's opening contention, that the Fifth Amendment governs police station confessions, is perhaps not an impermissible extension of the law but it has little to commend itself in the present circumstances. Historically, the privilege against self-incrimination did not bear at all on the use of extra-legal confessions, for which distinct standards evolved; indeed, "the *history* of the two principles is wide apart, differing by one hundred years in origin, and derived through separate lines of precedents . . ." 8 Wigmore, *Evidence* § 2266 at 401 (McNaughton rev. 1961) . . . Even those who would readily enlarge the privilege must concede some linguistic difficulties since the Fifth Amendment in terms proscribes only compelling any person "in any criminal case to be a witness against himself."

Though weighty, I do not say these points and similar ones are conclusive, for, as the Court reiterates, the privilege embodies basic principles always capable of expansion. Certainly the privilege does represent a protective concern for the accused and an emphasis upon accusatorial rather than inquisitorial values in law enforcement, although this is similarly true of other limitations such as the grand jury requirement and the reasonable doubt standard. Accusatorial values, however, have openly been absorbed into the due process standard governing confessions; this indeed is why at present "the kinship of the two rules [governing confessions and self-incrimination] is too apparent for denial." McCormick, *Evidence* 155 (1954). Since extension of the general principle has already occurred, to insist that the privilege applies as such serves only to carry over inapposite historical details and engaging rhetoric and to obscure the policy choices to be made in regulating confessions.

Having decided that the Fifth Amendment privilege does apply in the police station, the Court reveals that the privilege imposes more exacting restrictions than does the Fourteenth Amendment's voluntariness test . . .

The Fifth Amendment, however, has never been thought to forbid *all* pressure to incriminate one's self in the situations covered by it. On the contrary, it has been held that failure to incriminate one's self can result in denial of removal of one's case from state to federal court, in refusal of a military commission, in denial of a discharge in bankruptcy, and in numerous other adverse consequences. This is not to say that short of jail or torture any sanction is permissible in any case; policy and history alike may impose sharp limits. However, the Court's unspoken assumption that *any* pressure violates the privilege is not supported by the precedents and it has failed to show why the Fifth Amendment prohibits that relatively mild pressure the Due Process Clause permits . . .

A closing word must be said about the Assistance of Counsel Clause of the Sixth Amendment, which is never expressly relied on by the Court but whose judicial precedents turn out to be linchpins of the confession rules announced today . . .

The only attempt in this Court to carry the right to counsel into the station house occurred in *Escobedo* [v. *Illinois*, 378 U.S. 478], the Court repeating several times that that stage was no less "critical" than trial itself. See 378 U.S. 485–488. This is hardly persuasive when we consider that a grand jury inquiry, the filing of a certiorari petition, and certainly the purchase of narcotics by an undercover agent from a prospective defendant may all be equally "critical" yet provision of counsel and advice on that score have never been thought compelled by the Constitution in such cases. The sound reason why this right is so freely extended for a criminal trial is the severe injustice risked by confronting an untrained defendant with a range of technical points of law, evidence, and tactics familiar to the prosecutor but not to himself. This danger shrinks markedly in the police station where indeed the lawyer in fulfilling his professional responsibilities of necessity may become an obstacle to truthfinding. The Court's summary citation of the Sixth Amendment cases here seems to me best described as "the domino method of constitutional adjudication . . . wherein every explanatory statement in a previous opinion is made the basis for extension to a wholly different situation." [Friendly, "The Bill of Rights as a Code of Criminal Procedure," 53 *Calif. L. Rev.* 929, 950 (1965).]

III. Policy Considerations

Examined as an expression of public policy, the Court's new regime proves so dubious that there can be no due compensation for its weakness in constitutional law . . .

Without at all subscribing to the generally black picture of police conduct painted by the Court, I think it must be frankly recognized at the outset that police questioning allowable under due process precedents may inherently entail some pressure on the suspect and may seek advantage in his ignorance or weaknesses. The atmosphere and questioning techniques, proper and fair though they be, can in themselves exert a tug on the suspect to confess, and in this light "to speak of any confessions of crime made after arrest as being 'voluntary' or 'uncoerced' is somewhat inaccurate, although traditional. A confession is wholly and incontestably voluntary only if a guilty person gives himself up to the law and becomes his own accuser." *Ashcraft* v. *Tennessee*, 322 U.S. 143, 161 (Jackson, J., dissenting). Until today, the role of the Constitution has been only to sift out *undue* pressure, not to assure spontaneous confessions.

The Court's new rules aim to offset these minor pressures and disadvantages intrinsic to any kind of police interrogation. The rules do not serve due process interests in preventing blatant coercion since, as I noted earlier, they do nothing to contain the policeman who is prepared to lie from the start. The rules work for reliability in confessions almost only in the Pickwickian sense that they can prevent some from being given at all.[6] In short, the benefit of this

---

[6] The Court's vision of a lawyer "mitigat[ing] the dangers of untrustworthiness" by witnessing coercion and assisting accuracy in the confession is largely a fancy; for if counsel arrives, there is rarely going to be a police station confession . . .

new regime is simply to lessen or wipe out the inherent compulsion and inequalities to which the Court devotes some nine pages of description.

What the Court largely ignores is that its rules impair, if they will not eventually serve wholly to frustrate, an instrument of law enforcement that has long and quite reasonably been thought worth the price paid for it.[7] There can be little doubt that the Court's new code would markedly decrease the number of confessions. To warn the suspect that he may remain silent and remind him that his confession may be used in court are minor obstructions. To require also an express waiver by the suspect and an end to questioning whenever he demurs must heavily handicap questioning. And to suggest or provide counsel for the suspect simply invites the end of the interrogation.

How much harm this decision will inflict on law enforcement cannot fairly be predicted with accuracy. Evidence on the role of confessions is notoriously incomplete, and little is added by the Court's reference to the FBI experience and the resources believed wasted in interrogation. We do know that some crimes cannot be solved without confessions, that ample expert testimony attests to their importance in crime control, and that the Court is taking a real risk with society's welfare in imposing its new regime on the country. The social costs of crime are too great to call the new rules anything but a hazardous experimentation.

While passing over the costs and risks of its experiment, the Court portrays the evils of normal police questioning in terms which I think are exaggerated. Albeit stringently confined by the due process standards interrogation is no doubt often inconvenient and unpleasant for the suspect. However, it is no less so for a man to be arrested and jailed, to have his house searched, or to stand trial in court, yet all this may properly happen to the most innocent given probable cause, a warrant, or an indictment. Society has always paid a stiff price for law and order, and peaceful interrogation is not one of the dark moments of the law . . .

In closing this necessarily truncated discussion of policy consid-

---

[7] This need is, of course, what makes so misleading the Court's comparison of a probate judge readily setting aside as involuntary the will of an old lady badgered and beleaguered by the new heirs. With wills, there is no public interest save in a totally free choice; with confessions, the solution of crime is a countervailing gain, however the balance is resolved.

erations attending the new confession rules, some reference must be made to their ironic untimeliness. There is now in progress in this country a massive re-examination of criminal law enforcement procedures on a scale never before witnessed. Participants in this undertaking include a Special Committee of the American Bar Association, under the chairmanship of Chief Judge Lumbard of the Court of Appeals for the Second Circuit; a distinguished study group of the American Law Institute, headed by Professors Vorenberg and Bator of the Harvard Law School; and the President's Commission on Law Enforcement and Administration of Justice, under the leadership of the Attorney General of the United States. Studies are also being conducted by the District of Columbia Crime Commission, the Georgetown Law Center, and by others equipped to do practical research. There are also signs that legislatures in some of the States may be preparing to re-examine the problem before us.

It is no secret that concern has been expressed lest long-range and lasting reforms be frustrated by this Court's too rapid departure from existing constitutional standards. Despite the Court's disclaimer, the practical effect of the decision made today must inevitably be to handicap seriously sound efforts at reform, not least by removing options necessary to a just compromise of competing interests. Of course legislative reform is rarely speedy or unanimous, though this Court has been more patient in the past. But the legislative reforms when they come would have the vast advantage of empirical data and comprehensive study, they would allow experimentation and use of solutions not open to the courts, and they would restore the initiative in criminal law reform to those forums where it truly belongs . . .

In conclusion: Nothing in the letter or the spirit of the Constitution or in the precedents squares with the heavy-handed and one-sided action that is so precipitously taken by the Court in the name of fulfilling its constitutional responsibilities. The foray which the Court makes today brings to mind the wise and farsighted words of Mr. Justice Jackson in *Douglas* v. *Jeannette,* 319 U.S. 157, 181 (separate opinion): "This Court is forever adding new stories to the temples of constitutional law, and the temples have a way of collapsing when one story too many is added."

C

The Relation Between
the State and Federal
Judicial Systems

Fay v. Noia

372 U.S. 391, 448 (1963)

In 1942, Charles Noia, Santo Caminito, and Frank Bonino were jointly tried and convicted of felony murder in a New York state court. Their signed confessions constituted the state's entire case. Caminito and Bonino appealed, and their convictions were affirmed.[1] For reasons that are not entirely clear, Noia did not appeal. Over ten years later, Caminito was discharged by a federal court on a writ of habeas corpus on the ground that his confessions had been obtained in violation of his Fourteenth Amendment rights.[2] Bonino's conviction was then set aside on the same ground by the New York Court of Appeals on a motion by Bonino for reargument of his original appeal.[3] Noia, still in jail, then sought relief in the state court on the ground that his confession also had been unconstitutionally obtained, but the state court refused to reach the merits, holding that "[Noia's] failure to pursue the usual and accepted appellate procedure to gain a review of the conviction does not entitle him later to utilize . . . [a method of collateral attack]. And this is so even though the asserted error or irregularity relates to a violation of constitutional right."[4]

[1] People v. Bonino, People v. Caminito, 291 N.Y. 540, 50 N.E.2d 654.
[2] United States ex rel Caminito v. Murphy, 222 F.2d 698 (2d Cir.).
[3] People v. Bonino, 1 N.Y.2d 752, 135 N.E.2d 51.
[4] People v. Caminito, 3 N.Y.2d 596, 601, 148 N.E.2d 139.

Noia then brought the present petition for a writ of habeas corpus in a federal district court. The state stipulated that Noia's confession was involuntary but urged that Noia's original failure to appeal, which would bar direct Supreme Court review of the conviction, also barred collateral attack in this habeas corpus proceeding. Unhappy as Noia's plight undoubtedly was, the state appeared to be on firm ground. It was established that a petitioner for federal habeas corpus could obtain review of a constitutional claim if his detention by state authorities pursuant to a conviction rested on the state's rejection of that claim on its merits.[5] But the Supreme Court's decisions at least strongly indicated that such review was not available when the state courts had an adequate and independent nonfederal ground—for example, a failure to raise the question properly under state procedural rules—for refusing to consider the claim.[6]

After the federal district court denied Noia relief, the Court of Appeals for the Second Circuit reversed, 2–1, relying heavily on the exceptional circumstances.

The Supreme Court, 6–3, affirmed the decision in Noia's favor, but on considerably broader grounds. Justice Brennan, writing for the Court, held in part that "the doctrine under which state procedural defaults are held to constitute an adequate and independent state law ground barring direct Supreme Court review is not to be extended to limit the power granted the federal courts under the federal habeas statute," and that "Noia's failure to appeal cannot under the circumstances be deemed an intelligent and understanding waiver of his right to appeal such as to justify the withholding of federal habeas corpus relief."

In his dissent, Justice Harlan attacked both of these holdings. The issues presented by this case may seem technical, at least in contrast to the cases that precede it in this volume, but the opinion is included because of the rich insight it affords into the Justice's view of the federal system and the nature of our constitutional government.

Mr. Justice Harlan, whom Mr. Justice Clark and Mr. Justice Stewart join, dissenting.

This decision, both in its abrupt break with the past and in its consequences for the future, is one of the most disquieting that the Court has rendered in a long time.

Section 2241 of the Judicial Code, 28 U.S.C. § 2241, entitled "Power to grant writ," which is part of the federal habeas corpus statute, provides among other things:

---

[5] E.g., Brown v. Allen, 344 U.S. 443.
[6] See, e.g., Daniels v. Allen, 344 U.S. 443, 482–487. Cf. Irvin v. Dowd, 359 U.S. 394.

"(c) The writ of habeas corpus shall not extend to a prisoner unless— . . .

"(3) He is in custody in violation of the Constitution or laws or treaties of the United States."

I dissent from the Court's opinion and judgment for the reason that the federal courts have no *power,* statutory or constitutional, to release the respondent Noia from state detention. This is because his custody by New York does not violate any federal right, since it is pursuant to a conviction whose validity rests upon an adequate and independent state ground which the federal courts are required to respect . . .[7]

The true significance of today's decision can perhaps best be laid bare in terms of a hypothetical case presenting questions of the powers of this Court on direct review, and of a Federal District Court on habeas corpus.

1. *On direct review.*—Assume that a man is indicted, and held for trial in a state court, by a grand jury from which members of his race have been systematically excluded. Assume further that the State requires any objection to the composition of the grand jury to be raised prior to the verdict, that no such objection is made, and that the defendant seeks to raise the point for the first time on appeal from his conviction. If the state appellate court refuses to consider the claim because it was raised too late, and if certiorari is sought and granted, the initial question before this Court will be whether there was an adequate state ground for the judgment below. If the petitioner was represented by counsel not shown to be incompetent, and if the necessary information to make the objection is not shown to have been unavailable at the time of trial, it is certain that the judgment of conviction will stand, despite the fact the indictment was obtained in violation of the petitioner's constitutional rights.

What is the reason for the rule that an adequate and independent state ground of decision bars Supreme Court review of that decision—a rule which, of course, is as applicable to procedural as to substantive grounds? . . .

---

[7] An extended discussion of the history and development of habeas corpus is omitted. The reader is referred to the full opinion, and to the opinion of the majority, for conflicting interpretations of that development. [Ed.]

An examination of the alternatives that might conceivably be followed will, I submit, confirm that the rule is one of constitutional dimensions going to the heart of the division of judicial powers in a federal system.

One alternative to the present rule would be for the Court to review and decide any federal questions in the case, even if the determination of nonfederal questions were adequate to sustain the judgment below, and then to send the case back to the state court for further consideration. But it needs no extended analysis to demonstrate that such action would exceed this Court's powers under Article III. As stated in *Herb* v. *Pitcairn*, 324 U.S. 117, 126:

> Our power is to correct wrong judgments, not to revise opinions. We are not permitted to render an advisory opinion, and if the same judgment would be rendered by the state court after we corrected its views of federal laws, our review could amount to nothing more than an advisory opinion.

Another alternative, which would avoid the problem of advisory opinions, would be to take the entire case and to review on the merits the state court's decision of *every* question in it. For example, in our hypothetical case the Court might consider on its merits the question whether the state court correctly ruled that under state law objections to the composition of the grand jury must be made prior to the verdict.

To a limited extent, of course, this procedural ruling of the state court raises federal as well as state questions. It is clear that a State may not preclude Supreme Court review of federal claims by discriminating against or evading the assertion of a federal right, and indeed that state procedural grounds for refusal to consider a federal claim must rest on a "fair or substantial basis" [*Lawrence* v. *State Tax Comm'n.*, 286 U.S. 276, 282]. Occasionally this means that a state procedural rule which may properly preclude the raising of state claims in a state court cannot thwart review of federal claims in this Court. These principles are inherent in the concept that a state ground, to be of sufficient breadth to support the judgment, must be *both* "adequate" and "independent."

But determination of the adequacy and independence of the state ground, I submit, marks the constitutional limit of our power in this sphere. The reason why this is so was perhaps most articulately expressed in a different but closely related context by Mr. Justice Field in his opinion in *Baltimore & O. R. Co.* v. *Baugh,* 149 U.S. 368, 401. He stated, in a passage quoted with approval by the Court in the historic decision in *Erie R. Co.* v. *Tompkins,* 304 U.S. 64, 78–79:

> The Constitution of the United States . . . recognizes and pre-serves the autonomy and independence of the States—inde-pendence in their legislative and independence in their judicial departments. Supervision over either the legislative or the judicial action of the States is in no case permissible except as to matters by the Constitution specifically authorized or delegated to the United States. Any interference with either, except as thus per-mitted, is an invasion of the authority of the State and, to that extent, a denial of its independence.

For this Court to go beyond the adequacy of the state ground and to review and determine the correctness of that ground on its merits would, in our hypothetical case, be to assume full control over a State's procedures for the administration of its own criminal justice. This is and must be beyond our power if the federal system is to exist in substance as well as form. The right of the State to regulate its own procedures governing the conduct of litigants in its courts, and its interest in supervision of those procedures, stand on the same constitutional plane as its right and interest in framing "substantive" laws governing other aspects of the conduct of those within its borders.

There is still a third possible course this Court might follow if it were to reject the adequate state ground rule. The Act of 1867, which in § 1 extended the habeas corpus jurisdiction to state prisoners detained in violation of federal law, in § 2 gave the Su-preme Court the authority, in cases coming from the state courts, to order execution directly without remanding the case. That authority, which has been exercised at least once, remained unim-paired through the modifications of appellate and certiorari jurisdic-tion, and exists today. Acting pursuant to that authority in our hypothetical case, this Court might grant certiorari, "ignore" the state ground of decision, decide the federal question, and, instead of merely remanding the case, issue a writ requiring the petitioner's release from custody. By this simple device, the Court, it might be argued, would avoid problems of advisory opinions while at the same time refraining from consideration of questions of state law.

But apart from the unseemliness of such a disposition, it is apparent that what the Court would actually be doing would be to decide the state law question *sub silentio* and to reverse the state court judgment on that question. For if the petitioner is detained pursuant to the judgment, and his detention is to be terminated, that must mean that the state ground is not adequate to support the only purpose for which the judgment was rendered. The judgment, in other words, becomes a nullity.

Moreover, the future effect of such a disposition is precisely the same as a reversal on the merits of the question of state law. If noncompliance with a state rule requiring a particular constitutional claim to be raised before verdict does not preclude consideration of the claim by this Court, then the rule is invalid in every significant sense, since no judgment based on its application can ever be effective.

In short, the constitutional infirmities of such a disposition by this Court are the same as those inherent in review of the state question on its merits. The vice, however, is greater because the Court would, in actuality, be invalidating a state rule without even purporting to consider it.

2. *On habeas corpus.*—The adequate state ground doctrine thus finds its source in basic constitutional principles, and the question before us is whether this is as true in a collateral attack in habeas corpus as on direct review. Assume, then, that after dismissal of the writ of certiorari in our hypothetical case, the prisoner seeks habeas corpus in a Federal District Court, again complaining of the composition of the grand jury that indicted him. Is that federal court constitutionally more free than the Supreme Court on direct review to "ignore" the adequate state ground, proceed to the federal question, and order the prisoner's release?

The answer must be that it is not. Of course, as the majority states, a judgment is not a "jurisdictional prerequisite" to a habeas corpus application, but that is wholly irrelevant. The point is that if the applicant is detained *pursuant* to a judgment, termination of the detention necessarily nullifies the judgment. The fact that a District Court on habeas has fewer choices than the Supreme Court, since it can *only* act on the body of the prisoner, does not alter the significance of the exercise of its power. In habeas as on direct review, ordering the prisoner's release invalidates the judgment of conviction and renders ineffective the state rule relied upon to sustain that judgment. Try as the majority does to turn habeas corpus into a roving commission of inquiry into every possible invasion of the applicant's civil rights that may ever have occurred, it cannot divorce the writ from a judgment of conviction if that judgment is the basis of the detention.

Thus in the present case if this Court had granted certiorari to review the State's denial of *coram nobis,* had considered the coerced confession claim, and had ordered Noia's release, the necessary effects of that disposition would have been (1) to set aside the conviction and (2) to invalidate application of the New York rule requiring the claim to be raised on direct appeal in order to be preserved. It is, I think, beyond dispute that the Court does exactly the same thing by affirming the decision below in this case. In doing so, the Court exceeds its constitutional power if in fact the state ground relied upon to sustain the judgment of conviction is an adequate one. The effect of the approach adopted by the Court is, indeed, to do away with the adequate state ground rule entirely in every state case, involving a federal question, in which detention follows from a judgment.

The majority seems to recognize at least some of the consequences of its decision when it attempts to fill the void created by abolition of the adequate state ground rule in state criminal cases. But the substitute it has fashioned—that of "conscious waiver" or "deliberate bypassing" of state procedures—is, as I shall next try to show, wholly unsatisfactory.

Apparently on the basis of a doctrine analogous to that of "unclean hands," the Court states that a federal judge, in his discretion, may deny relief on habeas corpus to one who has understandingly and knowingly refused to avail himself of state procedures. But such a test, if it is meant to constitute a limitation on interference with state administration of criminal justice, falls far short of the mark. In fact, as explained and applied in this case, it amounts to no limitation at all.

First, the Court explains that the test is one calling for the exercise of the district judge's *discretion,* that the judge may, in other words, grant relief even when a conscious waiver has been shown. Thus the Court does not merely tell the States that, if they wish to detain those whom they convict, they must revamp their entire systems of criminal procedures so that no forfeiture may be imposed in the absence of deliberate choice; the States are also warned that even a deliberate, explicit, intelligent choice not to assert a constitutional right may not preclude its assertion on federal habeas.

Second, the Court states (as it must if it is to adhere to its definition) that "[a] choice made by counsel not participated in by the petitioner does not automatically bar relief." It is true that there are cases in which the adequacy of the state ground necessarily turns on the question whether the defendant himself expressly and intelligently waived a constitutional right. Foremost among these are the cases involving right to counsel, for the Court has made it clear that this right cannot be foregone without deliberate choice by the defendant. But to carry this principle over in full force to cases in which a defendant is represented by counsel not shown to be incompetent is to undermine the entire representational system. We have manifested an ever-increasing awareness of the fundamental importance of representation by counsel, and yet today the Court suggests that the State may no more have a rule of forfeiture for one who is competently represented than for one who is not. The effect on state procedural rules may be disastrous.

Third, when it comes to apply the "waiver" test in this case, the Court then in effect reads its own creation out of existence. Recognizing that Noia himself decided not to appeal, and that he apparently made this choice after consultation with counsel, the Court states that his decision was nevertheless not a "waiver." Since a new trial might have resulted in a death sentence, Noia was, in the majority's view, confronted with a "grisly choice," and he quite properly declined to play "Russian roulette" by appealing his conviction.

Does the Court mean by these colorful phrases that it would be unconstitutional for the State to impose a heavier sentence in a second trial for the same offense?[8] Apparently not, since the majority assures us that there may be some cases in which a risk of a

[8] This question, not answered by the majority in Fay v. Noia, was pending before the Court in another case when this volume went to press. See North Carolina v. Pearce, 397 F.2d 253 (4th Cir.), *cert. granted,* 89 S. Ct. 258. [Ed.]

heavier sentence must be run. What distinguishes this case, we are told, is that the risk of the death sentence on a new trial was substantial in view of the trial judge's statement that Noia's past record and his involvement in the crime almost led the judge to disregard the jury's recommendation against a death sentence.

What the Court seems to be saying in this exercise in fine distinctions is that no waiver of a right can be effective if some adverse consequence might reasonably be expected to follow from exercise of that right. Under this approach, of course, there could never be a binding waiver, since only an incompetent would give up a right without any good reason, and an incompetent cannot make an intelligent waiver. The Court wholly ignores the question whether the choice made by the defendant is one that the State could constitutionally require.

Looked at from any angle, the concept of waiver which the Court has created must be found wanting. Of gravest importance, it carries this Court into a sphere in which it has no proper place in the context of the federal system. The true limitations on our constitutional power are those inherent in the rule requiring that a judgment resting on an adequate state ground must be respected . . .

New York asserts that a claim of the kind involved here must be raised on timely appeal if it is to be preserved, and contends that in permitting an appeal it has provided a reasonable opportunity for the claim to be made. The collateral post-conviction writ of *coram nobis*, the State has said, remains a remedy only for the calling up of facts unknown at the time of the judgment. In other words, the State claims that it may constitutionally detain a man pursuant to a judgment of conviction, regardless of any error that may have led to that conviction, if the relevant facts were reasonably available and an appeal was not taken.

Under the circumstances here—particularly the fact that Noia was represented by counsel whose competence is not challenged—is this a reasonable ground for barring collateral assertion of the federal claim? Certainly the State has a vital interest in requiring that appeals be taken on the basis of facts known at the time, since the first assertion of a claim many years later might otherwise require release long after it was feasible to hold a new trial . . .

Moreover, we should be slow to reject—as an invalid barrier to the raising of a federal right—a state determination that one forum rather than another must be resorted to for the assertion of that right. A far more rigid restriction of federal forums was upheld in *Yakus* v. *United States*, 321 U.S. 414. In that case, the Court sustained a federal statute permitting an attack on the validity of an administrative price regulation to be made only on timely review of the administrative order, and precluding the defense of invalidity in a later criminal prosecution for violation of the regulation. What the Court there said bears repetition here:

> No procedural principle is more familiar to this Court than that a constitutional right may be forfeited in criminal as well as civil cases by the failure to make timely assertion of the right before a tribunal having jurisdiction to determine it. 321 U.S. at 444.

But is there some special circumstance here that operates to invalidate the nonfederal ground? Certainly it cannot be that the claim of a coerced confession is of such a nature that a State is constitutionally compelled to permit its assertion at any time even if it could have been, but was not, raised on appeal. Many federal decisions have held that a federal prisoner held pursuant to a federal conviction may not assert such a claim in collateral proceedings when it was not, but could have been, asserted on appeal.

Is it then a basis for invalidating the nonfederal ground that Noia's two codefendants are today free from custody on facts which Noia says are identical to those in his case? Does the nonfederal ground fall when the federal claim appears to have obvious merit? There may be some question whether the facts in Noia's case and those in Bonino's and Caminito's are identical, but assuming that they are, I think it evident that the nonfederal ground must still stand.

Again, there is highly relevant precedent dealing with federal prisoners. In *Sunal* v. *Large*, 332 U.S. 174, Sunal and Kulick had been prosecuted for violation of the Selective Service Act, and both had sought to raise a defense the court had refused to consider. Both were convicted and sentenced to imprisonment but took no appeal, quite evidently because such an appeal would have been to no avail under the existing state of the law. Subsequently, in another case, this Court held on comparable facts that the defense in question must be permitted. *Estep* v. *United States*, 327 U.S. 114. Sunal and Kulick then sought relief on habeas corpus, and this relief was denied. The opinion of the Court observed that there had been no barrier to the perfection of appeals by these prisoners and no facts which were not then known. That an appeal may have appeared futile at the time (indeed, far more futile than was the case here) was held not a sufficient basis for collateral relief. The present case, I submit, would be less troublesome than *Sunal* even had it involved a federal prisoner.

Surely, the state ground is not rendered inadequate because on a new trial for the same offense, Noia might have received the death sentence. The State is well within constitutional limits in permitting such a sentence to be imposed. Of particular relevance here is the decision in *Larson* v. *United States*, 275 F.2d 673. Two criminal defendants had been tried and sentenced to imprisonment by a federal court. One defendant, Juelich, had moved for a continuance or a change of venue, on the ground of community prejudice, and his motion had been denied. Both defendants were convicted; Juelich appealed from his conviction; and the Court of Appeals reversed, *Juelich* v. *United States*, 214 F.2d 950, holding that the constitutional requirement of a fair trial had been violated by the refusal to grant a change of venue or a continuance. Larson, the other defendant, had chosen not to appeal, apparently because he feared that the death sentence might be imposed in a new trial, but after his codefendant's success, he sought collateral relief under § 2255. That relief was denied by the District Court, and the Court of Appeals affirmed, stating:

> We do not say . . . that in every instance, before resort can be had to Section 2255 there must be an appeal. We say only that, in the circumstances of this case, Larson, taking a calculated risk, made a free choice not to jeopardize his life, and he is bound by that decision. . . . Whatever errors there were in his trial were known to Larson and to his counsel—for the same errors formed the basis for Juelich's appeal. Manifest justice to an accused person requires only that he have an opportunity to correct errors that may have led to an unfair trial. The orderly administration of justice requires that even a criminal case some day come to an end. 275 F.2d at 679–680.

This Court denied certiorari. 363 U.S. 849.

Decisions such as *Sunal* and *Larson* are reasoned expressions by the federal judiciary of its views on the fair and proper administration of federal criminal justice. We cannot turn around and tell the State of New York that it is constitutionally prohibited from being governed by the same considerations.

I recognize that Noia's predicament may well be thought one that strongly calls for correction. But the proper course to that end lies with the New York Governor's powers of executive clemency, not with the federal courts. Since Noia is detained pursuant to a state judgment whose validity rests on an adequate and independent state ground, the judgment below should be reversed.

Henry v. *Mississippi*
379 U.S. 443, 457 (1964)

This case is a fascinating sequel to *Fay* v. *Noia* (see above). There the Court held that a state procedural ground adequate to bar direct review of a federal constitutional claim would not bar consideration of the claim in federal habeas corpus. A natural question to ask after *Noia* was whether there might now be some way for the federal claim to be considered on *direct review*, despite the adequate state ground, and the *Henry* case seems addressed to just that question.

Aaron Henry, a Negro civil rights leader, was convicted in a Mississippi state court of disturbing the peace by making indecent proposals to an eighteen-year-old hitchhiker. Certain evidence, which Henry later alleged was the product of an unconstitutional search, was introduced without objection, but the receipt of this evidence was included among the grounds on which Henry's attorneys based a motion for a directed verdict of acquittal. The Mississippi Supreme Court, affirming the conviction, held that the failure to make an objection to the evidence at the time of its introduction at trial barred consideration of the constitutional claim.

In a 5–4 decision, the United States Supreme Court vacated the judgment and remanded the case. Justice Brennan, the author of *Fay* v. *Noia*, spoke for the majority. He strongly suggested that the state procedural ground for refusing to hear the federal claim was not "adequate" under traditional standards to bar direct review. But this point did not need to be reached, he held, because the record suggested that Henry's counsel had "deliberately bypassed the opportunity to make timely objection in the state court." The state courts should have an opportunity to consider this question of waiver and to receive extrinsic evidence, since such a "deliberate choice"

57

of strategy by counsel, unlike other adequate state grounds, would bar consideration of the federal claim on direct review *and* on habeas corpus.[1] Thus state consideration of the waiver point might eliminate the need for further federal litigation.

Justice Harlan filed a dissent for himself and Justices Clark and Stewart.[2] He took issue with the majority's suggestion of inadequacy, bringing his own knowledge of the trial process to bear on the problem, and argued that the real purpose of the decision was to carry one step further the assault on state procedural practices begun in *Fay* v. *Noia*.

Mr. Justice Harlan, with whom Mr. Justice Clark and Mr. Justice Stewart join, dissenting.

Flying banners of federalism, the Court's opinion actually raises storm signals of a most disquieting nature. While purporting to recognize the traditional principle that an adequate procedural, as well as substantive, state ground of decision bars direct review here of any federal claim asserted in the state litigation, the Court, unless I wholly misconceive what is lurking in today's opinion, portends a severe dilution, if not complete abolition, of the concept of "adequacy" as pertaining to state procedural grounds.

In making these preliminary observations I do not believe I am seeing ghosts. For I cannot account for the remand of this case in the face of what is a demonstrably adequate state procedural ground of decision by the Mississippi Supreme Court except as an early step toward extending in one way or another the doctrine of *Fay* v. *Noia*, 372 U.S. 391, to direct review. In that case, decided only two Terms ago, the Court turned its back on history, and did away with the adequate state ground doctrine in federal habeas corpus proceedings.

Believing that any step toward extending *Noia* to direct review should be flushed out and challenged at its earliest appearance in an opinion of this Court, I respectfully dissent.

---

[1] The Court here made it clear that there were at least some occasions—perhaps most—when a decision by counsel not to raise a point would bind the defendant as much as would his own waiver.

[2] Justice Black also dissented, but on a different ground. He argued that while there was no real issue as to waiver, the state ground of decision was inadequate under traditional standards.

I

The Mississippi Supreme Court did not base its ultimate decision upon petitioner's federal claim that his wife's consent could not validate an otherwise improper police search of the family car, but on the procedural ground that petitioner (who was represented by three experienced lawyers) had not objected at the time the fruits of this search were received in evidence. This Court now strongly implies, but does not decide (in view of its remand on the "waiver" issue) that enforcement of the State's "contemporaneous-objection" rule was inadequate as a state ground of decision because the petitioner's motion for a directed verdict of acquittal afforded the trial judge a satisfactory opportunity to take "appropriate corrective action" with reference to the allegedly inadmissible evidence. Thus, it is suggested, this may be a situation where "giving effect to the contemporaneous-objection rule for its own sake 'would be to force resort to an arid ritual of meaningless form.'"

From the standpoint of the realities of the courtroom, I can only regard the Court's analysis as little short of fanciful. The petitioner's motion for a verdict could have provoked one of three courses of action by the trial judge, none of which can reasonably be considered as depriving the State's contemporaneous-objection rule of its capacity to serve as an adequate state ground.

1. The trial judge might have granted the directed verdict. But had this action been appropriate, the Supreme Court of Mississippi, in its first opinion, would have ordered the prosecution dismissed. Since it did not, and the matter is entirely one of state law, further speculation by this Court should be foreclosed.

2. The trial judge might have directed a mistrial. The State's interest in preventing mistrials through the contemporaneous-objection requirement is obvious.

3. The remaining course of action is the example given by the Court; the trial judge could have denied the motion for a directed verdict, but, *sua sponte*, called for elaboration of the argument, determined that the search of the automobile was unconstitutional, and given cautionary instructions to the jury to disregard the inadmissible evidence when the case was submitted to it.

The practical difficulties with this approach are manifestly sufficient to show a substantial state interest in their avoidance, and thus to show an "adequate" basis for the State's adherence to the contemporaneous-objection rule . . .

[*After quoting the defendant's directed verdict motion in full, the opinion continued:*] As every trial lawyer of any experience knows, motions for directed verdicts are generally made as a matter of course at the close of the prosecution's case, and are generally denied without close consideration unless the case is clearly border-line. It is simply unrealistic in this context to have expected the trial judge to pick out the single vague sentence from the directed verdict motion and to have acted upon it with the refined imagination the Court would require of him. Henry's three lawyers apparently regarded the search and seizure claim as make-weight. They had not mentioned it earlier in the trial and gave no explanation for their laxity in raising it. And when they did mention it, they did so in a cursory and conclusional sentence placed in a secondary position in a directed verdict motion. The theory underlying the search and seizure argument—that a wife's freely given permission to search the family car is invalid—is subtle to say the very least, and as the matter was presented to the trial judge it would have been extraordinary had he caught it, or even realized that there was a serious problem to catch. But this is not all the Court would require of him. He must, in addition, realize that despite the inappropriateness of granting the directed verdict requested of him, he could partially serve the cause of the defense by taking it upon himself to frame and give cautionary instructions to the jury to disregard the evidence obtained as fruits of the search.[3]

Contrast with this the situation presented by a contemporaneous objection. The objection must necessarily be directed to the single question of admissibility; the judge must inevitably focus on it; there would be no doubt as to the appropriate form of relief, and the effect of the trial judge's decision would be immediate rather than remote. Usually the proper timing of an objection will force an

[3] Furthermore, even if counsel had fully elaborated the argument and had made it in the context of a motion to strike rather than a motion for directed verdict, the trial judge could properly have exercised his discretion (as the Mississippi Supreme Court did) and denied any relief. This power is recognized in trial judges in the federal system in order to prevent the "ambushing" of a trial through the withholding of an objection that should have been made when questionable evidence was first introduced. Federalism is turned upside down if it is denied to judges in the state systems.

elaboration of it. Had objection been made in this case during the officer's testimony about the search, it would have called forth of its own force the specific answer that the wife had given her permission and, in turn, the assertion that the permission was ineffective. The issue, in short, would have been advertently faced by the trial judge and the likelihood of achieving a correct result maximized.

Thus the state interest which so powerfully supports the contemporaneous-objection rule is that of maximizing correct decisions and concomitantly minimizing errors requiring mistrials and retrials. The alternative for the State is to reverse a trial judge who, from a long motion, fails to pick out and act with remarkable imagination upon a single vague sentence relating to admissibility of evidence long since admitted. A trial judge is a decision-maker, not an advocate. To force him out of his proper role by requiring him to coax out the arguments and imaginatively reframe the requested remedies for the counsel before him is to place upon him more responsibility than a trial judge can be expected to discharge.

There was no "appropriate corrective action" that could have realistically satisfied the purposes of the contemporaneous-objection rule. Without question the State had an interest in maintaining the integrity of its procedure, and thus without doubt reliance on the rule in question is "adequate" to bar direct review of petitioner's federal claim by this Court.

II

The real reason for remanding this case emerges only in the closing pages of the Court's opinion. It is pointed out that even were the contemporaneous-objection rule considered to be an adequate state ground, this would not, under *Fay* v. *Noia*, preclude consideration of Henry's federal claim in federal habeas corpus unless it were made to appear that Henry had deliberately waived his federal claim in the state proceedings. It is then said that in the interest of "efficient administration of criminal justice" and "harmonious" relations between the federal and state judiciaries the Mississippi courts should be given the opportunity to pass, in the first instance, on the waiver issue; the prospect is entertained that such action on the part of this Court will encourage the States to grasp the "opportunity" afforded by *Fay* v. *Noia* and *Townsend* v. *Sain* [372 U.S. 293] by providing "state procedures, direct or collateral, for a full airing of federal claims." It is "suggested" that were this to be done "irritation" and "friction" respecting the exercise of federal habeas corpus power *vis-à-vis* state convictions "might be ameliorated."

What does all this signify? The States are being invited to voluntarily obliterate all state procedures, however conducive they may be to the orderly conduct of litigation, which might thwart state-court consideration of federal claims. But what if the States do not accept the invitation? Despite the Court's soft-spoken assertion that "settled principles" will be applied in the future, I do not think the intimation will be missed by any discerning reader of the Court's opinion that at the least a substantial dilution of the adequate state-ground doctrine may be expected. A contrary prediction is belied by the implication of the opinion that under "settled principles," the contemporaneous-objection rule relied upon in this case could be declared inadequate.

To me this would not be a move toward "harmonious" federalism; any further disrespect for state procedures, no longer cognizable at all in federal habeas corpus, would be the very antithesis of it. While some may say that, given *Fay* v. *Noia*, what the Court is attempting to do is justifiable as a means of promoting "efficiency" in the administration of criminal justice, it is the sort of efficiency which, though perhaps appropriate in some watered-down form of federalism, is not congenial to the kind of federalism I had supposed was ours. I venture to say that to all who believe the federal system as we have known it to be a priceless aspect of our Constitutionalism, the spectre implicit in today's decision will be no less disturbing than what the Court has already done in *Fay* v. *Noia*.

Believing that the judgment below rests on an adequate independent state ground, I would dismiss the writ issued in this case as improvidently granted.[4]

---

[4] For a further illustration of Justice Harlan's concern that the Court is interfering improperly with the operation of state procedural systems, see his dissent in Chapman v. California, 386 U.S. 18, 45. The Court held in this case that the harmlessness of a trial error in a state criminal prosecution must be determined by a rule of federal law when the error involves the denial of a federal constitutional right. [Ed.]

D

Substantive Aspects of Due Process and Equal Protection—Herein of "One Man, One Vote"

Reynolds v. Sims

377 U.S. 533, 589 (1964)

In 1962 the Supreme Court, speaking through Justice Brennan, distinguished a long line of precedents and held that claims of legislative malapportionment are within the competence of the federal courts to adjudicate.[1] Vigorous dissents were filed by Justices Frankfurter and Harlan, with Justice Harlan addressing himself not only to the question of justiciability but also to the merits of the plaintiffs' claim under the equal protection clause of the Fourteenth Amendment. Despite protestations to the contrary, particularly in Justice Stewart's concurring opinion, many saw this decision as the first step toward the announcement of a rule that each vote in each district in a state must, insofar as practicable, be given the same weight as every other vote in that state—that "one man" is constitutionally entitled to "one vote." These predictions were given added impetus in the next two years by the decisions in *Gray* v. *Sanders*,[2] striking down the Georgia county unit system in a case involving elections for statewide office (that of U.S. senator), and *Wesberry* v. *Sanders*,[3] holding that under Article I,

---

[1] Baker v. Carr, 369 U.S. 186.
[2] 372 U.S. 368.
[3] 376 U.S. 1 (see below).

Section 2, of the Constitution,[4] the states must select members in the federal House of Representatives either by elections at large or in districts composed "as nearly as is practicable" of equal population.

Justice Harlan dissented in both these cases, but he did not stop the tide. In *Reynolds* v. *Sims*, a suit challenging Alabama's legislative apportionment, and five other cases decided the same day,[5] the Court held that the legislatures of the six states involved would have to be reapportioned to bring them into conformity with the requirements of the equal protection clause. The governing principle was that each house of a state legislature must be apportioned on a population basis and each member must represent substantially the same number of people. The Chief Justice wrote for a majority of six in each case. Justice Clark, who dissented in the New York and Colorado cases, concurred in the judgments in the other cases on the basis that there was invidious discrimination against some voters resulting from a "crazy quilt" of apportionment. Justice Stewart, who also dissented in the New York and Colorado cases, concurred in the judgment in the Alabama, Delaware, and Virginia cases on the basis of the irrationality of the apportionment, and would have remanded the Maryland case for consideration of the issue whether the Maryland apportionment systematically prevented effective majority rule. Justice Harlan, speaking only for himself, filed a single dissenting opinion applicable to all six cases.

Like Justice Frankfurter,[6] Justice Harlan has been convinced from the outset that this new undertaking by the Court has seriously endangered the federal system and the principle of separation of powers, and his conviction has not diminished as the Court has grown more deeply involved in the electoral process. Though many of the opinions in this line of cases might be chosen as representative of his views, the *Reynolds* dissent is perhaps his most forceful statement.

Mr. Justice Harlan, dissenting.

In these cases the Court holds that seats in the legislatures of six States are apportioned in ways that violate the Federal Constitution. Under the Court's ruling it is bound to follow that the legislatures in all but a few of the other 44 States will meet the same

---

[4] "The House of Representatives shall be composed of Members chosen every second Year by the People of the several States, and the Electors in each State shall have the Qualifications requisite for Electors of the most numerous Branch of the State Legislature."

[5] WMCA, Inc. v. Lomenzo, 377 U.S. 633 (New York); Maryland Committee for Fair Representation v. Tawes, 377 U.S. 656 (Maryland); Davis v. Mann, 377 U.S. 678 (Virginia); Roman v. Sincock, 377 U.S. 695 (Delaware); Lucas v. Forty-Fourth General Assembly, 377 U.S. 713 (Colorado).

[6] See Baker v. Carr, 369 U.S. 186, 266 (dissenting opinion).

fate. These decisions, with *Wesberry* v. *Sanders,* 376 U.S. 1, involving congressional districting by the States, and *Gray* v. *Sanders,* 372 U.S. 368, relating to elections for statewide office, have the effect of placing basic aspects of state political systems under the pervasive overlordship of the federal judiciary. Once again, I must register my protest.

Preliminary Statement

Today's holding is that the Equal Protection Clause of the Fourteenth Amendment requires every State to structure its legislature so that all the members of each house represent substantially the same number of people; other factors may be given play only to the extent that they do not significantly encroach on this basic "population" principle. Whatever may be thought of this holding as a piece of political ideology—and even on that score the political history and practices of this country from its earliest beginnings leave wide room for debate—I think it demonstrable that the Fourteenth Amendment does not impose this political tenet on the States or authorize this Court to do so.

The Court's constitutional discussion, found in its opinion in the Alabama cases, is remarkable . . . for its failure to address itself at all to the Fourteenth Amendment as a whole or to the legislative history of the Amendment pertinent to the matter at hand. Stripped of aphorisms, the Court's argument boils down to the assertion that appellees' right to vote has been invidiously "debased" or "diluted" by systems of apportionment which entitle them to vote for fewer legislators than other voters, an assertion which is tied to the Equal Protection Clause only by the constitutionally frail tautology that "equal" means "equal."

Had the Court paused to probe more deeply into the matter, it would have found that the Equal Protection Clause was never intended to inhibit the States in choosing any democratic method they pleased for the apportionment of their legislatures. This is shown by the language of the Fourteenth Amendment taken as a whole, by the understanding of those who proposed and ratified it, and by the political practices of the States at the time the Amendment was adopted. It is confirmed by numerous state and congressional actions since the adoption of the Fourteenth Amendment, and by the common understanding of the Amendment as evidenced by subsequent constitutional amendments and decisions of this Court before *Baker* v. *Carr* [369 U.S. 186], made an abrupt break with the past in 1962.

The failure of the Court to consider any of these matters cannot be excused or explained by any concept of "developing" constitutionalism. It is meaningless to speak of constitutional "development" when both the language and history of the controlling provisions of the Constitution are wholly ignored. Since it can, I think, be shown beyond doubt that state legislative apportionments, as such, are wholly free of constitutional limitations, save such as may be imposed by the Republican Form of Government Clause (Const., Art. IV, § 4), the Court's action now bringing them within the purview of the Fourteenth Amendment amounts to nothing less than an exercise of the amending power by this Court.

So far as the Federal Constitution is concerned, the complaints in these cases should all have been dismissed below for failure to state a cause of action, because what has been alleged or proved shows no violation of any constitutional right . . .

I

A. *The Language of the Fourteenth Amendment*

The Court relies exclusively on that portion of § 1 of the Fourteenth Amendment which provides that no State shall "deny to any person within its jurisdiction the equal protection of the laws," and disregards entirely the significance of § 2, which reads:

> Representatives shall be apportioned among the several States according to their respective numbers, counting the whole number of persons in each State, excluding Indians not taxed. *But when the right to vote at any election for* the choice of electors for President and Vice President of the United States, Representatives in Congress, *the Executive and Judicial officers of a State, or the members of the Legislature thereof, is denied* to any of the male inhabitants of such State, being twenty-one years of age, and citizens of the United States, *or in any way abridged*, except for participation in rebellion, or other crime, the basis of representation therein shall be reduced in the proportion which the number of such male citizens shall bear to the whole number of male citizens twenty-one years of age in such State. (Emphasis added.)

The Amendment is a single text. It was introduced and discussed as such in the Reconstruction Committee, which reported it to the Congress. It was discussed as a unit in Congress and proposed as a unit to the States, which ratified it as a unit. A proposal to split up the Amendment and submit each section to the States as a separate amendment was rejected by the Senate. Whatever one might take to be the application to these cases of the Equal Protection Clause if it stood alone, I am unable to understand the Court's utter disregard of the second section which expressly recognizes the States' power to deny "or in any way" abridge the right of their inhabitants to vote for "the members of the [State] Legislature," and its express provision of a remedy for such denial or abridgment. The comprehensive scope of the second section and its particular reference to the state legislatures preclude the suggestion that the first section was intended to have the result reached by the Court today. If indeed the words of the Fourteenth Amendment speak for themselves, as the majority's disregard of history seems to imply, they speak as clearly as may be against the construction which the majority puts on them. But we are not limited to the language of the Amendment itself.

B. *Proposal and Ratification of the Amendment*

The history of the adoption of the Fourteenth Amendment provides conclusive evidence that neither those who proposed nor those who ratified the Amendment believed that the Equal Protection Clause limited the power of the States to apportion their legislatures as they saw fit. Moreover, the history demonstrates that the intention to leave this power undisturbed was deliberate and was widely believed to be essential to the adoption of the Amendment . . .[7]

The facts recited above show beyond any possible doubt:

(1) that Congress, with full awareness of and attention to the possibility that the States would not afford full equality in voting rights to all their citizens, nevertheless deliberately chose not to interfere with the States' plenary power in this regard when it proposed the Fourteenth Amendment;

(2) that Congress did not include in the Fourteenth Amendment restrictions on the States' power to control voting rights

[7] The opinion's extensive discussion of the legislative history of the Fourteenth Amendment, and of ratification by the several states, is omitted. The conclusions drawn from that discussion are set forth in the following paragraph. [Ed.]

because it believed that if such restrictions were included, the Amendment would not be adopted; and

(3) that at least a substantial majority, if not all, of the States which ratified the Fourteenth Amendment did not consider that in so doing, they were accepting limitations on their freedom, never before questioned, to regulate voting rights as they chose.

Even if one were to accept the majority's belief that it is proper entirely to disregard the unmistakable implications of the second section of the Amendment in construing the first section, one is confounded by its disregard of all this history. There is here none of the difficulty which may attend the application of basic principles to situations not contemplated or understood when the principles were framed. The problems which concern the Court now were problems when the Amendment was adopted. By the deliberate choice of those responsible for the Amendment, it left those problems untouched.

C. *After 1868*

The years following 1868, far from indicating a developing awareness of the applicability of the Fourteenth Amendment to problems of apportionment, demonstrate precisely the reverse: that the States retained and exercised the power independently to apportion their legislatures . . .

D. *Today*

Since the Court now invalidates the legislative apportionments in six States, and has so far upheld the apportionment in none, it is scarcely necessary to comment on the situation in the States today, which is, of course, as fully contrary to the Court's decision as is the record of every prior period in this Nation's history. As of 1961, the Constitutions of all but 11 States, roughly 20% of the total, recognized bases of apportionment other than geographic spread of population, and to some extent favored sparsely populated areas by a variety of devices, ranging from straight area representation or guaranteed minimum area representation to complicated schemes of the kind exemplified by the provisions of New York's Constitution of 1894, still in effect until struck down by the Court today in No. 20. Since Tennessee, which was the subject of *Baker* v. *Carr,* and

Virginia, scrutinized and disapproved today in No. 69, are among the 11 States whose own Constitutions are sound from the standpoint of the Federal Constitution as construed today, it is evident that the actual practice of the States is even more uniformly than their theory opposed to the Court's view of what is constitutionally permissible.

E. *Other Factors*

In this summary of what the majority ignores, note should be taken of the Fifteenth and Nineteenth Amendments. The former prohibited the States from denying or abridging the right to vote "on account of race, color, or previous condition of servitude." The latter, certified as part of the Constitution in 1920, added sex to the prohibited classifications . . .

If constitutional amendment was the only means by which all men and, later, women, could be guaranteed the right to vote at all, even for *federal* officers, how can it be that the far less obvious right to a particular kind of apportionment of *state* legislatures—a right to which is opposed a far more plausible conflicting interest of the State than the interest which opposes the general right to vote—can be conferred by judicial construction of the Fourteenth Amendment? Yet, unless one takes the highly implausible view that the Fourteenth Amendment controls methods of apportionment but leaves the right to vote itself unprotected, the conclusion is inescapable that the Court has, for purposes of these cases, relegated the Fifteenth and Nineteenth Amendments to the same limbo of constitutional anachronisms to which the second section of the Fourteenth Amendment has been assigned.

Mention should be made finally of the decisions of this Court which are disregarded or, more accurately, silently overruled today . . .

Each of these recent cases is distinguished on some ground or other in *Baker* v. *Carr.* Their summary dispositions prevent consideration whether these after-the-fact distinctions are real or imaginary. The fact remains, however, that between 1947 and 1957, four cases raising issues precisely the same as those decided today were presented to the Court. Three were dismissed because the issues presented were thought insubstantial and in the fourth the lower court's dismissal was affirmed.

I have tried to make the catalogue complete, yet to keep it within the manageable limits of a judicial opinion. In my judgment, today's decisions are refuted by the language of the Amendment which they construe and by the inference fairly to be drawn from subsequently enacted Amendments. They are unequivocally refuted by history and by consistent theory and practice from the time of the adoption of the Fourteenth Amendment until today.

II

The Court's elaboration of its new "constitutional" doctrine indicates how far—and how unwisely—it has strayed from the appropriate bounds of its authority. The consequence of today's decision is that in all but the handful of States which may already satisfy the new requirements the local District Court or, it may be, the state courts, are given blanket authority and the constitutional duty to supervise apportionment of the State Legislatures. It is difficult to imagine a more intolerable and inappropriate interference by the judiciary with the independent legislatures of the States.

In the Alabama cases, the District Court held invalid not only existing provisions of the State Constitution—which this Court lightly dismisses with a wave of the Supremacy Clause and the remark that "it makes no difference whether a State's apportionment scheme is embodied in its constitution or in statutory provisions,"—but also a proposed amendment to the Alabama Constitution which had never been submitted to the voters of Alabama for ratification, and "standby" legislation which was not to become effective unless the amendment was rejected (or declared unconstitutional) and in no event before 1966. Both of these measures had been adopted only nine days before, at an Extraordinary Session of the Alabama Legislature, convened pursuant to what was very nearly a directive of the District Court. The District Court formulated its own plan for the apportionment of the Alabama Legislature, by picking and choosing among the provisions of the legislative measures. Beyond that, the court warned the legislature that there would be still further judicial reapportionment unless the legislature, like it or not, undertook the task for itself. This Court now states that the District Court acted in "a most proper and commendable manner," and approves the District Court's avowed intention of taking "some further action" unless the State Legislature acts by 1966 . . .[8]

Records such as these in the cases decided today are sure to be duplicated in most of the other States if they have not been already. They present a jarring picture of courts threatening to take action in an area which they have no business entering, inevitably on the basis of political judgments which they are incompetent to make. They show legislatures of the States meeting in haste and deliberating and deciding in haste to avoid the threat of judicial interference. So far as I can tell, the Court's only response to this unseemly state of affairs is ponderous insistence that "a denial of constitutionally protected rights demands judicial protection." By thus refusing to recognize the bearing which a potential for conflict of this kind may have on the question whether the claimed rights are in fact constitutionally entitled to judicial protection, the Court assumes, rather than supports, its conclusion.

It should by now be obvious that these cases do not mark the end of reapportionment problems in the courts. Predictions once made that the courts would never have to face the problem of actually working out an apportionment have proved false. This Court, however, continues to avoid the consequences of its decisions, simply assuring us that the lower courts "can and . . . will work out more concrete and specific standards." Deeming it "expedient" not to spell out "precise constitutional tests," the Court contents itself with stating "only a few rather general considerations."

Generalities cannot obscure the cold truth that cases of this type are not amenable to the development of judicial standards. No set of standards can guide a court which has to decide how many legislative districts a State shall have, or what the shape of the districts shall be, or where to draw a particular district line. No judicially manageable standard can determine whether a State should have single-member districts or multimember districts or some combination of both. No such standard can control the balance between keeping up with population shifts and having stable districts. In all these respects, the courts will be called upon to make particular decisions with respect to which a principle of equally populated districts will be of no assistance whatsoever. Quite ob-

---

[8] Similar discussion of the Maryland, Virginia, and Delaware cases is omitted. [Ed.]

viously, there are limitless possibilities for districting consistent with such a principle. Nor can these problems be avoided by judicial reliance on legislative judgments so far as possible. Reshaping or combining one or two districts, or modifying just a few district lines, is no less a matter of choosing among many possible solutions, with varying political consequences, than reapportionment broadside.[9]

The Court ignores all this, saying only that "what is marginally permissible in one State may be unsatisfactory in another, depending on the particular circumstances of the case." It is well to remember that the product of today's decisions will not be readjustment of a few districts in a few States which most glaringly depart from the principle of equally populated districts. It will be a redetermination, extensive in many cases, of legislative districts in all but a few States.

Although the Court—necessarily, as I believe—provides only generalities in elaboration of its main thesis, its opinion nevertheless fully demonstrates how far removed these problems are from fields of judicial competence. Recognizing that "indiscriminate districting" is an invitation to "partisan gerrymandering," the Court nevertheless excludes virtually every basis for the formation of electoral districts other than "indiscriminate districting." In one or another of today's opinions, the Court declares it unconstitutional for a State to give effective consideration to any of the following in establishing legislative districts:

(1) history;

(2) "economic or other sorts of group interests";

(3) area;

(4) geographical considerations;

(5) a desire "to insure effective representation for sparsely settled areas";

(6) "availability of access of citizens to their representatives";

(7) theories of bicameralism (except those approved by the Court);

(8) occupation;

(9) "an attempt to balance urban and rural power";

(10) the preference of a majority of voters in the State.

[9] It is not mere fancy to suppose that in order to avoid problems of this sort, the Court may one day be tempted to hold that all state legislators must be elected in statewide elections.

72

So far as presently appears, the *only* factor which a State may consider, apart from numbers, is political subdivisions. But even "a clearly rational state policy" recognizing this factor is unconstitutional if "population is submerged as the controlling consideration . . ."[10]

I know of no principle of logic or practical or theoretical politics, still less any constitutional principle, which establishes all or any of these exclusions. Certain it is that the Court's opinion does not establish them. So far as the Court says anything at all on this score, it says only that "legislators represent people, not trees or acres"; that "citizens, not history or economic interests, cast votes"; that "people, not land or trees or pastures, vote." All this may be conceded. But it is surely equally obvious, and, in the context of elections, more meaningful to note that people are not ciphers and that legislators can represent their electors only by speaking for their interests—economic, social, political—many of which do reflect the place where the electors live. The Court does not establish, or indeed even attempt to make a case for the proposition that conflicting interests within a State can only be adjusted by disregarding them when voters are grouped for purposes of representation.

Conclusion

With these cases the Court approaches the end of the third round set in motion by the complaint filed in *Baker* v. *Carr*. What is done today deepens my conviction that judicial entry into this realm is profoundly ill-advised and constitutionally impermissible. As I have said before, I believe that the vitality of our political system, on which in the last analysis all else depends, is weakened by reliance on the judiciary for political reform; in time a complacent body politic may result.

These decisions also cut deeply into the fabric of our federalism. What must follow from them may eventually appear to be the product of state legislatures. Nevertheless, no thinking person can fail to recognize that the aftermath of these cases, however desirable it may be thought in itself, will have been achieved at the cost of a radical alteration in the relationship between the States and the Federal Government, more particularly the Federal Judiciary. Only one who has an overbearing impatience with the federal system and

[10] Cf. Swann v. Adams, 385 U.S. 440, decided in 1967. [Ed.]

its political processes will believe that that cost was not too high or was inevitable.

Finally, these decisions give support to a current mistaken view of the Constitution and the constitutional function of this Court. This view, in a nutshell, is that every major social ill in this country can find its cure in some constitutional "principle," and that this Court should "take the lead" in promoting reform when other branches of government fail to act. The Constitution is not a panacea for every blot upon the public welfare, nor should this Court, ordained as a judicial body, be thought of as a general haven for reform movements. The Constitution is an instrument of government, fundamental to which is the premise that in a diffusion of governmental authority lies the greatest promise that this Nation will realize liberty for all its citizens. This Court, limited in function in accordance with that premise, does not serve its high purpose when it exceeds its authority, even to satisfy justified impatience with the slow workings of the political process. For when, in the name of constitutional interpretation, the Court *adds* something to the Constitution that was deliberately excluded from it, the Court in reality substitutes its view of what should be so for the amending process.

I dissent in each of these cases, believing that in none of them have the plaintiffs stated a cause of action . . .[11]

Avery v. Midland County

390 U.S. 474, 486 (1968)

One of the questions left after *Reynolds* v. *Sims* (see above) was whether the principles declared in that case would be applied to units of local government within the states. The Court's ruling in 1967, upholding a procedure for choosing a local school board in a manner that gave certain localities substantially greater per capita representation than others,[1] made

[11] In an excellent study of the reapportionment decisions, the author says of this opinion: "Justice Harlan, in lonely isolation, wrote a fitting epilogue to Justice Frankfurter's monumental dissenting opinion in *Baker* . . . His historical and textual argument is overpowering, all the more so because not rebutted by Chief Justice Warren's opinions for the Court. But like the history he used, his opinion seems destined to become history." R. Dixon, *Democratic Representation* 265 (1968). Among Professor Dixon's principal themes is the inadequacy of mathematical equality in assuring adequate representation of interests. [Ed.]

[1] Sailors v. Board of Education of Kent County, 387 U.S. 105. See also Dusch v. Davis, 387 U.S. 112.

the question a very live one. But a year later, in *Avery,* the Court laid the question to rest, distinguishing the prior case on the basis of "the administrative nature of the area school board's functions and the essentially appointive form of the scheme employed," and holding that:

> The Constitution permits no substantial variation from equal population in drawing districts for units of local government having general governmental powers over the entire geographic area served by the body.

Separate dissenting opinions were filed by Justices Harlan, Stewart, and Fortas. The excerpt from Justice Harlan's dissent included here omits the argument that the case was not within the Court's appellate jurisdiction, and focuses on the Justice's attack upon what he believed to be a far too facile extension of the "one man, one vote" rule below the state level.

Mr. Justice Harlan, dissenting . . .

I consider this decision, which extends the state apportionment rule of *Reynolds* v. *Sims,* 377 U.S. 533, to an estimated 80,000 units of local government throughout the land, both unjustifiable and ill-advised.

I continue to think that these adventures of the Court in the realm of political science are beyond its constitutional powers, for reasons set forth at length in my dissenting opinion in *Reynolds.* However, now that the Court has decided otherwise, judicial self-discipline requires me to follow the political dogma now constitutionally embedded in consequence of that decision. I am not foreclosed, however, from remonstrating against the extension of that decision to new areas of government. At the present juncture I content myself with stating two propositions which, in my view, stand strongly against what is done today. The first is that the "practical necessities" which have been thought by some to justify the profound break with history that was made in 1962 by this Court's decision in *Baker* v. *Carr,* 369 U.S. 186, are not present here. The second is that notwithstanding *Reynolds* the "one man, one vote" ideology does not provide an acceptable formula for structuring local governmental units.

A

The argument most generally heard for justifying the entry of the federal courts into the field of state legislative apportionment is that since state legislatures had widely failed to correct serious malapportionments in their own structure, and since no other means of redress had proved available through the political process, this Court was entitled to step into the picture. While I continue to reject that thesis as furnishing an excuse for the federal judiciary's straying outside its proper constitutional role, and while I continue to believe that it bodes ill for the country and the entire federal judicial system if this Court does not firmly set its face against this loose and short-sighted point of view, the important thing for present purposes is that no such justification can be brought to bear in this instance.

No claim is made in this case that avenues of political redress are not open to correct any malapportionment in elective local governmental units, and it is difficult to envisage how such a situation could arise. Local governments are creatures of the States, and they may be reformed either by the state legislatures, which are now required to be apportioned according to *Reynolds,* or by amendment of state constitutions. In these circumstances, the argument of practical necessity has no force. The Court, then, should withhold its hand until such a supposed necessity does arise, before intruding itself into the business of restructuring local governments across the country.

There is another reason why the Court should at least wait for a suitable period before applying the *Reynolds* dogma to local governments. The administrative feasibility of judicial application of the "one man, one vote" rule to the apportionment even of state legislatures has not yet been demonstrated. A number of significant administrative questions remain unanswered,[2] and the burden on the federal courts has been substantial. When this has thus far been the outcome of applying the rule to 50 state legislatures, it seems most unwise at this time to extend it to some 80,000 units of local government, whose bewildering variety is sure to multiply the problems which have already arisen and to cast further burdens, of imponderable dimension, on the federal courts. I am frankly astonished at the ease with which the Court has proceeded to fasten upon the entire country at its lowest political levels the strong arm of the federal judiciary, let alone a particular political ideology which has been the subject of wide debate and differences from the beginnings of our Nation.

[2] One such question is the extent to which an apportionment may take into account population changes which occur between decennial censuses. Another is the degree of population variation which is constitutionally permissible.

B

There are also convincing functional reasons why the *Reynolds* rule should not apply to local governmental units at all. The effect of *Reynolds* was to read a long debated political theory—that the only permissible basis for the selection of state legislators is election by majority vote within areas which are themselves equal in population—into the United States Constitution, thereby foreclosing the States from experimenting with legislatures rationally formed in other ways. Even assuming that this result could be justified on the state level, because of the substantial identity in form and function of the state legislatures, and because of the asserted practical necessities for federal judicial interference referred to above, the "one man, one vote" theory is surely a hazardous generalization on the local level. As has been noted previously, no "practical necessity" has been asserted to justify application of the rule to local governments. More important, the greater and more varied range of functions performed by local governmental units implies that flexibility in the form of their structure is even more important than at the state level, and that by depriving local governments of this needed adaptability the Court's holding may indeed defeat the very goals of *Reynolds.*

The present case affords one example of why the "one man, one vote" rule is especially inappropriate for local governmental units. The Texas Supreme Court held as a matter of Texas law:

Theoretically, the commissioners court is the governing body of the county and the commissioners represent all the residents, both urban and rural, of the county. But developments during the years have greatly narrowed the scope of the functions of the commissioners court and limited its major responsibilities to the nonurban areas of the county. It has come to pass that the city government . . . is the major concern of the city dwellers and the administration of the affairs of the county is the major concern of the rural dwellers. 406 S.W.2d 422, 428.

Despite the specialized role of the commissioners court, the majority has undertaken to bring it within the ambit of *Reynolds* simply by classifying it as "a unit of local government with general responsibility and power for local affairs." Although this approach is intended to afford "equal protection" to all voters in Midland

County, it would seem that it in fact discriminates against the county's rural inhabitants. The commissioners court, as found by the Texas Supreme Court, performs more functions in the area of the county outside Midland City than it does within the city limits. Therefore, each rural resident has a greater interest in its activities than each city dweller. Yet under the majority's formula the urban residents are to have a dominant voice in the county government, precisely proportional to their numbers, and little or no allowance may be made for the greater stake of the rural inhabitants in the county government.

This problem is not a trivial one and is not confined to Midland County. It stems from the fact that local governments, unlike state governments, are often specialized in function. Application of the *Reynolds* rule to such local governments prevents the adoption of apportionments which take into account the effect of this specialization, and therefore may result in a denial of equal treatment to those upon whom the exercise of the special powers has unequal impact. Under today's decision, the only apparent alternative is to classify the governmental unit as other than "general" in power and responsibility, thereby, presumably, avoiding application of the *Reynolds* rule. Neither outcome satisfies *Reynolds'* avowed purpose: to assure "equality" to all voters. The result also deprives localities of the desirable option of establishing slightly specialized, elective units of government, such as Texas' county commissioners court, and varying the size of the constituencies so as rationally to favor those whom the government affects most. The majority has chosen explicitly to deny local governments this alternative by rejecting even the solution of the Texas Supreme Court, which held that the present county apportionment was impermissible but would have allowed the new apportionment to reflect factors related to the special functions of the county commissioners court, such as "land areas, geography, miles of county roads and taxable values," 406 S.W.2d at 428, as well as population.

Despite the majority's declaration that it is not imposing a "straitjacket" on local governmental units, its solution is likely to have other undesirable "freezing" effects on local government. One readily foreseeable example is in the crucial field of metropolitan government. A common pattern of development in the Nation's urban areas has been for the less affluent citizens to migrate to or remain within the central city, while the more wealthy move to the suburbs and come into the city only to work. The result has been to impose a relatively heavier tax burden upon city taxpayers and to fragmentize governmental services in the metropolitan area. An oft-proposed solution to these problems has been the institution of an integrated government encompassing the entire metropolitan area. In many instances, the suburbs may be included in such a metropolitan unit only by majority vote of the voters in each suburb. As a practical matter, the suburbanites often will be reluctant to join the metropolitan government unless they receive a share in the government proportional to the benefits they bring with them and not merely to their numbers. The city dwellers may be ready to concede this much, in return for the ability to tax the suburbs. Under the majority's pronouncements, however, this rational compromise would be forbidden: the metropolitan government must be apportioned solely on the basis of population if it is a "general" government.

These functional considerations reinforce my belief that the "one man, one vote" rule, which possesses the simplistic defects inherent in any judicially imposed solution of a complex social problem, is entirely inappropriate for determining the form of the country's local governments . . .

Harper v. *Virginia State Board of Elections*
383 U.S. 663, 680 (1966)

Perhaps the most significant constitutional development of recent decades has been the increased willingness of the Court to rely on the equal protection clause of the Fourteenth Amendment as a basis for striking down state substantive laws as well as procedural rules. The apportionment decisions are only one illustration; this case and the *Levy* case, which follows in this collection, are also notable examples.

The shift away from due process and toward equal protection as a basis for sustaining challenges to state action may have several explanations. Certainly the Court is anxious to forget its use of the due process clause before 1937 to strike down so many legislative efforts to alleviate social ills. Perhaps too the concept of equal protection is one that at least appears to rest on objective criteria rather than on the subjective preferences of the particular judge. Whatever the reasons, the development is plain, and is bound to affect the course of future constitutional litigation.

In *Harper*, the Court, speaking through Justice Douglas in a 6–3 decision, relied on the equal protection clause to invalidate a state requirement of payment of a $1.50 poll tax as a qualification for voting in state elections. Justice Black's dissenting opinion attacked reliance on this clause:

> [The Court] seems to be using the old "natural-law-due-process formula" to justify striking down state laws as violations of the Equal Protection Clause . . . [There is not in my opinion any] constitutional support whatever for this Court to use the Equal Protection Clause, as it has today, to write into the Constitution its notions of what it thinks is good governmental policy.

Justice Harlan in his dissent took issue with the majority in strikingly similar terms.

Mr. Justice Harlan, whom Mr. Justice Stewart joins, dissenting.

The final demise of state poll taxes, already totally proscribed by the Twenty-Fourth Amendment with respect to federal elections and abolished by the States themselves in all but four States with respect to state elections, is perhaps in itself not of great moment. But the fact that the *coup de grace* has been administered by this Court instead of being left to the affected States or to the federal political process should be a matter of continuing concern to all interested in maintaining the proper role of this tribunal under our scheme of government.

I do not propose to retread ground covered in my dissents in *Reynolds* v. *Sims*, 377 U.S. 533, 589, and *Carrington* v. *Rash*, 380 U.S. 89, 97, and will proceed on the premise that the Equal Protection Clause of the Fourteenth Amendment now reaches both state apportionment (*Reynolds*) and voter-qualification (*Carrington*) cases. My disagreement with the present decision is that in holding the Virginia poll tax violative of the Equal Protection Clause the Court has departed from long-established standards governing the application of that clause.

The Equal Protection Clause prevents States from arbitrarily treating people differently under their laws. Whether any such differing treatment is to be deemed arbitrary depends on whether or not it reflects an appropriate differentiating classification among those affected; the clause has never been thought to require equal treatment of all persons despite differing circumstances. The test evolved by this Court for determining whether an asserted justifying classification exists is whether such a classification can be deemed to be founded on some rational and otherwise constitutionally permissible state policy. This standard reduces to a minimum the likelihood that the federal judiciary will judge state policies in terms of the individual notions and predilections of its own members, and until recently it has been followed in all kinds of "equal protection" cases.[1]

Reynolds v. *Sims, supra,* among its other breaks with the past, also marked a departure from these traditional and wise principles. Unless its "one man, one vote" thesis of state legislative apportionment is to be attributed to the unsupportable proposition that "Equal Protection" simply means indiscriminate equality, it seems inescapable that what *Reynolds* really reflected was but this Court's own views of how modern American representative government should be run. For it can hardly be thought that no other method of apportionment may be considered rational.

Following *Reynolds* the Court in *Carrington* v. *Rash,* 380 U.S. 89, applied the traditional equal protection standard in striking down a Texas statute disqualifying as voters in state elections certain members of the Armed Forces of the United States. But today in holding unconstitutional state poll taxes and property qualifications for voting and *pro tanto* overruling *Breedlove* v. *Suttles,* 302 U.S. 277, and *Butler* v. *Thompson,* 341 U.S. 937, the Court reverts to the highly subjective judicial approach manifested by *Reynolds.* In substance the Court's analysis of the equal protection issue goes no further than to say that the electoral franchise is "precious" and "fundamental," and to conclude that "to introduce wealth or payment of a fee as a measure of a voter's qualifications is to introduce

[1] I think the somewhat different application of the Equal Protection Clause to racial discrimination cases finds justification in the fact that insofar as that clause may embody a particular value in addition to rationality, the historical origins of the Civil War Amendments might attribute to racial equality this special status.

A similar characterization to indigency as a "neutral fact," irrelevant or suspect for purposes of legislative classification, has never been accepted by this Court. Griffin v. Illinois, 351 U.S. 12, requiring free trial transcripts for indigent appellants, and Douglas v. California, 372 U.S. 353, requiring the appointment of counsel for such appellants, cannot fairly be so interpreted for although reference was made indiscriminately to both equal protection and due process the analysis was cast primarily in terms of the latter . . .

a capricious or irrelevant factor." These are of course captivating phrases, but they are wholly inadequate to satisfy the standard governing adjudication of the equal protection issue: Is there a rational basis for Virginia's poll tax as a voting qualification? I think the answer to that question is undoubtedly "yes."[2]

Property qualifications and poll taxes have been a traditional part of our political structure. In the Colonies the franchise was generally a restricted one. Over the years these and other restrictions were gradually lifted, primarily because popular theories of political representation had changed. Often restrictions were lifted only after wide public debate. The issue of woman suffrage, for example, raised questions of family relationships, of participation in public affairs, of the very nature of the type of society in which Americans wished to live; eventually a consensus was reached, which culminated in the Nineteenth Amendment no more than 45 years ago.

Similarly with property qualifications, it is only by fiat that it can be said, especially in the context of American history, that there can be no rational debate as to their advisability. Most of the early Colonies had them; many of the States have had them during much of their histories; and, whether one agrees or not, arguments have been and still can be made in favor of them. For example, it is certainly a rational argument that payment of some minimal poll tax promotes civic responsibility, weeding out those who do not care enough about public affairs to pay $1.50 or thereabouts a year for the exercise of the franchise. It is also arguable, indeed it was probably accepted as sound political theory by a large percentage of Americans through most of our history, that people with some property have a deeper stake in community affairs, and are consequently more responsible, more educated, more knowledgeable, more worthy of confidence, than those without means, and that the

---

[2] I have no doubt that poll taxes that deny the right to vote on the basis of race or color violate the Fifteenth Amendment and can be struck down by this Court. That question is presented to us in Butts v. Harrison, No. 655, the companion case decided today. The Virginia poll tax is on its face applicable to all citizens, and there was no allegation that it was discriminatorily enforced. The District court explicitly found "no racial discrimination . . . in its application as a condition to voting." 240 F.Supp. 270, 271. Appellant in *Butts, supra,* argued first, that the Virginia Constitutional Convention of 1902, which framed the poll-tax provision, was guided by a desire to reduce Negro suffrage, and second, that because of the generally lower economic standard of Negroes as contrasted with whites in Virginia the tax does in fact operate as a significant obstacle to voting by Negroes. The Court does not deal with this Fifteenth Amendment argument, and it suffices for me to say that on the record here I do not believe that the factors alluded to are sufficient to invalidate this $1.50 tax whether under the Fourteenth or Fifteenth Amendment.

community and nation would be better managed if the franchise were restricted to such citizens.[3] Nondiscriminatory and fairly applied literacy tests, upheld by this Court in *Lassiter* v. *Northampton Election Board*, 360 U.S. 45, find justification on very similar grounds.

These viewpoints, to be sure, ring hollow on most contemporary ears. Their lack of acceptance today is evidenced by the fact that nearly all of the States, left to their own devices, have eliminated property or poll-tax qualifications; by the cognate fact that Congress and three-quarters of the States quickly ratified the Twenty-Fourth Amendment; and by the fact that rules such as the "pauper exclusion" in Virginia law, Va. Const. § 23, Va. Code § 24–18, have never been enforced.

Property and poll-tax qualifications, very simply, are not in accord with current egalitarian notions of how a modern democracy should be organized. It is of course entirely fitting that legislatures should modify the law to reflect such changes in popular attitudes. However, it is all wrong, in my view, for the Court to adopt the political doctrines popularly accepted at a particular moment of our history and to declare all others to be irrational and invidious, barring them from the range of choice by reasonably minded people acting through the political process. It was not too long ago that Mr. Justice Holmes felt impelled to remind the Court that the Due Process Clause of the Fourteenth Amendment does not enact the *laissez-faire* theory of society, *Lochner* v. *New York*, 198 U.S. 45, 75–76. The times have changed, and perhaps it is appropriate to observe that neither does the Equal Protection Clause of that Amendment rigidly impose upon America an ideology of unrestrained egalitarianism.[4]

I would affirm the decision of the District Court.

[3] At the Constitutional Convention, for example, there was some sentiment to prescribe a freehold qualification for federal elections under Art. IV, § 1. The proposed amendment was defeated, in part because it was thought suffrage qualifications were best left to the States. See II *Records of the Federal Convention* 201–210 (Farrand ed. 1911). Madison's views were expressed as follows: "Whether the Constitutional qualification ought to be a freehold, would with him depend much on the probable reception such a change would meet with in States where the right was now exercised by every description of people. In several of the States a freehold was now the qualification. Viewing the subject in its merits alone, the freeholders of the Country would be the safest depositories of Republican liberty." *Id.* at 203.

[4] In Shapiro v. Thompson, 89 S.Ct. 1322, 1342, decided in 1969, the Justice sharply dissented from a judgment holding invalid under the equal protection clause state laws conditioning welfare assistance on one-year state residence. "Resurgence of the expansive view of 'equal protection,' " he said, "carries the seeds of more judicial interference with the State and federal legislative process." Id. at 1354. [Ed.]

Levy v. Louisiana

391 U.S. 68, 76 (1968)

A Louisiana statute permits actions for wrongful death to be brought by certain surviving relatives.[1] This statute had been construed by Louisiana's courts not to permit an action by an unacknowledged illegitimate child for the wrongful death of a parent, or to permit an action by the parent for the wrongful death of such a child. In *Levy* and a companion case, *Glona* v. *American Guarantee & Liability Ins. Co.*,[2] both limitations were declared to be invalid under the equal protection clause.

Justice Douglas, writing for the Court, upheld the illegitimate child's right to sue by starting with the indisputable premise that even a bastard is a "person" within the meaning of the Fourteenth Amendment and then concluding with almost blinding speed that the distinction between legitimate and illegitimate children was "invidious." On the right of the parent of an illegitimate child to bring suit, Justice Douglas was unable to find any rational basis for the state's exclusion:

> A law which creates an open season on illegitimates in the area of automobile accidents gives a windfall to tortfeasors. But it hardly has a causal connection with the "sin" which is, we are told, the historic reason for the creation of the disability.

Justice Harlan dissented in both cases. His opinion, joined by Justices Black and Stewart, combines grace and style with an instinct for the jugular. The forcefulness of the dissent is particularly striking in view of the inherent appeal of the result reached by the majority.

Mr. Justice Harlan, whom Mr. Justice Black and Mr. Justice Stewart join, dissenting.

These decisions can only be classed as constitutional curiosities.

At common law, no person had a legally cognizable interest in the wrongful death of another person, and no person could inherit the personal right of another to recover for tortious injuries to his body. By statute, Louisiana has created both rights in favor of certain classes of persons. The question in these cases is whether the way in which Louisiana has defined the classes of persons who

---

[1] La. Civ. Code Ann. Art. 2315.
[2] 391 U.S. 73.

may recover is constitutionally permissible. The Court has reached a negative answer to this question by a process that can only be described as brute force.

One important reason why recovery for wrongful death had everywhere to await statutory delineation is that the interest one person has in the life of another is inherently intractable. Rather than hear offers of proof of love and affection and economic dependence from every person who might think or claim that the bell had tolled for him, the courts stayed their hands pending legislative action. Legislatures, responding to the same diffuseness of interests, generally defined classes of proper plaintiffs by highly arbitrary lines based on family relationships, excluding issues concerning the actual effect of the death on the plaintiff.

Louisiana has followed the traditional pattern. There the actions lie in favor of the surviving spouse and children of the deceased, if any; if none, then in favor of the surviving parents of the deceased, if any; if none, then in favor of the deceased's brothers and sisters, if any; if none, then no action lies. According to this scheme, a grown man may sue for the wrongful death of parents he did not love,[3] even if the death relieves him of a great economic burden or entitles him to a large inheritance. But an employee who loses a job because of the death of his employer has no cause of action, and a minor child cared for by neighbors or relatives "as if he were their own son" does not therefore have a right to sue for their death. Perhaps most dramatic, a surviving parent, for example, of a Louisiana deceased may sue if and only if there is no surviving spouse or child: it does not matter who loved or depended on whom, or what the economic situation of any survivor may be, or even whether the spouse or child elects to sue.[4] In short, the whole scheme of the Louisiana wrongful death statute, which is similar

[3] He may even, like Shakespeare's Edmund, have spent his life contriving treachery against his family. Supposing that the Bard had any views on the law of legitimacy, they might more easily be discerned from Edmund's character than from the words he utters in defense of the only thing he cares for, himself. [The reference in this footnote was an answer to the majority's quotation from Edmund's speech in Shakespeare's *King Lear*, Act I, Scene ii: "Why bastard, wherefore base? When my dimensions are as well compact, my mind as generous, and my shape as true."]

[4] The court speaks in *Levy* of tortfeasors going free. However, the deceased in that case left a legitimate parent. Under the Court's opinion, the right of legitimate and perhaps dependent parents to sue will henceforth be cut off by the mere existence of an illegitimate child, though the child be a self-supporting adult, and though the child elect not to sue . . .

in this respect to that of most other States, makes everything the Court says about affection and nurture and dependence altogether irrelevant. The only question in any case is whether the plaintiff falls within the classes of persons to whom the State has accorded a right of action for the death of another.

Louisiana has chosen, as have most other States in one respect or another, to define these classes of proper plaintiffs in terms of their legal rather than their biological relation to the deceased. A man may recover for the death of his wife, whether he loved her or not, but may not recover for the death of his paramour. A child may recover for the death of his adopted parents. An illegitimate may recover for the wrongful death of a parent who has taken a few hours to acknowledge him formally, but not for the death of a person who he claims is his parent but who has not acknowledged him. A parent may recover for the death of an illegitimate child he has acknowledged, but not for the death of an illegitimate child whom he did not bother to acknowledge until the possibility of tort recovery arose.

The Court today, for some reason which I am at a loss to understand, rules that the State must base its arbitrary definition of the plaintiff class on biological rather than legal relationships. Exactly how this makes the Louisiana scheme even marginally more "rational" is not clear, for neither a biological relationship nor legal acknowledgment is indicative of the love or economic dependence that may exist between two persons. It is, frankly, preposterous to suggest that the State has made illegitimates into "nonpersons," or that, by analogy with what Louisiana has done here it might deny illegitimates constitutional rights or the benefits of doing business in corporate form.[5] The rights at issue here stem from the existence of a family relationship, and the State has decided only that it will not recognize the family relationship unless the formalities of marriage, or of the acknowledgment of children by the parent in question, have been complied with.

There is obvious justification for this decision. If it be conceded, as I assume it is, that the State has power to provide that people who choose to live together should go through the formalities of

[5] A more obvious analogy from the law of corporations than the rather farfetched example the Court has suggested is the elementary rule that the benefits of doing business in corporate form may be denied, to the willful, the negligent, and the innocent alike, if the formalities of incorporation have not been properly complied with.

marriage and, in default, that people who bear children should acknowledge them, it is logical to enforce these requirements by declaring that the general class of rights that are dependent upon family relationships shall be accorded only when the formalities as well as the biology of those relationships are present. Moreover, and for many of the same reasons why a State is empowered to require formalities in the first place, a State may choose to simplify a particular proceeding by reliance on formal papers rather than a contest of proof.[6] That suits for wrongful death, actions to determine the heirs of intestates, and the like, must as a constitutional matter deal with every claim of biological paternity or maternity on its merits is an exceedingly odd proposition.

The Equal Protection Clause states a complex and difficult principle. Certain classifications are "inherently suspect," which I take to mean that any reliance upon them in differentiating legal rights requires very strong affirmative justification. The difference between a child who has been formally acknowledged and one who has not is hardly one of these. Other classifications are impermissible because they bear no intelligible proper relation to the consequences that are made to flow from them. This does not mean that any classification this Court thinks could be better drawn is unconstitutional. But even if the power of this Court to improve on the lines that Congress and the States have drawn were very much broader than I consider it to be, I could not understand why a State which bases the right to recover for wrongful death strictly on family relationships could not demand that those relationships be formalized.

I would affirm the decisions of the state court and the Court of Appeals for the Fifth Circuit.[7]

---

[6]Even where liability arises under a federal statute defining rights in terms of a family relationship to the deceased, federal courts have generally looked to the law and the formalities of the appropriate State . . . In De Sylva v. Ballentine, 351 U.S. 570, arising under the Copyright Act, 61 Stat. 652, 17 U.S.C. § 1 *et seq.*, we held that the word "children" in § 24 of that federal statute should be defined by reference to California law; California law provided that an illegitimate who had been acknowledged in writing by his father could inherit from him; since the illegitimate involved in *De Sylva* had been acknowledged, we held he was included within the statutory term. Two justices, concurring in the unanimous result, argued that it was not proper to look to state law for a definition of the federal statutory term "children." Nowhere, however, was it suggested that we look to the Constitution . . .

[7] A number of cases have been argued before the Court by the Justice's former law clerks. *Levy* and *Gault* (see above), both argued for the prevailing party by Norman Dorsen, are the only ones in the present volume. [Ed.]

Poe v. *Ullman*

367 U.S. 497, 522 (1961)

Connecticut statutes on the books since 1879 made it a crime for any person to use any contraceptive drug or device or to be an accessory to such a use. Only one criminal prosecution had been brought under this law up to the time of *Poe*.[1] In that action the state courts had upheld the constitutionality of the law, and the prosecution had then been discontinued. The present case consisted of three declaratory judgment suits—two by certain married persons (using fictitious names) who alleged that the statutes prevented them from receiving medical advice on birth control, and the third by Dr. C. Lee Buxton, alleging his inability to give advice because of the statute. The suits were brought against Abraham Ullman, a state's attorney, in a state court. The plaintiffs, who were seeking a declaration of the invalidity of the statutes, appealed to the Supreme Court from state court determinations sustaining demurrers to the complaints.

The Supreme Court, 5–4, dismissed the appeals. Justice Frankfurter, writing for himself and three others, voted to dismiss on the ground that there was no justiciable controversy—the fact of only one prosecution in all the years the statute had been in effect indicated a lack of "the immediacy which is an indispensable condition of constitutional adjudication." Justice Brennan concurred, saying that there was no "real and substantial controversy" in view of the indications that the state was interested only in preventing the opening of birth control clinics on a large scale.

Justices Black, Stewart, Douglas, and Harlan noted their dissents separately. While the first two did not reach the merits, the last two did, and both argued that the statute was unconstitutional.

A reading of Justice Harlan's dissent is indispensable to a full understanding of his judicial philosophy. While it demonstrates great respect for the principles of justiciability and of deference to state legislative judgments, it reveals with equal clarity an impatience with what he regarded as a labored refusal to reach the merits, as well as a willingness to strike out in new directions in constitutional litigation. The opinion is thus perhaps the best illustration of the measured boldness of the Justice's view of the role of the Court.

The length of the dissent has required extensive editing in order to bring it within the limits necessitated by this volume, but it is hoped that the essence of the Justice's line of argument has been retained.

[1] State v. Nelson, 126 Conn. 412, 11 A.2d 856.

Mr. Justice Harlan, dissenting.

I am compelled, with all respect, to dissent from the dismissal of these appeals. In my view the course which the Court has taken does violence to established concepts of "justiciability," and unjustifiably leaves these appellants under the threat of unconstitutional prosecution . . .

In my view of these cases a present determination of the Constitutional issues is the only course which will advance justice, and I can find no sound reason born of considerations as to the possible inadequacy or ineffectiveness of the judgment that might be rendered which justifies the Court's contrary disposition. While ordinarily I would not deem it appropriate to deal, in dissent, with Constitutional issues which the Court has not reached, I shall do so here because such issues, as I see things, are entangled with the Court's conclusion as to the nonjusticiability of these appeals.

Justiciability

There can be no quarrel with the plurality opinion's statement that "Justiciability is of course not a legal concept with a fixed content or susceptible of scientific verification," but, with deference, the fact that justiciability is not precisely definable does not make it ineffable. Although a large number of cases are brought to bear on the conclusion that is reached, I think it is fairly demonstrable that the authorities fall far short of compelling dismissal of these appeals. Even so, it is suggested that the cases do point the way to a "rigorous insistence on exigent adversity" and a "policy against premature constitutional decision," which properly understood does indeed demand that result.

The policy referred to is one to which I unreservedly subscribe. Without undertaking to be definitive, I would suppose it is a policy the wisdom of which is woven of several strands: (1) Due regard for the fact that the source of the Court's power lies ultimately in its duty to decide, in conformity with the Constitution, the particular controversies which come to it, and does not arise from some generalized power of supervision over state and national legislatures; (2) therefore it should insist that litigants bring to the Court interests and rights which require present recognition and controversies demanding immediate resolution; (3) also it follows that the controversy must be one which is in truth and fact the litigant's own, so that the clash of adversary contest which is needed to sharpen and illuminate issues is present and gives that aid on which our adjudicatory system has come to rely; (4) finally, it is required that other means of redress for the particular right claimed be unavailable, so that the process of the Court may not become overburdened and conflicts with other courts or departments of government may not needlessly be created, which might come about if either those truly affected are not the ones demanding relief, or if the relief we can give is not truly needed . . .

The precise failing in these proceedings which is said to justify refusal to exercise our mandatory appellate jurisdiction [is] that there has been but one recorded Connecticut case dealing with a *prosecution* under the statute. The significance of this lack of recorded evidence of prosecutions is said to make the presentation of appellants' rights too remote, too contingent, too hypothetical for adjudication in the light of the policies already considered. In my view it is only as a result of misconceptions both about the purport of the record before us and about the nature of the rights appellants put forward that this conclusion can be reached.

As far as the record is concerned, I think it is pure conjecture, and indeed conjecture which to me seems contrary to realities, that an open violation of the statute by a doctor (or more obviously still by a birth-control clinic) would not result in a substantial threat of prosecution. Crucial to the opposite conclusion is the description of the 1940 prosecution instituted in *State* v. *Nelson*, 126 Conn. 412, 11 A.2d 856, as a "test case" which, as it is viewed, scarcely even punctuates the uniform state practice of nonenforcement of this statute. I read the history of Connecticut enforcement in a very different light. The *Nelson* case, as appears from the state court's opinion, was a prosecution of two doctors and a nurse for aiding and abetting violations of this statute by married women in prescribing and advising the use of contraceptive materials by them. It is true that there is evidence of a customary unwillingness to enforce the statute prior to *Nelson*, for in that case the prosecutor stated to the trial court in a later motion to discontinue the prosecutions that "When this Waterbury clinic [operated by the defendants] was opened there were in open operation elsewhere in the State at least eight other contraceptive clinics which had been in existence for a long period of time and no questions as to their right to operate had been raised . . ."

What must also be noted is that the prosecutor followed this statement with an explanation that the primary purpose of the prosecution was to provide clear warning to all those who, like Nelson, might rely on this practice of nonenforcement . . . Thus the respect in which *Nelson* was a test case is only that it was brought for the purpose of making entirely clear the State's power and willingness to enforce against "*any* person, whether a physician or layman" (emphasis supplied), the statute and to eliminate from future cases the very doubt about the existence of these elements which had resulted in eight open birth-control clinics, and which would have made unfair the conviction of Nelson.

The plurality opinion now finds, and the concurring opinion must assume, that the only explanation of the absence of recorded prosecutions subsequent to the *Nelson* case is that Connecticut has renounced that intention to prosecute and punish "*any* person . . . in accordance with the literal provisions of the law" which it announced in *Nelson*. But if renunciation of the purposes of the *Nelson* prosecution is consistent with a lack of subsequent prosecutions, success of that purpose is no less consistent with this lack. I find it difficult to believe that doctors generally—and not just those operating specialized clinics—would continue openly to disseminate advice about contraceptives after *Nelson* in reliance on the State's supposed unwillingness to prosecute, or to consider that high-minded members of the profession would in consequence of such inaction deem themselves warranted in disrespecting this law so long as it is on the books. Nor can I regard as "chimerical" the fear of enforcement of these provisions that seems to have caused the disappearance of at least nine birth-control clinics. In short, I fear that the Court has indulged in a bit of sleight of hand to be rid of this case. It has treated the significance of the absence of prosecutions during the twenty years since *Nelson* as identical with that of the absence of prosecutions during the years before *Nelson*. It has ignored the fact that the very purpose of the *Nelson* prosecution was to change defiance into compliance. It has ignored the very possibility that this purpose may have been successful.[2] The result is to postulate a security from prosecution for open defiance of the statute which I do not believe the record supports . . .

But even if Dr. Buxton were not in the litigation and appellants the Poes and Doe were seeking simply to use contraceptives without any need of consulting a physician beforehand—which is not the case we have, although it is the case which the plurality opinion of the Court is primarily concerned to discuss—even then I think that it misconceives the concept of justiciability and the nature of these appellants' rights to say that the failure of the State to carry through any criminal prosecution requires dismissal of their appeals.

The Court's disposition assumes that to decide the case now, in the absence of any consummated prosecutions, is unwise because it forces a difficult decision in advance of any exigent necessity therefor. Of course it is abundantly clear that this requisite necessity can exist prior to any actual prosecution, for that is the theory of anticipatory relief, and is by now familiar law. What must be relied on, therefore, is that the historical absence of prosecutions in some way leaves these appellants free to violate the statute without fear of prosecution, whether or not the law is Constitutional, and thus absolves us from the duty of deciding if it is. Despite the suggestion of a "tougher and truer law" of immunity from criminal prosecution and despite speculation as to a "tacit agreement" that this law will not be enforced, there is, of course, no suggestion of an estoppel against the State if it should attempt to prosecute appellants. Neither the plurality nor the concurring opinion suggests that appellants have some legally cognizable right not to be prosecuted if the statute is Constitutional. What is meant is simply that the appellants are more or less free to act without fear of prosecution because the prosecuting authorities of the State, in their discretion and at their whim, are, as a matter of prediction, unlikely to decide to prosecute.

---

[2] . . . The strong implication of the concurring opinion that a suit for anticipatory relief brought by a birth-control clinic (though it would raise no different issues and present a record no less "skimpy") would succeed in invoking our jurisdiction where these suits fail, exposes the fallacy underlying the Court's disposition: the unprecedented doctrine that a suit for anticipatory relief will be entertained at the instance of one who is forced to violate a statute flagrantly, but not at the urging of one who may violate it surreptitiously with a high probability of avoiding detection.

Here is the core of my disagreement with the present disposition. As I will develop later in this opinion, the most substantial claim which these married persons press is their right to enjoy the privacy of their marital relations free of the enquiry of the criminal law, whether it be in a prosecution of them or of a doctor whom they have consulted. And I cannot agree that their enjoyment of this privacy is not substantially impinged upon, when they are told that if they use contraceptives, indeed whether they do so or not, the only thing which stands between them and being forced to render criminal account of their marital privacy is the whim of the prosecutor. Connecticut's highest court has told us in the clearest terms that, given proof, the prosecutor will succeed if he decides to bring a proceeding against one of the appellants for taking the precise actions appellants have announced they intend to take . . . All that stands between the appellants and jail is the legally unfettered whim of the prosecutor and the Constitutional issue this Court today refuses to decide . . .

Constitutionality

I consider that this Connecticut legislation, as construed to apply to these appellants, violates the Fourteenth Amendment. I believe that a statute making it a criminal offense for *married couples* to use contraceptives is an intolerable and unjustifiable invasion of privacy in the conduct of the most intimate concerns of an individual's personal life. I reach this conclusion, even though I find it difficult and unnecessary at this juncture to accept appellants' other argument that the judgment of policy behind the statute, so applied, is so arbitrary and unreasonable as to render the enactment invalid for that reason alone. Since both the contentions draw their basis from no explicit language of the Constitution, and have yet to find expression in any decision of this Court, I feel it desirable at the outset to state the framework of Constitutional principles in which I think the issue must be judged.

I

In reviewing state legislation, whether considered to be in the exercise of the State's police powers, or in provision for the health, safety, morals, or welfare of its people, it is clear that what is

93

concerned are "the powers of government inherent in every sovereignty." *The License Cases*, 5 How. 504, 583. Only to the extent that the Constitution so requires may this Court interfere with the exercise of this plenary power of government. But precisely because it is the Constitution alone which warrants judicial interference in sovereign operations of the State, the basis of judgment as to the Constitutionality of state action must be a rational one, approaching the text which is the only commission for our power not in a literalistic way, as if we had a tax statute before us, but as the basic charter of our society, setting out in spare but meaningful terms the principles of government. But as inescapable as is the rational process in Constitutional adjudication in general, nowhere is it more so than in giving meaning to the prohibitions of the Fourteenth Amendment and, where the Federal Government is involved, the Fifth Amendment, against the deprivation of life, liberty or property without due process of law . . .

Were due process merely a procedural safeguard it would fail to reach those situations where the deprivation of life, liberty, or property was accomplished by legislation which by operating in the future could, given even the fairest possible procedure in application to individuals, nevertheless destroy the enjoyment of all three. Thus the guaranties of due process, though having their roots in Magna Carta's *"per legem terrae"* and considered as procedural safeguards "against executive usurpation and tyranny," have in this country "become bulwarks also against arbitrary legislation." *Hurtado* v. *California,* 110 U.S. 516 at 532.

However it is not the particular enumeration of rights in the first eight Amendments which spells out the reach of Fourteenth Amendment due process, but rather, as was suggested in another context long before the adoption of that Amendment, those concepts which are considered to embrace those rights "which are . . . *fundamental; which belong . . . to the citizens of all free governments," Corfield* v. *Coryell,* 4 Wash. C.C. 371, 380, for "the purposes [of securing] which men enter into society," *Calder* v. *Bull,* 3 Dall. 386, 388. Again and again this Court has resisted the notion that the Fourteenth Amendment is no more than a shorthand reference to what is explicitly set out elsewhere in the Bill of Rights. Indeed the fact that an identical provision limiting federal action is found among the first eight Amendments, applying to the Federal Government, suggests that due process is a discrete concept which subsists as an independent guaranty of liberty and procedural fairness, more general and inclusive than the specific prohibitions.

Due process has not been reduced to any formula; its content cannot be determined by reference to any code. The best that can be said is that through the course of this Court's decisions it has represented the balance which our Nation, built upon postulates of respect for the liberty of the individual, has struck between that liberty and the demands of organized society. If the supplying of content to this Constitutional concept has of necessity been a rational process, it certainly has not been one where judges have felt free to roam where unguided speculation might take them. The balance of which I speak is the balance struck by this country, having regard to what history teaches are the traditions from which it developed as well as the traditions from which it broke. That tradition is a living thing. A decision of this Court which radically departs from it could not long survive, while a decision which builds on what has survived is likely to be sound. No formula could serve as a substitute, in this area, for judgment and restraint . . .

Each new claim to Constitutional protection must be considered against a background of Constitutional purposes, as they have been rationally perceived and historically developed. Though we exercise limited and sharply restrained judgment, yet there is no "mechanical yardstick," no "mechanical answer." The decision of an apparently novel claim must depend on grounds which follow closely on well-accepted principles and criteria. The new decision must take "its place in relation to what went before and further [cut] a channel for what is to come." *Irvine* v. *California*, 347 U.S. 128, 147 (dissenting opinion). The matter was well put in *Rochin* v. *California*, 342 U.S. 165, 170–171:

> The vague contours of the Due Process Clause do not leave judges at large. We may not draw on our merely personal and private notions and disregard the limits that bind judges in their judicial function. Even though the concept of due process of law is not final and fixed, these limits are derived from considerations that are fused in the whole nature of our judicial process . . . These are considerations deeply rooted in reason and in the compelling traditions of the legal profession.

On these premises I turn to the particular Constitutional claim in this case.

II

Appellants contend that the Connecticut statute deprives them, as it unquestionably does, of a substantial measure of liberty in carrying on the most intimate of all personal relationships, and that it does so arbitrarily and without any rational, justifying purpose. The State, on the other hand, asserts that it is acting to protect the moral welfare of its citizenry, both directly, in that it considers the practice of contraception immoral in itself, and instrumentally, in that the availability of contraceptive materials tends to minimize "the disastrous consequence of dissolute action," that is fornication and adultery.

It is argued by appellants that the judgment, implicit in this statute—that the use of contraceptives by married couples is immoral—is an irrational one, that in effect it subjects them in a very important matter to the arbitrary whim of the legislature, and that it does so for no good purpose. Where, as here, we are dealing with what must be considered "a basic liberty," cf. *Skinner* v. *Oklahoma* [316 U.S. 535] at 541, "There are limits to the extent to which the presumption of constitutionality can be pressed," *id.* at 544 (concurring opinion), and the mere assertion that the action of the State finds justification in the controversial realm of morals cannot justify alone any and every restriction it imposes.

Yet the very inclusion of the category of morality among state concerns indicates that society is not limited in its objects only to the physical well-being of the community, but has traditionally concerned itself with the moral soundness of its people as well. Indeed to attempt a line between public behavior and that which is purely consensual or solitary would be to withdraw from community concern a range of subjects with which every society in civilized times has found it necessary to deal. The laws regarding marriage which provide both when the sexual powers may be used and the legal and societal context in which children are born and brought up, as well as laws forbidding adultery, fornication and homosexual practices which express the negative of the proposition, confining sexuality to lawful marriage, form a pattern so deeply pressed into the substance of our social life that any Constitutional doctrine in this area must build upon that basis.

It is in this area of sexual morality, which contains many proscriptions of consensual behavior having little or no direct impact on others, that the State of Connecticut has expressed its moral judgment that all use of contraceptives is improper. Appellants cite an impressive list of authorities who, from a great variety of points of view, commend the considered use of contraceptives by married couples. What they do not emphasize is that not too long ago the current of opinion was very probably quite the opposite, and that even today the issue is not free of controversy. Certainly, Connecticut's judgment is no more demonstrably correct or incorrect than are the varieties of judgment, expressed in law, on marriage and divorce, on adult consensual homosexuality, abortion, and sterilization, or euthanasia and suicide. If we had a case before us which required us to decide simply, and in abstraction, whether the moral judgment implicit in the application of the present statute to married couples was a sound one, the very controversial nature of these questions would, I think, require us to hesitate long before concluding that the Constitution precluded Connecticut from choosing as it has among these various views.

But, as might be expected, we are not presented simply with this moral judgment to be passed on as an abstract proposition. The secular state is not an examiner of consciences: it must operate in the realm of behavior, of overt actions, and where it does so operate, not only the underlying, moral purpose of its operations, but also the *choice of means* becomes relevant to any Constitutional judgment on what is done. The moral presupposition on which appellants ask us to pass judgment could form the basis of a variety of legal rules and administrative choices, each presenting a different issue for adjudication. For example, one practical expression of the moral view propounded here might be the rule that a marriage in which only contraceptive relations had taken place had never been consummated and could be annulled. Again, the use of contraceptives might be made a ground for divorce, or perhaps tax benefits and subsidies could be provided for large families. Other examples also readily suggest themselves.

III

Precisely what is involved here is this: the State is asserting the right to enforce its moral judgment by intruding upon the most intimate details of the marital relation with the full power of the criminal law. Potentially, this could allow the deployment of all the incidental machinery of the criminal law, arrests, searches and seizures; inevitably, it must mean at the very least the lodging of criminal charges, a public trial, and testimony as to the *corpus delicti*. Nor could any imaginable elaboration of presumptions, testimonial privileges, or other safeguards, alleviate the necessity for testimony as to the mode and manner of the married couples' sexual relations, or at least the opportunity for the accused to make denial of the charges. In sum, the statute allows the State to enquire into, prove and punish married people for the private use of their marital intimacy.

This, then, is the precise character of the enactment whose Constitutional measure we must take. The statute must pass a more rigorous Constitutional test than that going merely to the plausibility of its underlying rationale. This enactment involves what, by common understanding throughout the English-speaking world, must be granted to be a most fundamental aspect of "liberty," the privacy of the home in its most basic sense, and it is this which requires that the statute be subjected to "strict scrutiny." *Skinner* v. *Oklahoma, supra* at 541 . . .

It is clear, of course, that this Connecticut statute does not invade the privacy of the home in the usual sense, since the invasion involved here may, and doubtless usually would, be accomplished without any physical intrusion whatever into the home. What the statute undertakes to do, however, is to create a crime which is grossly offensive to this privacy, while the Constitution refers only to methods of ferreting out substantive wrongs, and the procedure it requires presupposes that substantive offenses may be committed and sought out in the privacy of the home. But such an analysis forecloses any claim to Constitutional protection against this form of deprivation of privacy, only if due process in this respect is limited to what is explicitly provided in the Constitution, divorced from the rational purposes, historical roots, and subsequent developments of the relevant provisions . . .

I think the sweep of the Court's decisions, under both the Fourth and Fourteenth Amendments, amply shows that the Constitution protects the privacy of the home against all unreasonable intrusion of whatever character. "[These] principles . . . affect the very essence of constitutional liberty and security. They reach farther than [a] concrete form of the case . . . before the court, with its adventitious circumstances; they apply to all invasions on the part of the government and its employés of the sanctity of a man's home and the privacies of life . . ." *Boyd* v. *United States,* 116 U.S. 616, 630. "The security of one's privacy against arbitrary intrusion by the police—which is at the core of the Fourth Amendment—is basic to a free society." *Wolf* v. *Colorado* [338 U.S.] at 27.

It would surely be an extreme instance of sacrificing substance to form were it to be held that the Constitutional principle of privacy against arbitrary official intrusion comprehends only physical invasions by the police. To be sure, the times presented the Framers with two particular threats to that principle, the general warrant and the quartering of soldiers in private homes. But though "Legislation, both statutory and constitutional, is enacted, . . . from an experience of evils, . . . its general language should not, therefore, be necessarily confined to the form that evil had theretofore taken . . . [A] principle to be vital must be capable of wider application than the mischief which gave it birth." *Weems* v. *United States,* 217 U.S. 349, 373.

Although the form of intrusion here—the enactment of a substantive offense—does not, in my opinion, preclude the making of a claim based on the right of privacy embraced in the "liberty" of the Due Process Clause, it must be acknowledged that there is another sense in which it could be argued that this intrusion on privacy differs from what the Fourth Amendment, and the similar concept of the Fourteenth, were intended to protect: here we have not an intrusion into the home so much as on the life which characteristically has its place in the home. But to my mind such a distinction is so insubstantial as to be captious: if the physical curtilage of the home is protected, it is surely as a result of solicitude to protect the privacies of the life within. Certainly the safeguarding of the home does not follow merely from the sanctity of property rights. The home derives its pre-eminence as the seat of family life. And the integrity of that life is something so fundamental that it has been found to draw to its protection the principles of more than one explicitly granted Constitutional right . . .

Of this whole "private realm of family life" it is difficult to imagine what is more private or more intimate than a husband and wife's marital relations. We would indeed be straining at a gnat and swallowing a camel were we to show concern for the niceties of property law involved in our recent decision, under the Fourth Amendment, in *Chapman* v. *United States*, 365 U.S. 610, and yet fail at least to see any substantial claim here.

Of course, just as the requirement of a warrant is not inflexible in carrying out searches and seizures, so there are countervailing considerations at this more fundamental aspect of the right involved. "The family . . . is not beyond regulation," *Prince* v. *Massachusetts* [321 U.S. 158 at 166] and it would be an absurdity to suggest either that offenses may not be committed in the bosom of the family or that the home can be made a sanctuary for crime. The right of privacy most manifestly is not an absolute. Thus, I would not suggest that adultery, homosexuality, fornication, and incest are immune from criminal enquiry, however privately practiced. So much has been explicitly recognized in acknowledging the State's rightful concern for its people's moral welfare. But not to discriminate between what is involved in this case and either the traditional offenses against good morals or crimes which, though they may be committed anywhere, happen to have been committed or concealed in the home, would entirely misconceive the argument that is being made.

Adultery, homosexuality, and the like are sexual intimacies which the State forbids altogether, but the intimacy of husband and wife is necessarily an essential and accepted feature of the institution of marriage, an institution which the State not only must allow, but which always and in every age it has fostered and protected. It is one thing when the State exerts its power either to forbid extra-marital sexuality altogether, or to say who may marry, but it is quite another when, having acknowledged a marriage and the intimacies inherent in it, it undertakes to regulate by means of the criminal law the details of that intimacy.

In sum, even though the State has determined that the use of contraceptives is as iniquitous as any act of extra-marital sexual immorality, the intrusion of the whole machinery of the criminal law into the very heart of marital privacy, requiring husband and wife to render account before a criminal tribunal of their uses of that intimacy, is surely a very different thing indeed from punishing those who establish intimacies which the law has always forbidden and which can have no claim to social protection.

In my view the appellants have presented a very pressing claim for Constitutional protection. Such difficulty as the claim presents lies only in evaluating it against the State's countervailing contention that it be allowed to enforce, by whatever means it deems appropriate, its judgment of the immorality of the practice this law condemns. In resolving this conflict a number of factors compel me to conclude that the decision here must most emphatically be for the appellants. Since, as it appears to me, the statute marks an abridgment of important fundamental liberties protected by the Fourteenth Amendment, it will not do to urge in justification of that abridgment simply that the statute is rationally related to the effectuation of a proper state purpose. A closer scrutiny and stronger justification than that are required.

Though the State has argued the Constitutional permissibility of the moral judgment underlying this statute, neither its brief, nor its argument, nor anything in any of the opinions of its highest court in these or other cases even remotely suggests a justification for the obnoxiously intrusive means it has chosen to effectuate that policy. To me the very circumstance that Connecticut has not chosen to press the enforcement of this statute against individual users, while it nevertheless persists in asserting its right to do so at any time—in effect a right to hold this statute as an imminent threat to the privacy of the households of the State—conduces to the inference either that it does not consider the policy of the statute a very important one, or that it does not regard the means it has chosen for its effectuation as appropriate or necessary.

But conclusive, in my view, is the utter novelty of this enactment. Although the Federal Government and many States have at one time or other had on their books statutes forbidding or regulating the distribution of contraceptives, none, so far as I can find, has made the *use* of contraceptives a crime. Indeed, a diligent search has revealed that no nation, including several which quite evidently share Connecticut's moral policy, has seen fit to effectuate that policy by the means presented here.

Though undoubtedly the States are and should be left free to reflect a wide variety of policies, and should be allowed broad scope in experimenting with various means of promoting those policies, I must agree with Mr. Justice Jackson that "There are limits to the extent to which a legislatively represented majority may conduct

... experiments at the expense of the dignity and personality" of the individual. *Skinner* v. *Oklahoma, supra.* In this instance these limits are, in my view, reached and passed . . .

Griswold v. *Connecticut*

381 U.S. 479, 499 (1965)

Four years after *Poe* v. *Ullman* (see above), the Court was forced to deal with the merits of the Connecticut legislation prohibiting the use of contraceptives. Apparently anxious for a determination on the merits, the state had prosecuted Estelle Griswold and Dr. C. Lee Buxton, officers of The Planned Parenthood League, on charges of having violated the law as accessories by giving information, instruction, and advice to married persons on the use of contraceptives.[1] On their appeal to the Supreme Court from affirmance of their convictions, the judgment was reversed, 7–2, Justices Black and Stewart dissenting. Six separate opinions were written, highlighting the novelty of the issues presented. Justice Douglas, speaking for five members of the Court, found that the state law interfered unduly with a "zone of privacy created by several fundamental constitutional guarantees"—notably the First, Third, Fourth, Fifth, and Ninth Amendments. Justice Goldberg, who joined this opinion, wrote to emphasize the relevance of the Ninth Amendment to his conclusion that the statute deprived the appellants of liberty without due process, while Justice White, concurring in the judgment, spoke in terms of substantive due process, arguing that the statute lacked a rational relationship to a permissible purpose.

Justice Harlan, whose views on the merits had been detailed in his dissent in *Poe*, limited his separate concurring opinion to the question whether the "incorporation" doctrine can or should be used to limit the reach of Fourteenth Amendment due process. Thus his opinion here is not only a sequel to *Poe*, but an appropriate conclusion to the materials in this volume dealing with the substantive aspects of due process and equal protection. The last paragraph may well be the sharpest and most forceful statement of the Justice's view of the nature and sources of judicial restraint.

Mr. Justice Harlan, concurring in the judgment.

I fully agree with the judgment of reversal, but find myself unable to join the Court's opinion. The reason is that it seems to me to

[1] Dr. Buxton, a professor at Yale Medical School, was serving as Medical Director of a center operated by the League in New Haven. The center had been open for only ten days when Dr. Buxton and Mrs. Griswold, Executive Director of the League, were arrested.

evince an approach to this case very much like that taken by my Brothers Black and Stewart in dissent, namely: the Due Process Clause of the Fourteenth Amendment does not touch this Connecticut statute unless the enactment is found to violate some right assured by the letter or penumbra of the Bill of Rights.

In other words, what I find implicit in the Court's opinion is that the "incorporation" doctrine may be used to *restrict* the reach of Fourteenth Amendment Due Process. For me this is just as unacceptable constitutional doctrine as is the use of the "incorporation" approach to *impose* upon the States all the requirements of the Bill of Rights as found in the provisions of the first eight amendments and in the decisions of this Court interpreting them.

In my view, the proper constitutional inquiry in this case is whether this Connecticut statute infringes the Due Process Clause of the Fourteenth Amendment because the enactment violates basic values "implicit in the concept of ordered liberty," *Palko* v. *Connecticut,* 302 U.S. 319, 325. For reasons stated at length in my dissenting opinion in *Poe* v. *Ullman* [367 U.S. 497, 522] I believe that it does. While the relevant inquiry may be aided by resort to one or more of the provisions of the Bill of Rights, it is not dependent on them or any of their radiations. The Due Process Clause of the Fourteenth Amendment stands, in my opinion, on its own bottom.

A further observation seems in order respecting the justification of my Brothers Black and Stewart for their "incorporation" approach to this case. Their approach does not rest on historical reasons . . . but on the thesis that by limiting the content of the Due Process Clause of the Fourteenth Amendment to the protection of rights which can be found elsewhere in the Constitution, in this instance in the Bill of Rights, judges will thus be confined to "interpretation" of specific constitutional provisions, and will thereby be restrained from introducing their own notions of constitutional right and wrong into the "vague contours of the Due Process Clause." *Rochin* v. *California,* 342 U.S. 165, 170.

While I could not more heartily agree that judicial "self restraint" is an indispensable ingredient of sound constitutional adjudication, I do submit that the formula suggested for achieving it is more hollow than real. "Specific" provisions of the Constitution, no less than "due process," lend themselves as readily to "personal" interpretations by judges whose constitutional outlook is simply to keep the Constitution in supposed "tune with the times." Need one go further than to recall last Term's reapportionment cases, *Wesberry* v. *Sanders*, 376 U.S. 1, and *Reynolds* v. *Sims*, 377 U.S. 533, where a majority of the Court "interpreted" "by the People" (Art. I, § 2) and "equal protection" (Amdt. 14) to command "one person, one vote," an interpretation that was made in the face of irrefutable and still unanswered history to the contrary?

Judicial self-restraint will not, I suggest, be brought about in the "due process" area by the historically unfounded incorporation formula long advanced by my Brother Black, and now in part espoused by my Brother Stewart. It will be achieved in this area, as in other constitutional areas, only by continual insistence upon respect for the teachings of history, solid recognition of the basic values that underlie our society, and wise appreciation of the great roles that the doctrines of federalism and separation of powers have played in establishing and preserving American freedoms. Adherence to these principles will not, of course, obviate all constitutional differences of opinion among judges, nor should it. Their continued recognition will, however, go farther toward keeping most judges from roaming at large in the constitutional field than will the interpolation into the Constitution of an artificial and largely illusory restriction on the content of the Due Process Clause.

II

The First Amendment
and the Fourteenth:
The Delicate Balance

The strains inherent in any effort to accommodate the freedoms of the individual and the interests of society, which were explored in Part I in many contexts, are brought to even sharper focus in cases touching on speech and religion. Indeed the problem of determining whether particular governmental action infringes on these rights, particularly that of free expression, may well have been the most litigated constitutional issue in the Supreme Court in recent decades. All the cases in Part II bear on that problem, and, with the exception of the first, center on the question of the meaning of the constitutional guarantees relating to speech and expression.

Throughout his service on the Court, Justice Harlan has stood firmly in opposition to those who would give these interests absolute protection against the exercise of governmental power—who would, for example, deny the ability of government to impose sanctions for obscenity or defamation or to investigate associational relationships. Moreover, he has on many occasions, as in *Lathrop* v. *Donohue* and *NAACP* v. *Button,* manifested a greater regard than have other members of the Court for the legitimacy of the government's interest in achieving a regulatory objective. Also frequently evident is his insistence on separating questions of constitutionality from questions of the wisdom or desirability of a particular legislative policy.

But study of the Justice's opinions in this area leaves no doubt of the

105

depth of his concern for the protection of individual rights—for example, of his willingness to avoid broad statutory constructions that might threaten those rights, as in *Yates* v. *United States* and *Scales* v. *United States;* of his concern that federal power to curb obscenity be strictly confined; and of his recognition, as in *NAACP* v. *Alabama* and *Garner* v. *Louisiana,* that many forms of expression other than pure speech are deserving of constitutional protection from subtle as well as direct governmental assault. The balancing of interests, in his view, is not a responsibility that can be evaded by any simple or mechanical formula.

The Free Exercise
of Religion

Sherbert v. Verner

374 U.S. 398, 418 (1963)

The Court has been continually concerned with the application of the constitutional provisions prohibiting an establishment of religion and guaranteeing religious freedom. But the number of cases touching on these issues in recent years has not been great, and Justice Harlan's opinions in the area have been infrequent. In the school prayer cases in 1962 and 1963, perhaps the most widely discussed of all these decisions, the Justice did not write; rather, he joined the majority opinion in the first[1] and joined Justice Goldberg in his concurrence in the second.[2]

But the opportunity to write did present itself in *Sherbert* v. *Verner*, a less noted though perhaps equally important case, handed down during the same Term as the second prayer decision. Adell Sherbert was a Seventh-day Adventist who because of her religious convictions refused to work on Saturday. The jobs that were available in her locality required Saturday work, and since she would not take them, the state of South Carolina denied her unemployment compensation in accordance with the governing law on the ground that she would not accept suitable work. Mrs. Sherbert

[1] Engel v. Vitale, 370 U.S. 421.
[2] School District of Abington Township v. Schempp, 374 U.S. 203, 305.

argued that the denial of benefits was unconstitutional because it interfered with the free exercise of her religion, and the Supreme Court agreed. Justice Harlan's dissent for himself and Justice White states in compelling and concise terms his understanding of the state's constitutional obligation of neutrality with respect to religion. It also reveals the disturbing implications of the majority's opinion in this little-known case.

Mr. Justice Harlan, whom Mr. Justice White joins, dissenting.

Today's decision is disturbing both in its rejection of existing precedent and in its implications for the future. The significance of the decision can best be understood after an examination of the state law applied in this case.

South Carolina's Unemployment Compensation Law was enacted in 1936 in response to the grave social and economic problems that arose during the depression of that period. As stated in the statute itself:

> Economic insecurity due to unemployment is a serious menace to health, morals and welfare of the people of this State; *involuntary unemployment* is therefore a subject of general interest and concern . . . ; the achievement of social security requires protection against this greatest hazard of our economic life; this can be provided by encouraging the employers *to provide more stable employment and by the systematic accumulation of funds during periods of employment to provide benefits for periods of unemployment,* thus maintaining purchasing power and limiting the serious social consequences of poor relief assistance. § 68–38. (Emphasis added.)

Thus the purpose of the legislature was to tide people over, and to avoid social and economic chaos, during periods when *work was unavailable.* But at the same time there was clearly no intent to provide relief for those who for purely personal reasons were or became *unavailable for work.* In accordance with this design, the legislature provided, in § 68–113, that "an unemployed insured worker shall be eligible to receive benefits with respect to any week *only* if the Commission finds that . . . he is able to work and is available for work . . ." (Emphasis added.)

The South Carolina Supreme Court has uniformly applied this law in conformity with its clearly expressed purpose. It has consistently held that one is not "available for work" if his unemployment has resulted not from the inability of industry to provide a job but rather from personal circumstances, no matter how compelling. The reference to "involuntary unemployment" in the legislative statement of policy, whatever a sociologist, philosopher, or theologian might say, has been interpreted not to embrace such personal circumstances. See, e.g., *Judson Mills* v. *South Carolina Unemployment Compensation Comm'n*, 204 S.C. 37, 28 S.E.2d 535 (claimant was "unavailable for work" when she became unable to work the third shift, and limited her availability to the other two, because of the need to care for her four children).

In the present case all that the state court has done is to apply these accepted principles. Since virtually all of the mills in the Spartanburg area were operating on a six-day week, the appellant was "unavailable for work," and thus ineligible for benefits, when personal considerations prevented her from accepting employment on a full-time basis in the industry and locality in which she had worked. The fact that these personal considerations sprang from her religious convictions was wholly without relevance to the state court's application of the law. Thus in no proper sense can it be said that the State discriminated against the appellant on the basis of her religious beliefs or that she was denied benefits *because* she was a Seventh-day Adventist. She was denied benefits just as any other claimant would be denied benefits who was not "available for work" for personal reasons.

With this background, this Court's decision comes into clearer focus. What the Court is holding is that if the State chooses to condition unemployment compensation on the applicant's availability for work, it is constitutionally compelled to *carve out an exception*—and to provide benefits—for those whose unavilability is due to their religious convictions.[3] Such a holding has particular significance in two respects.

First, despite the Court's protestations to the contrary, the deci-

---

[3] The Court does suggest, in a rather startling disclaimer, that its holding is limited in applicability to those whose religious convictions do not make them "nonproductive" members of society, noting that most of the Seventh-day Adventists in the Spartanburg area are employed. But surely this disclaimer cannot be taken seriously, for the Court cannot mean that the case would have come out differently if none of the Seventh-day Adventists in Spartanburg had been gainfully employed, or if the appellant's religion had prevented her from working on Tuesdays instead of Saturdays. Nor can the Court be suggesting that it will make a value judgment in each case as to whether a particular individual's religious convictions prevent him from being "productive." I can think of no more inappropriate function for this Court to perform.

sion necessarily overrules *Braunfeld* v. *Brown*, 366 U.S. 599, which held that it did not offend the "Free Exercise" Clause of the Constitution for a State to forbid a Sabbatarian to do business on Sunday. The secular purpose of the statute before us today is even clearer than that involved in *Braunfeld*. And just as in *Braunfeld*—where exceptions to the Sunday closing laws for Sabbatarians would have been inconsistent with the purpose to achieve a uniform day of rest and would have required case-by-case inquiry into religious beliefs—so here, an exception to the rules of eligibility based on religious convictions would necessitate judicial examination of those convictions and would be at odds with the limited purpose of the statute to smooth out the economy during periods of industrial instability. Finally, the indirect financial burden of the present law is far less than that involved in *Braunfeld*. Forcing a store owner to close his business on Sunday may well have the effect of depriving him of a satisfactory livelihood if his religious convictions require him to close on Saturday as well. Here we are dealing only with temporary benefits, amounting to a fraction of regular weekly wages and running for not more than 22 weeks. Clearly, any differences between this case and *Braunfeld* cut against the present appellant.

Second, the implications of the present decision are far more troublesome than its apparently narrow dimensions would indicate at first glance. The meaning of today's holding, as already noted, is that the State must furnish unemployment benefits to one who is unavailable for work if the unavailability stems from the exercise of religious convictions. The State, in other words, must *single out* for financial assistance those whose behavior is religiously motivated, even though it denies such assistance to others whose identical behavior (in this case, inability to work on Saturdays) is not religiously motivated.

It has been suggested that such singling out of religious conduct for special treatment may violate the constitutional limitations on state action. My own view, however, is that at least under the circumstances of this case it would be a permissible accommodation of religion for the State, if it *chose* to do so, to create an exception to its eligibility requirements for persons like the appellant. The constitutional obligation of "neutrality," see *School District of Abington Township* v. *Schempp* [374 U.S. 203, 222], is not so narrow a channel that the slightest deviation from an absolutely straight course leads to condemnation. There are too many instances in which no such course can be charted, too many areas in which the pervasive activities of the State justify some special provision for religion to prevent it from being submerged by an all-embracing secularism. The State violates its obligation of neutrality when, for example, it mandates a daily religious exercise in its public schools, with all the attendant pressures on the school children that such an exercise entails. But there is, I believe, enough flexibility in the Constitution to permit a legislative judgment accommodating an unemployment compensation law to the exercise of religious beliefs such as appellant's.

For very much the same reasons, however, I cannot subscribe to the conclusion that the State is constitutionally *compelled* to carve out an exception to its general rule of eligibility in the present case. Those situations in which the Constitution may require special treatment on account of religion are, in my view, few and far between, and this view is amply supported by the course of constitutional litigation in this area. Such compulsion in the present case is particularly inappropriate in light of the indirect, remote, and insubstantial effect of the decision below on the exercise of appellant's religion and in light of the direct financial assistance to religion that today's decision requires.

For these reasons I respectfully dissent from the opinion and judgment of the Court.

B

The Dilemma of Obscenity

Roth v. United States

354 U.S. 476, 496 (1957)

Samuel Roth, the proprietor of a publishing business in New York, was convicted in a federal court on four counts of an indictment charging him with mailing obscene materials in violation of the federal "obscenity" statute.[1] David Alberts, the proprietor of a mail-order business in California, was convicted in a state court of lewdly keeping for sale obscene and indecent materials and publishing an obscene advertisement for them in violation of the California penal code. Both convictions were upheld on appeal and were reviewed by the Supreme Court during the 1956 Term. In a single opinion by Justice Brennan, the Supreme Court affirmed—7–2 in *Alberts* and 6–3 in *Roth*—with Justices Black and Douglas dissenting in both cases and Justice Harlan dissenting in *Roth*.

In considering the challenges to the constitutionality of the statutes under which Alberts and Roth were convicted, the majority viewed "the dispositive question"—squarely presented for the first time—to be "whether obscenity is utterance within the area of protected speech and press." Holding that it was not, the Court at the same time supplied a definition of obscene material: "material that deals with sex in a manner appealing

[1] 18 U.S.C. § 1461, first enacted in 1948.

112

to prurient interest."[2] Thus the Court filled the vacuum created by the absence of any definition in the statutes themselves and countered the argument that the statutes did not give adequate notice of what was prohibited.

Justice Harlan's opinion criticized the breadth of the majority's "unprotected speech" formula, and argued that wholly different criteria should be applied to federal and state efforts to cope with obscenity. Once again, the Justice's views of the nature of the federal system profoundly affected his conclusions about the constitutional limitations on governmental power.

Mr. Justice Harlan, concurring in the result in No. 61 [*Alberts*], and dissenting in No. 582 [*Roth*].

I regret not to be able to join the Court's opinion. I cannot do so because I find lurking beneath its disarming generalizations a number of problems which not only leave me with serious misgivings as to the future effect of today's decisions, but which also, in my view, call for different results in these two cases.

I

. . . The problem presented by these cases is how far, and on what terms, the state and federal governments have power to punish individuals for disseminating books considered to be undesirable because of their nature or supposed deleterious effect upon human conduct . . . The Court seems to assume that "obscenity" is a peculiar *genus* of "speech and press," which is as distinct, recognizable, and classifiable as poison ivy is among other plants. On this basis the *constitutional* question before us simply becomes, as the Court says, whether "obscenity," as an abstraction, is protected by the First and Fourteenth Amendments, and the question whether a *particular* book may be suppressed becomes a mere matter of classification, of "fact," to be entrusted to a fact-finder and insulated from independent constitutional judgment. But surely the problem cannot be solved in such a generalized fashion. Every communication has an individuality and "value" of its own. The suppression of a particular writing or other tangible form of expression is, therefore, an *individual* matter, and in the nature of things every

---

[2] As the Court noted, this definition was almost the same as that appearing in The American Law Institute's *Model Penal Code* § 207.10(2) (Tent. Draft No. 6, 1957).

such suppression raises an individual constitutional problem, in which a reviewing court must determine for *itself* whether the attacked expression is suppressable within constitutional standards. Since those standards do not readily lend themselves to generalized definitions, the constitutional problem in the last analysis becomes one of particularized judgments which appellate courts must make for themselves.

I do not think that reviewing courts can escape this responsibility by saying that the trier of the facts, be it a jury or a judge, has labeled the questioned matter as "obscene," for, if "obscenity" is to be suppressed, the question whether a particular work is of that character involves not really an issue of fact but a question of constitutional *judgment* of the most sensitive and delicate kind. Many juries might find that Joyce's "Ulysses" or Bocaccio's "Decameron" was obscene, and yet the conviction of a defendant for selling either book would raise, for me, the gravest constitutional problems, for no such verdict could convince me, without more, that these books are "utterly without redeeming social importance." In short, I do not understand how the Court can resolve the constitutional problems now before it without making its own independent judgment upon the character of the material upon which these convictions were based. I am very much afraid that the broad manner in which the Court has decided these cases will tend to obscure the peculiar responsibilities resting on state and federal courts in this field and encourage them to rely on easy labeling and jury verdicts as a substitute for facing up to the tough individual problems of constitutional judgment involved in every obscenity case.

My second reason for dissatisfaction with the Court's opinion is that the broad strides with which the Court has proceeded has led it to brush aside with perfunctory ease the vital constitutional considerations which, in my opinion, differentiate these two cases. It does not seem to matter to the Court that in one case we balance the power of a State in this field against the restrictions of the Fourteenth Amendment, and in the other the power of the Federal Government against the limitations of the First Amendment. I deal with this subject more particularly later.

Thirdly, the Court has not been bothered by the fact that the two cases involve different statutes. In California the book must have a "tendency to deprave or corrupt its readers"; under the federal statute it must tend "to stir sexual impulses and lead to sexually impure thoughts." The two statutes do not seem to me to present the same problems. Yet the Court compounds confusion when it superimposes on these two statutory definitions a third, drawn from the American Law Institute's Model Penal Code, Tentative Draft No. 6: "A thing is obscene if, considered as a whole, its predominant appeal is to prurient interest." The bland assurance that this definition is the same as the ones with which we deal flies in the face of the authors' express rejection of the "deprave and corrupt" and "sexual thoughts" tests . . .

There is a significant distinction between the definitions used in the prosecutions before us, and the American Law Institute formula. If, therefore, the latter is the correct standard, as my Brother BRENNAN elsewhere intimates [dissenting in *Kingsley Books, Inc.* v. *Brown*, 354 U.S. 436, 447], then these convictions should surely be reversed. Instead, the Court merely assimilates the various tests into one indiscriminate potpourri.

I now pass to the consideration of the two cases before us.

II

I concur in the judgment of the Court in No. 61, *Alberts* v. *California.*

The question in this case is whether the defendant was deprived of liberty without due process of law when he was convicted for selling certain materials found by the judge to be obscene because they would have a "tendency to deprave or corrupt its readers by exciting lascivious thoughts or arousing lustful desire."

In judging the constitutionality of this conviction, we should remember that our function in reviewing state judgments under the Fourteenth Amendment is a narrow one. We do not decide whether the policy of the State is wise, or whether it is based on assumptions scientifically substantiated. We can inquire only whether the state action so subverts the fundamental liberties implicit in the Due Process Clause that it cannot be sustained as a rational exercise of power . . .

What, then, is the purpose of this California statute? Clearly the state legislature has made the judgment that printed words *can* "deprave or corrupt" the reader—that words can incite to antisocial or immoral action. The assumption seems to be that the distribution of certain types of literature will induce criminal or immoral sexual conduct. It is well known, of course, that the validity of this assumption is a matter of dispute among critics, sociologists, psychiatrists, and penologists. There is a large school of thought, particularly in the scientific community, which denies any causal connection between the reading of pornography and immorality, crime, or delinquency. Others disagree. Clearly it is not our function to decide this question. That function belongs to the state legislature. Nothing in the Constitution requires California to accept as truth the most advanced and sophisticated psychiatric opinion. It seems to me clear that it is not irrational, in our present state of knowledge, to consider that pornography can induce a type of sexual conduct which a State may deem obnoxious to the moral fabric of society. In fact the very division of opinion on the subject counsels us to respect the choice made by the State.

Furthermore, even assuming that pornography cannot be deemed ever to cause, in an immediate sense, criminal sexual conduct, other interests within the proper cognizance of the States may be protected by the prohibition placed on such materials. The State can reasonably draw the inference that over a long period of time the indiscriminate dissemination of materials, the essential character of which is to degrade sex, will have an eroding effect on moral standards. And the State has a legitimate interest in protecting the privacy of the home against invasion of unsolicited obscenity.

Above all stands the realization that we deal here with an area where knowledge is small, data are insufficient, and experts are divided. Since the domain of sexual morality is pre-eminently a matter of state concern, this Court should be slow to interfere with state legislation calculated to protect that morality. It seems to me that nothing in the broad and flexible command of the Due Process Clause forbids California to prosecute one who sells books whose dominant tendency might be to "deprave or corrupt" a reader. I agree with the Court, of course, that the books must be judged as a whole and in relation to the normal adult reader.

What has been said, however, does not dispose of the case. It still remains for us to decide whether the state court's determination that this material should be suppressed is consistent with the Fourteenth Amendment; and that, of course, presents a federal question as to which we, and not the state court, have the ultimate responsibility. And so, in the final analysis, I concur in the judgment because, upon an independent perusal of the material involved, and in light of the considerations discussed above, I cannot say that its suppression would so interfere with the communication of "ideas" in any proper sense of that term that it would offend the Due Process Clause. I therefore agree with the Court that appellant's conviction must be affirmed.

III

I dissent in No. 582, *Roth* v. *United States*.

We are faced here with the question whether the federal obscenity statute, as construed and applied in this case, violates the First Amendment to the Constitution. To me, this question is of quite a different order than one where we are dealing with state legislation under the Fourteenth Amendment. I do not think it follows that state and federal powers in this area are the same, and that just because the State may suppress a particular utterance, it is automatically permissible for the Federal Government to do the same . . .

The Constitution differentiates between those areas of human conduct subject to the regulation of the States and those subject to the powers of the Federal Government. The substantive powers of the two governments, in many instances, are distinct. And in every case where we are called upon to balance the interest in free expression against other interests, it seems to me important that we should keep in the forefront the question of whether those other interests are state or federal. Since under our constitutional scheme the two are not necessarily equivalent, the balancing process must needs often produce different results. Whether a particular limitation on speech or press is to be upheld because it subserves a paramount governmental interest must, to a large extent, I think, depend on whether that government has, under the Constitution, a direct substantive interest, that is, the power to act, in the particular area involved.

The Federal Government has, for example, power to restrict seditious speech directed against it, because that Government certainly has the substantive authority to protect itself against revolution. But in dealing with obscenity we are faced with the converse situation, for the interests which obscenity statutes purportedly protect are primarily entrusted to the care, not of the Federal Government, but of the States. Congress has no substantive power over sexual morality. Such powers as the Federal Government has in this field are but incidental to its other powers, here the postal power, and are not of the same nature as those possessed by the States, which bear direct responsibility for the protection of the local moral fabric . . .

Not only is the federal interest in protecting the Nation against pornography attenuated, but the dangers of federal censorship in this field are far greater than anything the States may do. It has often been said that one of the great strengths of our federal system is that we have, in the forty-eight States, forty-eight experimental social laboratories. "State statutory law reflects predominantly this capacity of a legislature to introduce novel techniques of social control. The federal system has the immense advantage of providing forty-eight separate centers for such experimentation."[3] Different States will have different attitudes toward the same work of literature. The same book which is freely read in one State might be classed as obscene in another. And it seems to me that no overwhelming danger to our freedom to experiment and to gratify our tastes in literature is likely to result from the suppression of a borderline book in one of the States, so long as there is no uniform nation-wide suppression of the book, and so long as other States are free to experiment with the same or bolder books.

Quite a different situation is presented, however, where the Federal Government imposes the ban. The danger is perhaps not great if the people of one State, through their legislature, decide that "Lady Chatterley's Lover" goes so far beyond the acceptable standards of candor that it will be deemed offensive and nonsellable, for the State next door is still free to make its own choice. At least we do not have one uniform standard. But the dangers to free thought and expression are truly great if the Federal Government imposes a blanket ban over the Nation on such a book. The prerogative of the States to differ on their ideas of morality will be destroyed, the ability of States to experiment will be stunted. The fact that the people of one State cannot read some of the works of D. H. Lawrence seems to me, if not wise or desirable, at least

[3] Hart, "The Relations Between State and Federal Law," 54 *Colum. L. Rev.* 489, 493.

acceptable. But that no person in the United States should be allowed to do so seems to me to be intolerable, and violative of both the letter and spirit of the First Amendment.

I judge this case, then, in view of what I think is the attenuated federal interest in this field, in view of the very real danger of a deadening uniformity which can result from nation-wide federal censorship, and in view of the fact that the constitutionality of this conviction must be weighed against the First and not the Fourteenth Amendment. So viewed, I do not think that this conviction can be upheld. The petitioner was convicted under a statute which, under the judge's charge, makes it criminal to sell books which "tend to stir sexual impulses and lead to sexually impure thoughts." I cannot agree that any book which tends to stir sexual impulses and lead to sexually impure thoughts necessarily is "utterly without redeeming social importance." Not only did this charge fail to measure up to the standards which I understand the Court to approve, but as far as I can see, much of the great literature of the world could lead to conviction under such a view of the statute. Moreover, in no event do I think that the limited federal interest in this area can extend to mere "thoughts." The Federal Government has no business, whether under the postal or commerce power, to bar the sale of books because they might lead to any kind of "thoughts."

It is no answer to say, as the Court does, that obscenity is not protected speech. The point is that this statute, as here construed, defines obscenity so widely that it encompasses matters which might very well be protected speech. I do not think that the federal statute can be constitutionally construed to reach other than what the Government has termed as "hard-core" pornography. Nor do I think the statute can fairly be read as directed only at *persons* who are engaged in the business of catering to the prurient minded, even though their wares fall short of hard-core pornography. Such a statute would raise constitutional questions of a different order. That being so, and since in my opinion the material here involved cannot be said to be hard-core pornography, I would reverse this case with instructions to dismiss the indictment.

Ginzburg v. United States

383 U.S. 463, 493 (1966)

In the years since *Roth* (see above), the Court has struggled on many occasions with the problem of obscenity, often disposing of difficult cases with uninformative per curiam opinions. The definition in *Roth* seemed to undergo considerable tightening during this period, so that by 1966, when *Fanny Hill* was before the Court, it appeared that a majority would sustain a finding of obscenity only if it was established (1) that the dominant appeal of the material taken as a whole was to "prurient interest," (2) that the material was "patently offensive" in that it affronted current community standards,[1] and (3) that the material was utterly without redeeming social value.[2] Although there was no opinion for the Court in the *Fanny Hill* case, six Justices concluded that the book could not constitutionally be declared obscene.[3]

But in *Ginzburg*, decided the same day as *Fanny Hill*, something new was added. Ginzburg and three corporations controlled by him were convicted on twenty-eight counts of an indictment charging violation of the same federal statute as that involved in *Roth*.[4] The counts involved the mailing of three publications or of advertisements for those publications: *Eros* magazine, vol. 1, no. 4; *Liaison*, a bi-weekly newsletter, vol. 1, no. 1; and *The Housewife's Handbook on Selective Promiscuity*, a short book. In a 5–4 decision upholding the conviction, the majority, speaking through Justice Brennan, stated:

> We agree [with the prosecution] that the question of obscenity may include consideration of the setting in which the publications were presented as an aid to determining the question of obscenity, and assume without deciding that the prosecution could not have succeeded otherwise . . . We view the publications against a background of commercial exploitation of erotica solely for the sake of their prurient appeal. The record in that regard amply supports the decision of the trial judge that the mailing of all three publications offended the statute.

---

[1] This element was articulated by Justice Harlan in 1962, in his opinion announcing the judgment of the Court in Manual Enterprises, Inc. v. Day, 370 U.S. 478, 482.

[2] A Book Named "John Cleland's Memoirs of a Woman of Pleasure" v. Attorney General, 383 U.S. 413, 418. The definition stated in the text, however, did not itself command majority support in the *Fanny Hill* case.

[3] *Id.* Since the case involved the power of a state to deal with the problem of obscenity, Justice Harlan, adhering to his views in *Roth*, dissented. Justices Clark and White also dissented.

[4] 18 U.S.C. § 1461.

In his dissent, Justice Harlan took issue with this construction of the statute and adhered to the view, expressed in *Roth*, that the federal government can ban from the mails only "hard core pornography."[5]

Mr. Justice Harlan, dissenting.

I would reverse the convictions of Ginzburg and his three corporate co-defendants. The federal obscenity statute under which they were convicted, 18 U.S.C. § 1461, is concerned with unlawful shipment of "nonmailable" matter. In my opinion announcing the judgment of the Court in *Manual Enterprises, Inc.* v. *Day,* 370 U.S. 478, the background of the statute was assessed, and its focus was seen to be solely on the character of the material in question . . . I believe that under this statute the Federal Government is constitutionally restricted to banning from the mails only "hard-core pornography." Because I do not think it can be maintained that the material in question here falls within that narrow class, I do not believe it can be excluded from the mails.

The Court recognizes the difficulty of justifying these convictions; the majority refuses to approve the trial judge's "exegesis of *Roth*"; it declines to approve the trial court's "characterizations" of the *Handbook* "outside" the "setting" which the majority for the first time announces to be crucial to this conviction. Moreover, the Court accepts the Government's concession that the *Handbook* has a certain "worth" when seen in something labeled a "controlled, or even neutral, environment"; the majority notes that these are "publications which we have assumed . . . cannot themselves be adjudged obscene in the abstract." In fact, the Court in the last analysis sustains the convictions on the express assumption that the items held to be obscene are not, viewing them strictly, obscene at all.

This curious result is reached through the elaboration of a theory of obscenity entirely unrelated to the language, purposes, or history of the federal statute now being applied, and certainly different from the test used by the trial court to convict the defendants. While the precise holding of the Court is obscure, I take it that the objective test of *Roth*, which ultimately focuses on the material in

---

[5] This phrase, plainly narrower in scope than other definitions of "obscenity," is still somewhat vague in its contours. Writing in 1964, Justice Stewart conceded that "Perhaps I could never succeed in intelligibly defining [hard core pornography] . . . But I know it when I see it." Jacobellis v. Ohio, 378 U.S. 184, 197 (concurring opinion).

question, is to be supplemented by another test that goes to the question whether the mailer's aim is to "pander" to or "titillate" those to whom he mails questionable matter.

Although it is not clear whether the majority views the panderer test as a statutory gloss or as constitutional doctrine, I read the opinion to be in the latter category. The First Amendment, in the obscenity area, no longer fully protects material on its face nonobscene, for such material must now also be examined in the light of the defendant's conduct, attitude, motives. This seems to me a mere euphemism for allowing punishment of a person who mails otherwise constitutionally protected material just because a jury or a judge may not find him or his business agreeable. Were a State to enact a "panderer" statute under its police power, I have little doubt that—subject to clear drafting to avoid attacks on vagueness and equal protection grounds—such a statute would be constitutional. Possibly the same might be true of the Federal Government acting under its postal or commerce powers. What I fear the Court has done today is in effect to write a new statute, but without the sharply focused definitions and standards necessary in such a sensitive area. Casting such a dubious gloss over a straightforward 101-year-old statute is for me an astonishing piece of judicial improvisation . . .

If there is anything to this new pandering dimension to the mailing statute, the Court should return the case for a new trial, for petitioners are at least entitled to a day in court on the question on which their guilt has ultimately come to depend . . .

If a new trial were given in the present case, as I read the Court's opinion, the burden would be on the Government to show that the motives of the defendants were to pander to "the widespread weakness for titillation by pornography." I suppose that an analysis of the type of individuals receiving *Eros* and the *Handbook* would be relevant. If they were ordinary people, interested in purchasing *Eros* or the *Handbook* for one of a dozen personal reasons, this might be some evidence of pandering to the general public. On the other hand, as the Court suggests, the defendants could exonerate themselves by showing that they sent these works only or perhaps primarily (no standards are set) to psychiatrists and other serious-minded professional people. Also relevant would apparently be the nature of the mailer's advertisements or representations. Conceivably someone mailing to the public selective portions of a recognized classic with the avowed purpose of titillation would run the risk of conviction for mailing nonmailable matter. Presumably the Post Office under this theory might once again attempt to ban *Lady Chatterley's Lover*, which a lower court found not bannable in 1960 by an abstract application of *Roth*. I would suppose that if the Government could show that Grove Press is pandering to people who are interested in the book's sexual passages and not in D. H. Lawrence's social theories or literary technique, § 1461 could properly be invoked. Even the well-known opinions of Judge A. N. Hand in *United States* v. *One Book Entitled Ulysses*, 72 F.2d 705, and of Judge Woolsey in the District Court, 5 F.Supp. 182, might be rendered nugatory if a mailer of *Ulysses* is found to be titillating readers with its "coarse, blasphemous, and obscene" portions, 72 F.2d at 707, rather than piloting them through the intricacies of Joyce's stream of consciousness.

In the past, as in the trial of these petitioners, evidence as to a defendant's conduct was admissible only to show relevant intent.[6] Now evidence not only as to conduct, but also as to attitude and motive, is admissible on the primary question of whether the material mailed is obscene. I have difficulty seeing how these inquiries are logically related to the question whether a particular work is obscene. In addition, I think such a test for obscenity is impermissibly vague, and unwarranted by anything in the First Amendment or in 18 U.S.C. § 1461.

I would reverse the judgments below.

[6] To show pandering, the Court relies heavily on the fact that the defendants sought mailing privileges from the postmasters of Intercourse and Blue Ball, Pennsylvania, before settling upon Middlesex, New Jersey, as a mailing point. This evidence was admitted, however, only to show required *scienter* . . . The United States, in its brief in this Court, likewise viewed this evidence as relating solely to *scienter;* nowhere did the United States attempt to sustain these convictions on anything like a pandering theory.

C

Comment on Matters
of Public Interest

Time, Inc. v. Hill

385 U.S. 374, 402 (1967)

In 1964, in *New York Times Co.* v. *Sullivan*,[1] the Court held without dissent that unless actual malice is alleged and proved, the Constitution precludes a state from awarding damages for libel in actions brought by public officials against critics of their official conduct. In the few years since that decision it has become plain that the *New York Times* case marks only a beginning of a new and important constitutional development. This case and the next in this chapter are critical phases in that development. *Time, Inc.* v. *Hill* is particularly interesting because it involves an effort to accommodate the right of free speech and the individual's right to privacy—a right that is also one of constitutional dimensions.

James Hill and his family were held prisoner by three escaped convicts for some nineteen hours in 1952. A book entitled *The Desperate Hours* was published in 1953 and was made into a play in 1955. Also in 1955, *Life* magazine published a story headed "True Crime Inspires Tense Play," which stated that the Hill family's experience was the basis of the book and the play, and which contained photographs purporting to reenact the crime on the site where it occurred. Claiming that the article falsely

[1] 376 U.S. 254.

124

reported the family's experience—particularly in representing that the convicts had been guilty of violence—Hill brought suit in a New York state court against the publisher under provisions of the New York Civil Rights Law captioned "Right of Privacy."[2] At the first trial, the jury found for Hill, but on appeal a new trial was ordered on the issue of damages, and at the second trial $30,000 compensatory damages were awarded. After state court affirmances on appeal, the case was brought to the Supreme Court, which reversed by a 6–3 vote and remanded for a new trial. Justice Brennan, speaking for five members of the Court,[3] noted that the action was not one for defamation and recognized that, since the case related to a matter of public interest, it was different from a suit in which the defendant had intruded upon purely private affairs. Moreover, the case did not involve the appropriation and use in advertising or other promotion of a person's name or picture without his consent. Under all the circumstances, the Court held that the Constitution precluded liability in the absence of proof of "knowing or reckless falsity" on the part of the defendant. Since this was not the standard of liability used at the trial, the case had to be remanded.

Justice Harlan concurred in the remand, but argued that a better accommodation of the conflicting interests would be achieved if the defendant could be held liable for negligent as well as reckless or knowing misstatement of the facts.

Mr. Justice Harlan, concurring in part and dissenting in part . . .

Like the Court, I consider that only a narrow problem is presented by these facts. To me this is not "privacy" litigation in its truest sense. No claim is made that there was any intrusion upon the Hills' solitude or private affairs in order to obtain information for publication. The power of a State to control and remedy such intrusion for newsgathering purposes cannot de denied, but is not here asserted. Similarly it may be strongly contended that certain facts are of such limited public interest and so intimate and potentially embarrassing to an individual that the State may exercise its power to deter publication. But the instructions to the jury, the opinions in the New York appellate courts, and indeed the arguments advanced by both sides before this Court all recognize that

[2] New York Civil Rights Law §§ 50–51.

[3] Two of the five members, Justices Black and Douglas, joined Justice Brennan "in order for the Court to be able at this time to agree on an opinion," but expressed the view that the test announced in that opinion was inadequate to protect freedom of the press; they believed that total immunity from liability for defamation was required.

the theme of the article in question was a perfectly proper one and that an article of this type could have been prepared without liability. The record is replete with articles commenting on the genesis of *The Desperate Hours,* one of which was prepared by the author himself and used by appellee to demonstrate the supposed falsity of the *Life* piece. Finally no claim is made that appellant published the article to advance a commercial interest in the play. There is no evidence to show that Time, Inc., had any financial interest in the production or even that the article was published as an advertisement. Thus the question whether a State may apply more stringent limitations to the use of the personality in "purely commercial advertising" is not before the Court.

Having come this far in step with the Court's opinion, I must part company with its sweeping extension of the principles of *New York Times Co. v. Sullivan,* 376 U.S. 254. It was established in *New York Times* that mere falsity will not suffice to remove constitutional protection from published matter relating to the conduct of a public official that is of public concern. But that decision and those in which the Court has developed its doctrine, have never found independent value in false publications[4] nor any reason for their protection except to add to the protection of truthful communication. And the Court has been quick to note that where private actions are involved the social interest in individual protection from falsity may be substantial. Thus I believe that rigorous scrutiny of the principles underlying the rejection of the mere falsity criterion and the imposition of ancillary safeguards, as well as the interest which the State seeks to protect, is necessary to reach a proper resolution of this case.

Two essential principles seem to underlie the Court's rejection of the mere falsity criterion in *New York Times.* The first is the inevitability of some error in the situation presented in free debate especially when abstract matters are under consideration. Certainly that is illustrated here in the difficulty to be encountered in making

---

[4] The passage from Garrison v. Louisiana [379 U.S. 64], quoted in the opinion of the Court makes clear that the only interest in protecting falsehood is to give added "breathing space" to truth. It is undeniable that falsity may be published, especially in the political arena, with what may be considered "good" motives—for example, a good-faith belief in the absolute necessity of defeating an "evil" candidate. But the Court does not remove state power to control such conduct, thus underlining the strong social interest in discouraging false publication.

a precise description of the relationship between the Hill incident and *The Desperate Hours*. The second is the Court's recognition that in many areas which are at the center of public debate "truth" is not a readily identifiable concept, and putting to the pre-existing prejudices of a jury the determination of what is "true" may effectively institute a system of censorship. Any nation which counts the *Scopes* trial as part of its heritage cannot so readily expose ideas to sanctions on a jury finding of falsity. "The marketplace of ideas" where it functions still remains the best testing ground for truth.

But these arguments against suppressing what is found to be "false" on that ground alone do not negative a State's interest in encouraging the publication of well-researched materials more likely to be true. Certainly it is within the power of the State to use positive means—the provision of facilities and training of students—to further this end. The issue presented in this case is the constitutionality of a State's employment of sanctions to accomplish that same goal. The Court acknowledges that sanctions may be employed against knowing or reckless falsehoods but would seem to grant a "talismanic immunity" to all unintentional errors. However, the distinction between the facts presented to us here and the situation at issue in the *New York Times* case and its progeny casts serious doubt on that grant of immunity and calls for a more limited "breathing space" than that granted in criticism of public officials.

First, we cannot avoid recognizing that we have entered an area where the "marketplace of ideas" does not function and where conclusions premised on the existence of that exchange are apt to be suspect . . . Falsehood is more easily tolerated where public attention creates the strong likelihood of a competition among ideas. Here such competition is extremely unlikely for the scrutiny and discussion of the relationship of the Hill incident and the play is "occasioned by the particular charges in controversy" and the matter is not one in which the public has an "independent interest." It would be unreasonable to assume that Mr. Hill could find a forum for making a successful refutation of the *Life* material or that the public's interest in it would be sufficient for the truth to win out by comparison as it might in that area of discussion central to a free society. Thus the state interest in encouraging careful checking and preparation of published material is far stronger than in *New*

York Times. The dangers of unchallengeable untruth are far too well documented to be summarily dismissed.

Second, there is a vast difference in the state interest in protecting individuals like Mr. Hill from irresponsibly prepared publicity and the state interest in similar protection for a public official. In *New York Times* we acknowledged public officials to be a breed from whom hardiness to exposure to charges, innuendoes, and criticisms might be demanded and who voluntarily assumed the risk of such things by entry into the public arena. But Mr. Hill came to public attention through an unfortunate circumstance not of his making rather than his voluntary actions and he can in no sense be considered to have "waived" any protection the State might justifiably afford him from irresponsible publicity. Not being inured to the vicissitudes of journalistic scrutiny such an individual is more easily injured and his means of self-defense are more limited. The public is less likely to view with normal skepticism what is written about him because it is not accustomed to seeing his name in the press and expects only a disinterested report.

The coincidence of these factors in this situation leads me to the view that a State should be free to hold the press to a duty of making a reasonable investigation of the underlying facts and limiting itself to "fair comment" on the materials so gathered. Theoretically, of course, such a rule might slightly limit press discussion of matters touching individuals like Mr. Hill. But, from a pragmatic standpoint, until now the press, at least in New York, labored under the more exacting handicap of the existing New York privacy law and has certainly remained robust. Other professional activity of great social value is carried on under a duty of reasonable care and there is no reason to suspect the press would be less hardy than medical practitioners or attorneys for example. The "freedom of the press" guaranteed by the First Amendment, and as reflected in the Fourteenth, cannot be thought to insulate all press conduct from review and responsibility for harm inflicted. The majority would allow sanctions against such conduct only when it is morally culpable. I insist that it can also be reached when it creates a severe risk of irremediable harm to individuals involuntarily exposed to it and powerless to protect themselves against it. I would remand the case to the New York courts for possible retrial under that principle.

A constitutional doctrine which relieves the press of even this minimal responsibility in cases of this sort seems to me unnecessary and ultimately harmful to the permanent good health of the press itself. If the *New York Times* case has ushered in such a trend it will prove in its long-range impact to have done a disservice to the true values encompassed in the freedoms of speech and press.

Curtis Publishing Co. v. *Butts*

388 U.S. 130 (1967)

The issue in the *Butts* case was one of the questions reserved in *Hill* (see above): What is the constitutionally permissible standard of liability in a defamation action brought by a "public figure" who is not a "public official" within the meaning of that phrase as used in *New York Times* v. *Sullivan?*[1]

The *Butts* case was an action for defamation brought against the publisher of the *Saturday Evening Post* by a former football coach at the University of Georgia. Decided together with *Butts* was *Associated Press* v. *Walker*, a case in which retired General Edwin A. Walker had brought suit for defamation against the Associated Press for its reporting of his role in riots that occurred at the University of Mississippi. In both cases, substantial damage awards had been rendered.

The problem of sorting out the positions of each of the Justices in these two cases is virtually insurmountable. Suffice it to note here that the Court affirmed in *Butts*, 5–4, and reversed and remanded in *Walker*, 9–0; that five members of the Court agreed for purposes of the *Walker* decision that the "actual malice" standard of *New York Times* applied in defamation actions by any public figure;[2] and that the remaining four argued that liability could properly be based on "highly unreasonable conduct." The division of views in the *Butts* case was more complex.

There was no opinion for the Court in the two cases; Justice Harlan announced the judgments of the Court and delivered an opinion in which he elaborated on the theme introduced in his concurrence in *Hill*.

Mr. Justice Harlan announced the judgments of the Court and delivered an opinion in which Mr. Justice Clark, Mr. Justice Stewart and Mr. Justice Fortas join . . .

[1] 376 U.S. 254.

[2] Justices Black and Douglas, who believe that the Constitution requires total immunity from liability for defamation, joined in this narrower ground of decision in *Walker* to facilitate disposition of the case.

We fully recognize . . . that an accommodation between [competing considerations] is necessary not only in these cases, but in all libel actions arising from a publication concerning public issues. In *Time, Inc.* v. *Hill,* 385 U.S. 374, 388, we held that "the guarantees for speech and press are not the preserve of political expression or comment upon public affairs . . ." and affirmed that freedom of discussion "must embrace all issues about which information is needed or appropriate to enable the members of society to cope with the exigencies of their period." *Thornhill* v. *Alabama,* 310 U.S. 88, 102. This carries out the intent of the Founders who felt that a free press would advance "truth, science, morality, and arts in general" as well as responsible government. Letter to the Inhabitants of Quebec, 1 *Journals of the Continental Cong.* 108. From the point of view of deciding whether a constitutional interest of free speech and press is properly involved in the resolution of a libel question a rational distinction "cannot be founded on the assumption that criticism of private citizens who seek to lead in the determination of . . . policy will be less important to the public interest than will criticism of government officials." *Pauling* v. *Globe-Democrat Publishing Co.,* 362 F.2d 188, 196.

On the other hand, to take the rule found appropriate in *New York Times* to resolve the "tension" between the particular constitutional interest there involved and the interests of personal reputation and press responsibility, as being applicable throughout the realm of the broader constitutional interest, would be to attribute to this aspect of *New York Times* an unintended inexorability at the threshold of this new constitutional development. In *Time, Inc.* v. *Hill, supra* at 390, we counseled against "blind application of *New York Times Co.* v. *Sullivan*" and considered "the factors which arise in the particular context." Here we must undertake a parallel evaluation . . .

It is significant that the guarantee of freedom of speech and press falls between the religious guarantees and the guarantee of the right to petition for redress of grievances in the text of the First Amendment, the principles of which are carried to the States by the Fourteenth Amendment. It partakes of the nature of both, for it is as much a guarantee to individuals of their personal right to make their thoughts public and put them before the community, as it is a social necessity required for the "maintenance of our political system and an open society." *Time, Inc.* v. *Hill, supra* at 389. It is because of the personal nature of this right that we have rejected all manner of prior restraint on publication, despite strong arguments that if the material was unprotected the time of suppression was immaterial. The dissemination of the individual's opinions on matters of public interest is for us, in the historic words of the Declaration of Independence, an "unalienable right" that "governments are instituted among men to secure." History shows us that the Founders were not always convinced that unlimited discussion of public issues would be "for the benefit of all of us" [*Time, Inc.* v. *Hill, supra* at 389] but that they firmly adhered to the proposition that the "true liberty of the press" permitted "every man to publish his opinion." *Respublica* v. *Oswald*, 1 Dall. 319, 325 (Pa.).

The fact that dissemination of information and opinion on questions of public concern is ordinarily a legitimate, protected, and indeed cherished activity does not mean, however, that one may in all respects carry on that activity exempt from sanctions designed to safeguard the legitimate interests of others . . . Federal securities regulation, mail fraud statutes, and common-law actions for deceit and misrepresentation are only some examples of our understanding that the right to communicate information of public interest is not "unconditional." However, as our decision in *New York Times* makes explicit, while protected activity may in some respects be subjected to sanctions, it is not open to all forms of regulation. The guarantees of freedom of speech and press were not designed to prevent "the censorship of the press merely, but any action of the government by means of which it might prevent such free and general discussion of public matters as seems absolutely essential . . . ." 2 Cooley, *Constitutional Limitations* 886 (8th ed.). Our touchstones are that acceptable limitations must neither affect "the impartial distribution of news" and ideas, *Associated Press* v. *Labor Board* [301 U.S. 103, 133], nor because of their history or impact constitute a special burden on the press, nor deprive our free society of the stimulating benefit of varied ideas because their purveyors fear physical or economic retribution solely because of what they choose to think and publish.

The history of libel law leaves little doubt that it originated in soil entirely different from that which nurtured these constitutional values . . .

The law of libel has, of course, changed substantially since the early days of the Republic, and this change is "the direct consequence of the friction between it . . . and the highly cherished right of free speech." *State* v. *Browne*, 86 N.J.Super. 217, 228, 206 A.2d 591, 597. The emphasis has shifted from criminal to civil remedies, from the protection of absolute social values to the safeguarding of valid personal interests. Truth has become an absolute defense in almost all cases, and privileges designed to foster free communication are almost universally recognized. But the basic theory of libel has not changed, and words defamatory of another are still placed "in the same class with the use of explosives or the keeping of dangerous animals." Prosser, *The Law of Torts* § 108 at 792. Thus some antithesis between freedom of speech and press and libel actions persists, for libel remains premised on the content of speech and limits the freedom of the publisher to express certain sentiments, at least without guaranteeing legal proof of their substantial accuracy.

While the truth of the underlying facts might be said to mark the line between publications which are of significant social value and those which might be suppressed without serious social harm and thus resolve the antithesis on a neutral ground, we have rejected, in prior cases involving materials and persons commanding justified and important public interest, the argument that a finding of falsity alone should strip protections from the publisher. We have recognized "the inevitability of some error in the situation presented in free debate," *Time, Inc.* v. *Hill, supra* at 406 (opinion of this writer), and that "putting to the pre-existing prejudices of a jury the determination of what is 'true' may effectively institute a system of censorship."

Our resolution of *New York Times Co.* v. *Sullivan*, in the context of the numerous statutes and cases which allow ideologically neutral and generally applicable regulatory measures to be applied to publication, makes clear, however, that neither the interests of the publisher nor those of society necessarily preclude a damage award based on improper conduct which creates a false publication. It is the conduct element, therefore, on which we must principally focus if we are successfully to resolve the antithesis between civil libel actions and the freedom of speech and press. Impositions based on misconduct can be neutral with respect to content of the speech involved, free of historical taint, and adjusted to strike a fair balance between the interests of the community in free circulation of information and those of individuals in seeking recompense for harm done by the circulation of defamatory falsehood . . .

In the cases we decide today none of the particular considerations involved in *New York Times* is present. These actions cannot be analogized to prosecutions for seditious libel. Neither plaintiff has any position in government which would permit a recovery by him to be viewed as a vindication of governmental policy. Neither was entitled to a special privilege protecting his utterances against accountability in libel. We are prompted, therefore, to seek guidance from the rules of liability which prevail in our society with respect to compensation of persons injured by the improper performance of a legitimate activity by another. Under these rules, a departure from the kind of care society may expect from a reasonable man performing such activity leaves the actor open to a judicial shifting of loss. In defining these rules, and especially in formulating the standards for determining the degree of care to be expected in the circumstances, courts have consistently given much attention to the importance of defendants' activities. The courts have also, especially in libel cases, investigated the plaintiff's position to determine whether he has a legitimate call upon the court for protection in light of his prior activities and means of self-defense. We note that the public interest in the circulation of the materials here involved, and the publisher's interest in circulating them, is not less than that involved in *New York Times.* And both Butts and Walker commanded a substantial amount of independent public interest at the time of the publications; both, in our opinion, would have been labeled "public figures" under ordinary tort rules. Butts may have attained that status by position alone and Walker by his purposeful activity amounting to a thrusting of his personality into the "vortex" of an important public controversy, but both commanded sufficient continuing public interest and had sufficient access to the means of counterargument to be able "to expose through discussion the falsehood and fallacies" of the defamatory statements. *Whitney* v. *California,* 274 U.S. 357, 377 (Brandeis, J., dissenting).

These similarities and differences between libel actions involving persons who are public officials and libel actions involving those circumstanced as were Butts and Walker, viewed in light of the principles of liability which are of general applicability in our society, lead us to the conclusion that libel actions of the present kind cannot be left entirely to state libel laws, unlimited by any overriding constitutional safeguard, but that the rigorous federal requirements of *New York Times* are not the only appropriate accommodation of the conflicting interests at stake. We consider and would hold that a "public figure" who is not a public official may also recover damages for a defamatory falsehood whose substance makes substantial danger to reputation apparent, on a showing of highly unreasonable conduct constituting an extreme departure from the standards of investigation and reporting ordinarily adhered to by responsible publishers . . .

D

Association and Action as
Forms of Expression

NAACP v. Alabama

357 U.S. 449 (1958)

Alabama, like many states, requires a foreign corporation, except as exempted, to qualify before doing business by filing its charter and by designating a place of business and an agent to receive service of process. The National Association for the Advancement of Colored People, a nonprofit membership corporation organized under the laws of New York, has had chartered affiliates in Alabama since 1918 and its own regional office in that state since 1951. It never complied with the qualification statute, believing itself exempt.

In 1956, the Alabama Attorney General brought an action against the NAACP to oust it from the state, complaining among other things of its failure to comply with the qualification statute. In the course of the litigation, the court ordered the NAACP, on motion by the state, to produce various records, including the names and addresses of all Alabama members and agents of the Association. For failure to comply with the order, the Association was held in "civil contempt" and fined $10,000, subject to remission if the information were produced within five days and, if not, the fine was to be increased to $100,000. The Association, within the five-day period, produced substantially all the requested data except the membership lists, as to which it claimed constitutional protection. The fine was

135

then increased to $100,000, and when the Alabama Supreme Court refused review, the Association took the case to the United States Supreme Court, which unanimously reversed. Justice Harlan, speaking for the Court, articulated important principles governing the relationship between the rights of speech and of association, and emphasized the characteristics of both as aspects of the "liberty" assured by the Fourteenth Amendment.

Mr. Justice Harlan delivered the opinion of the Court.

We review from the standpoint of its validity under the Federal Constitution a judgment of civil contempt entered against petitioner, the National Association for the Advancement of Colored People, in the courts of Alabama. The question presented is whether Alabama, consistently with the Due Process Clause of the Fourteenth Amendment, can compel petitioner to reveal to the State's Attorney General the names and addresses of all its Alabama members and agents, without regard to their positions or functions in the Association. The judgment of contempt was based upon petitioner's refusal to comply fully with a court order requiring in part the production of membership lists. Petitioner's claim is that the order, in the circumstances shown by this record, violated rights assured to petitioner and its members under the Constitution . . .[1]

Petitioner argues that in view of the facts and circumstances shown in the record, the effect of compelled disclosure of the membership lists will be to abridge the rights of its rank-and-file members to engage in lawful association in support of their common beliefs. It contends that governmental action which, although not directly suppressing association, nevertheless carries this consequence, can be justified only upon some overriding valid interest of the State.

Effective advocacy of both public and private points of view, particularly controversial ones, is undeniably enhanced by group association, as this Court has more than once recognized by remarking upon the close nexus between the freedoms of speech and assembly. It is beyond debate that freedom to engage in association

---

[1] Before reaching the merits, the Court held that (1) the judgment of the Alabama Supreme Court did not rest on an independent nonfederal ground and (2) the NAACP had standing to assert the constitutional rights of its members to be protected from compelled disclosure. Discussion of both points is omitted here, but the reader who is interested in their resolution is urged to consult the detailed analysis in the full opinion. [Ed.]

for the advancement of beliefs and ideas is an inseparable aspect of the "liberty" assured by the Due Process Clause of the Fourteenth Amendment, which embraces freedom of speech. Of course, it is immaterial whether the beliefs sought to be advanced by association pertain to political, economic, religious or cultural matters, and state action which may have the effect of curtailing the freedom to associate is subject to the closest scrutiny.

The fact that Alabama, so far as is relevant to the validity of the contempt judgment presently under review, has taken no direct action to restrict the right of petitioner's members to associate freely, does not end inquiry into the effect of the production order. In the domain of these indispensable liberties, whether of speech, press, or association, the decisions of this Court recognize that abridgment of such rights, even though unintended, may inevitably follow from varied forms of governmental action. Thus in [*American Communications Ass'n. v. Douds*, 339 U.S. 382] the Court stressed that the legislation there challenged, which on its face sought to regulate labor unions and to secure stability in interstate commerce, would have the practical effect "of discouraging" the exercise of constitutionally protected political rights, 339 U.S. at 393, and it upheld the statute only after concluding that the reasons advanced for its enactment were constitutionally sufficient to justify its possible deterrent effect upon such freedoms. Similar recognition of possible unconstitutional intimidation of the free exercise of the right to advocate underlay this Court's narrow construction of the authority of a congressional committee investigating lobbying and of an Act regulating lobbying, although in neither case was there an effort to suppress speech. *United States* v. *Rumely*, 345 U.S. 41, 46–47; *United States* v. *Harriss*, 347 U.S. 612, 625–626. The governmental action challenged may appear to be totally unrelated to protected liberties. Statutes imposing taxes upon rather than prohibiting particular activity have been struck down when perceived to have the consequence of unduly curtailing the liberty of freedom of press assured under the Fourteenth Amendment. *Grosjean* v. *American Press Co.*, 297 U.S. 233.

It is hardly a novel perception that compelled disclosure of affiliation with groups engaged in advocacy may constitute as effective a restraint on freedom of association as the forms of governmental action in the cases above were thought likely to produce upon the particular constitutional rights there involved. This Court has recognized the vital relationship between freedom to associate and privacy in one's associations. When referring to the varied forms of governmental action which might interfere with freedom of assembly, it said in *American Communications Assn.* v. *Douds, supra* at 402: "A requirement that adherents of particular religious faiths or political parties wear identifying arm-bands, for example, is obviously of this nature." Compelled disclosure of membership in an organization engaged in advocacy of particular beliefs is of the same order. Inviolability of privacy in group association may in many circumstances be indispensable to preservation of freedom of association, particularly where a group espouses dissident beliefs.

We think that the production order, in the respects here drawn in question, must be regarded as entailing the likelihood of a substantial restraint upon the exercise by petitioner's members of their right to freedom of association. Petitioner has made an uncontroverted showing that on past occasions revelation of the identity of its rank-and-file members has exposed these members to economic reprisal, loss of employment, threat of physical coercion, and other manifestations of public hostility. Under these circumstances, we think it apparent that compelled disclosure of petitioner's Alabama membership is likely to affect adversely the ability of petitioner and its members to pursue their collective effort to foster beliefs which they admittedly have the right to advocate, in that it may induce members to withdraw from the Association and dissuade others from joining it because of fear of exposure of their beliefs shown through their associations and of the consequences of this exposure.

It is not sufficient to answer, as the State does here, that whatever repressive effect compulsory disclosure of names of petitioner's members may have upon participation by Alabama citizens in petitioner's activities follows not from *state* action but from *private* community pressures. The crucial factor is the interplay of governmental and private action, for it is only after the initial exertion of state power represented by the production order that private action takes hold.

We turn to the final question whether Alabama has demonstrated an interest in obtaining the disclosures it seeks from petitioner which is sufficient to justify the deterrent effect which we have concluded these disclosures may well have on the free exercise by petitioner's members of their constitutionally protected right of association . . .

The issues in the litigation commenced by Alabama by its bill in equity were whether the character of petitioner and its activities in Alabama had been such as to make petitioner subject to the registration statute, and whether the extent of petitioner's activities without qualifying suggested its permanent ouster from the State. Without intimating the slightest view upon the merits of these issues, we are unable to perceive that the disclosure of the names of petitioner's rank-and-file members has a substantial bearing on either of them. As matters stand in the state court, petitioner (1) has admitted its presence and conduct of activities in Alabama since 1918; (2) has offered to comply in all respects with the state qualification statute, although preserving its contention that the statute does not apply to it; and (3) has apparently complied satisfactorily with the production order, except for the membership lists, by furnishing the Attorney General with varied business records, its charter and statement of purposes, the names of all of its directors and officers, and with the total number of its Alabama members and the amount of their dues. These last items would not on this record appear subject to constitutional challenge and have been furnished, but whatever interest the State may have in obtaining names of ordinary members has not been shown to be sufficient to overcome petitioner's constitutional objections to the production order . . .

We hold that the immunity from state scrutiny of membership lists which the Association claims on behalf of its members is here so related to the right of the members to pursue their lawful private interests privately and to associate freely with others in so doing as to come within the protection of the Fourteenth Amendment. And we conclude that Alabama has fallen short of showing a controlling justification for the deterrent effect on the free enjoyment of the right to associate which disclosure of membership lists is likely to have. Accordingly, the judgment of civil contempt and the $100,000 fine which resulted from petitioner's refusal to comply with the production order in this respect must fall.[2]

[2] The Court's decision in this case has served as the basis for protection of the right of nondisclosure in other cases in which the Justice has found himself unable to join the Court's disposition. See, e.g., Gibson v. Florida Legislative Investigation Committee, 372 U.S. 539, 576; cf. Shelton v. Tucker, 364 U.S. 479, 496. But cf. Talley v. California, 362 U.S. 60, 66 (concurring opinion).

In Williams v. Rhodes, 89 S.Ct. 5, 15 (concurring opinion), the Justice relied heavily on the rights of association articulated in NAACP v. Alabama in his concurrence in the Court's invalidation of Ohio's application of its election laws. [Ed.]

Garner v. Louisiana

368 U.S. 157, 185 (1961)

For a number of years, until many of the questions were finally rendered academic by the public accommodations provisions of the Civil Rights Act of 1964,[1] the Supreme Court struggled with a series of "sit-in" cases arising out of efforts to desegregate public accommodations in the South. In each of these cases state authorities had prosecuted one or more civil rights workers for their efforts, usually on charges such as trespass or breach of the peace. In each case the ultimate questions—whether the Constitution prohibited privately operated but publicly licensed facilities from discriminating, or whether in any event state prosecution which had the effect of enforcing a private policy of discrimination was unconstitutional state action—were wondrously averted by a majority of the Court. *Garner* v. *Louisiana* is part of that history.

Garner actually involved three separate cases which were consolidated for purposes of argument and decision. The three defendants—John Garner, Mary Briscoe, and Jannette Hoston—had each been convicted in a Louisiana court of the offense of disturbing the peace. Although, as indicated in Justice Harlan's opinion, the facts of the three cases were not identical, each did involve a Negro defendant who had been arrested while sitting at a lunch counter set aside by the proprietor exclusively for the use of white customers. In each case, the defendant's behavior had been peaceful and orderly and the store or terminal had been one that admitted Negroes as customers and that maintained segregation only with respect to the service of food.

All three convictions were unanimously reversed by the Supreme Court. A majority of six, speaking through the Chief Justice, rested on the ground that "The convictions . . . were so totally devoid of evidentiary support as to render them unconstitutional under the Due Process Clause of the Fourteenth Amendment."[2] Concurring opinions were written by Justices Douglas, Frankfurter, and Harlan. The statement of Justice Harlan's reasons for being unable to accept the majority's ground of decision is omitted in the excerpt that follows; the emphasis is on the reasons for his concurrence, which are rooted in his belief that the defendants were engaged in a form of expression entitled to constitutional protection. The concurrence has been described by one observer as a "venture rich in imaginative daring."[3]

[1] 42 U.S.C. § 2000a *et seq.*
[2] The Court relied heavily on its earlier decision in Thompson v. Louisville, 362 U.S. 199.
[3] Kalven, *The Negro and the First Amendment* 132 (1965).

Mr. Justice Harlan, concurring in the judgment . . .

The Court's reversal for lack of evidence rests on two different views of [the controlling state statute].[4] First, it is said that the statute, as construed by the Louisiana courts, reaches at most only "violent," "boisterous," or "outwardly provocative" conduct that may foreseeably induce a public disturbance. On this view, these cases are found evidentially wanting because the petitioners' conduct, being entirely peaceful, was not of the character proscribed by the statute so construed. Alternatively, it is recognized that the statute is susceptible of a construction that would embrace as well other kinds of conduct having the above effect. On that view, the convictions are also found evidentially deficient, in that petitioners' conduct, so it is said, could not properly be taken as having any tendency to cause a public disturbance. In my opinion, the first of these holdings cannot withstand analysis with appropriate regard for the limitations upon our powers of review over state criminal cases; the second holding rests on untenable postulates as to the law of evidence . . .

Were there no more to these cases, I should have to vote to affirm. But in light of principles established by *Cantwell* v. *Connecticut*, 310 U.S. 296, and consistently since recognized, I think the convictions are subject to other constitutional infirmities.

At the outset it is important to focus on the precise factual situation in each of these cases. Common to all three are the circumstances that petitioners were given the invitation extended to the public at large to patronize these establishments; that they were told that they could be served food only at the Negro lunch counters; that their conduct was not unruly or offensive; and that none of them was ever asked by the owners or their agents to leave the establishments. While in *Briscoe*, there was some very slight, but in my view constitutionally adequate, evidence that those petitioners were expressly asked "to move" from the "white" lunch counter, and undisputed evidence that they did not do so, in *Garner*

[4] The Louisiana statute then in effect, La. Rev. Stat., 1950, § 14:103, provided in relevant part:

Disturbing the peace is the doing of any of the following in such a manner as would foreseeably disturb or alarm the public . . .

(7) Commission of any other act in such a manner as to unreasonably disturb or alarm the public. [Ed.]

141

and *Hoston* there was no evidence whatever of any express request to the petitioners in those cases that they move from the "white" lunch counters where they were sitting.

Nor do I think that any such request is fairly to be implied from the fact that petitioners were told by the management that they could not be served food at such counters. The premises in both instances housed merchandising establishments, a drugstore in *Garner,* a department store in *Hoston,* which solicited business from all comers to the stores. I think the reasonable inference is that the management did not want to risk losing Negro patronage in the stores by requesting these petitioners to leave the "white" lunch counters, preferring to rely on the hope that the irritations of white customers or the force of custom would drive them away from the counters. This view seems the more probable in circumstances when, as here, the "sitters'" behavior was entirely quiet and courteous, and, for all we know, the counters may have been only sparsely, if to any extent, occupied by white persons.

In short, I believe that in the *Garner* and *Hoston* cases the records should be taken as indicating that the petitioners remained at the "white" lunch counters with the implied consent of the management, even though a similar conclusion may not be warranted in the *Briscoe* case. Under these circumstances, applying principles announced in *Cantwell,* I would hold all these convictions offensive to the Fourteenth Amendment, in that: (1) in *Garner* and *Hoston* petitioners' conduct, occurring with the managements' implied consent, was a form of expression within the range of protections afforded by the Fourteenth Amendment which could in no event be punished by the State under a *general* breach of the peace statute; and (2) in *Briscoe,* while petitioners' "sitting," over the management's objection, cannot be deemed to be within the reach of such protections, their convictions must nonetheless fall because the Louisiana statute, as there applied (and *a fortiori* as applied in the other two cases), was unconstitutionally vague and uncertain.

In the *Cantwell* case a Jehovah's Witness had been convicted for breach of the peace under a Connecticut statute embracing what was considered to be the common-law concept of that offense. "The facts which were held to support the conviction . . . were that he stopped two men in the street, asked, and received, permission to play a phonograph record, and played the record 'Enemies,' which attacked the religion and church of the two men, who were Catholics. Both were incensed by the contents of the record and were tempted to strike Cantwell [the defendant] unless he went away. On being told to be on his way he left their presence. There was no evidence that he was personally offensive or entered into any argument with those he interviewed." 310 U.S. at 302–303.

Accepting the determination of the state courts that although the defendant himself had not been disorderly or provocative, his conduct under Connecticut law nonetheless constituted a breach of the peace because of its tendency to inflame others, this Court reversed. Starting from the premise that the "fundamental concept of liberty embodied in [the Fourteenth] Amendment embraces the liberties guaranteed by the First Amendment," the Court found that the defendant's activities fell within the protection granted to the "free exercise" of religion. Then recognizing the danger to such liberties of "leaving to the executive and judicial branches too wide a discretion" in the application of a statute "sweeping in a great variety of conduct under a general and indefinite characterization," the Court held that the defendant's activities could not constitutionally be reached under a general breach of the peace statute, but only under one specifically and narrowly aimed at such conduct. 310 U.S. at 307–308 . . .

I think these principles control the *Garner* and *Hoston* cases. There was more to the conduct of those petitioners than a bare desire to remain at the "white" lunch counter and their refusal of a police request to move from the counter. We would surely have to be blind not to recognize that petitioners were sitting at these counters, where they knew they would not be served, in order to demonstrate that their race was being segregated in dining facilities in this part of the country.

Such a demonstration, in the circumstances of these two cases, is as much a part of the "free trade in ideas," *Abrams* v. *United States,* 250 U.S. 616, 630 (Holmes, J., dissenting), as is verbal expression, more commonly thought of as "speech." It, like speech, appeals to good sense and to "the power of reason as applied through public discussion," *Whitney* v. *California,* 274 U.S. 357, 375 (Brandeis, J., concurring), just as much as, if not more than, a public oration delivered from a soapbox at a street corner. This Court has never limited the right to speak, a protected "liberty" under the Fourteenth Amendment, *Gitlow* v. *New York*, 268 U.S. 652, 666, to mere verbal expression. If the act of displaying a red flag as a symbol of opposition to organized government is a liberty encompassed within free speech as protected by the Fourteenth Amendment, the act of sitting at a privately owned lunch counter with the consent of the owner, as a demonstration of opposition to enforced segregation, is surely within the same range of protections. This is not to say, of course, that the Fourteenth Amendment reaches to demonstrations conducted on private property over the objection of the owner (as in *Briscoe*), just as it would surely not encompass verbal expression in a private home if the owner has not consented.

No one can deny the interest that a State has in preserving peace and harmony within its borders. Pursuant to this interest, a state legislature may enact a trespass statute, or a disturbance of the peace statute which either lists in detail the acts condemned by legitimate state policy or proscribes breaches of the peace generally, thus relating the offense to the already developed body of common law defining that crime. Or it may, as Louisiana has done, append to a specific enumeration in a breach of the peace statute a "catch-all" clause to provide for unforeseen but obviously disruptive and offensive behavior which cannot be justified, and which is not within the range of constitutional protection.

But when a State seeks to subject to criminal sanctions conduct which, except for a demonstrated paramount state interest, would be within the range of freedom of expression as assured by the Fourteenth Amendment, it cannot do so by means of a general and all-inclusive breach of the peace prohibition. It must bring the activity sought to be proscribed within the ambit of a statute or clause "narrowly drawn to define and punish specific conduct as constituting a clear and present danger to a substantial interest of the State." *Cantwell* v. *Connecticut, supra* at 311. And of course that interest must be a legitimate one. A State may not "suppress free communication of views, religious or other, under the guise of conserving desirable conditions." *Cantwell, supra* at 308.

These limitations exist not because control of such activity is beyond the power of the State, but because sound constitutional principles demand of the state legislature that it focus on the nature of the otherwise "protected" conduct it is prohibiting, and that it then make a legislative judgment as to whether that conduct presents so clear and present a danger to the welfare of the community that it may legitimately be criminally proscribed.

The Louisiana Legislature made no such judgment before the petitioners in *Garner* and *Hoston* engaged in their "sit-in" activity. In light of the *Cantwell* case, whose reasoning of course cannot be deemed limited to "expression" taking place on the public streets, Louisiana could not, in my opinion, constitutionally reach those petitioners' conduct under subsection (7)—the "catch-all clause" —of its then existing disturbance of the peace statute. In so concluding, I intimate no view as to whether Louisiana could by a specifically drawn statute constitutionally proscribe conduct of the kind evidenced in these two cases, or upon the constitutionality of the statute which the State has recently passed. I deal here only with these two cases, and the statute that is before us now.

Finally, I believe that the principles of *Cantwell* lead to the conclusion that this general breach of the peace provision must also be deemed unconstitutional for vagueness and uncertainty, *as applied* in the circumstances of all these cases. As to *Garner* and *Hoston* this affords an alternative ground for reversal. As to *Briscoe*, where the evidence falls short of establishing that those petitioners remained at the "white" lunch counter with the express or implied consent of the owner, I would rest reversal solely on this ground.

While *Cantwell* was not explicitly founded on that premise, it seems to me implicit in the opinion that a statute which leaves the courts in uncertainty as to whether it was intended to reach otherwise constitutionally protected conduct must by the same token be deemed inadequate warning to a defendant that his conduct has been condemned by the State. Such warning is, of course, a requirement of the Fourteenth Amendment.

This conclusion finds added support in the cases requiring of state legislatures more specificity in statutes impinging on freedom of expression than might suffice for other criminal enactments. To the extent that this Louisiana statute is explicit on the subject of expression it prohibits only that which is "unnecessarily loud, offensive, or insulting" or activity carried on "in a violent or tumultuous manner by any three or more persons." No charge was made or proved that petitioners' conduct met any of those criteria. Nor has the statute been elucidated in this respect before, or since, petitioners' conviction, by any decision of the Louisiana courts of which we have been advised . . .

In the absence of any Louisiana statute purporting to express the State's overriding interest in prohibiting petitioners' conduct as a clear and present danger to the welfare of the community, peaceful demonstration on public streets, and on private property with the consent of the owner, was constitutionally protected as a form of expression. Louisiana's breach of the peace statute drew no distinct line between presumably constitutionally protected activity and the conduct of the petitioners in *Briscoe*, as a criminal trespass statute might have done. The fact that in *Briscoe*, unlike *Garner* and *Hoston*, the management did not consent to the petitioners' remaining at the "white" lunch counter does not serve to permit the application of this general breach of the peace statute to the conduct shown in that case. For the statute by its terms appears to be as applicable to "incidents fairly within the protection of the guarantee of free speech," *Winters* v. *New York* [333 U.S. 507] at 509, as to that which is not within the range of such protection. Hence such a law gives no warning as to what may fairly be deemed to be within its compass.

For the foregoing reasons I dissent from the opinion of the Court, but join in the judgment.

E

Legitimate Governmental Interests as an Element in the Balance

Barenblatt v. United States

360 U.S. 109 (1959)

During much of Justice Harlan's term of service the Supreme Court has been troubled, and often deeply divided, by the cases of persons convicted for refusing to answer the questions of a legislative committee. Many of these cases resulted from the investigations of the House Un-American Activities Committee and served to provide the country with a grim aftertaste of the McCarthy era as they rose slowly to the highest court for review.

Barenblatt was such a case. In June 1954, Lloyd Barenblatt—a former graduate student and teaching fellow at the University of Michigan— appeared before the House Un-American Activities Committee, which was engaged in investigating alleged Communist infiltration into the field of education. Relying on a variety of constitutional provisions including the First, Ninth, and Tenth Amendments (but not the Fifth), Barenblatt refused to answer questions about his present or former membership in the Communist Party and related matters. As a result, he was convicted of a violation of federal law,[1] and his conviction was affirmed by the Court of Appeals and ultimately by the Supreme Court in a 5–4 decision.

[1] 2 U.S.C. § 192.

147

Writing for the Court, Justice Harlan, in portions of the opinion not included here, held that the House Committee had been duly authorized to conduct the investigations and that Barenblatt had been adequately informed of the pertinency of the questions he had refused to answer. The Justice then turned to the issue whether the questions asked by the committee transgressed constitutional limitations. He concluded that they did not only after a painstaking analysis of the competing interests of the individual and the government. The case serves as an excellent illustration of the Justice's conception of the proper role of the Court, in view of his apparent lack of sympathy for the tactics, strategy, and objectives of Barenblatt's interrogators.[2]

Mr. Justice Harlan delivered the opinion of the Court.

Once more the Court is required to resolve the conflicting constitutional claims of congressional power and of an individual's right to resist its exercise. The congressional power in question concerns the internal process of Congress in moving within its legislative domain; it involves the utilization of its committees to secure "testimony needed to enable it efficiently to exercise a legislative function belonging to it under the Constitution." *McGrain* v. *Daugherty*, 273 U.S. 135, 160. The power of inquiry has been employed by Congress throughout our history, over the whole range of the national interests concerning which Congress might legislate or decide upon due investigation not to legislate; it has similarly been utilized in determining what to appropriate from the national purse, or whether to appropriate. The scope of the power of inquiry, in short, is as penetrating and far-reaching as the potential power to enact and appropriate under the Constitution.

Broad as it is, the power is not, however, without limitations. Since Congress may only investigate into those areas in which it may potentially legislate or appropriate, it cannot inquire into matters which are within the exclusive province of one of the other branches of the Government. Lacking the judicial power given to the Judiciary, it cannot inquire into matters that are exclusively the concern of the Judiciary. Neither can it supplant the Executive in what exclusively belongs to the Executive. And the Congress, in common with all branches of the Government, must exercise its

---

[2] See Justice Harlan's address at Brandeis (Part VI, below).

powers subject to the limitations placed by the Constitution on governmental action, more particularly in the context of this case the relevant limitations of the Bill of Rights.

The congressional power of inquiry, its range and scope, and an individual's duty in relation to it, must be viewed in proper perspective. The power and the right of resistance to it are to be judged in the concrete, not on the basis of abstractions. In the present case congressional efforts to learn the extent of a nation-wide, indeed world-wide, problem have brought one of its investigating committees into the field of education. Of course, broadly viewed, inquiries cannot be made into the teaching that is pursued in any of our educational institutions. When academic teaching-freedom and its corollary learning-freedom, so essential to the well-being of the Nation, are claimed, this Court will always be on the alert against intrusion by Congress into this constitutionally protected domain. But this does not mean that the Congress is precluded from interrogating a witness merely because he is a teacher. An educational institution is not a constitutional sanctuary from inquiry into matters that may otherwise be within the constitutional legislative domain merely for the reason that inquiry is made of someone within its walls.

In the setting of this framework of constitutional history, practice and legal precedents, we turn to the particularities of this case . . .

Petitioner's various contentions resolve themselves into three propositions: First, the compelling of testimony by the Subcommittee was neither legislatively authorized nor constitutionally permissible because of the vagueness of Rule XI of the House of Representatives, Eighty-third Congress, the charter of authority of the parent Committee. Second, petitioner was not adequately apprised of the pertinency of the Subcommittee's questions to the subject matter of the inquiry. Third, the questions petitioner refused to answer infringed rights protected by the First Amendment . . .[3]

Constitutional Contentions

Our function, at this point, is purely one of constitutional adjudication in the particular case and upon the particular record before us, not to pass judgment upon the general wisdom or efficacy of

---

[3] Those portions of the opinion rejecting the first two of these contentions are omitted. [Ed.]

the activities of this Committee in a vexing and complicated field.

The precise constitutional issue confronting us is whether the Subcommittee's inquiry into petitioner's past or present membership in the Communist Party transgressed the provisions of the First Amendment, which of course reach and limit congressional investigations.

The Court's past cases establish sure guides to decision. Undeniably, the First Amendment in some circumstances protects an individual from being compelled to disclose his associational relationships. However, the protections of the First Amendment, unlike a proper claim of the privilege against self-incrimination under the Fifth Amendment, do not afford a witness the right to resist inquiry in all circumstances. Where First Amendment rights are asserted to bar governmental interrogation resolution of the issue always involves a balancing by the courts of the competing private and public interests at stake in the particular circumstances shown. These principles were recognized in the *Watkins* case [*Watkins* v. *United States*, 354 U.S. 178], where, in speaking of the First Amendment in relation to congressional inquiries, we said (at p. 198): "It is manifest that despite the adverse effects which follow upon compelled disclosure of private matters, not all such inquiries are barred . . . The critical element is the existence of, and the weight to be ascribed to, the interest of the Congress in demanding disclosures from an unwilling witness." More recently in *National Association for the Advancement of Colored People* v. *Alabama,* 357 U.S. 449, 463–466, we applied the same principles in judging state action claimed to infringe rights of association assured by the Due Process Clause of the Fourteenth Amendment, and stated that the "'subordinating interest of the State must be compelling'" in order to overcome the individual constitutional rights at stake. In light of these principles we now consider petitioner's First Amendment claims.

The first question is whether this investigation was related to a valid legislative purpose, for Congress may not constitutionally require an individual to disclose his political relationships or other private affairs except in relation to such a purpose.

That Congress has wide power to legislate in the field of Communist activity in this Country, and to conduct appropriate investigations in aid thereof, is hardly debatable. The existence of such power has never been questioned by this Court, and it is sufficient to say, without particularization, that Congress has enacted or considered in this field a wide range of legislative measures, not a few of which have stemmed from recommendations of the very Committee whose actions have been drawn in question here. In the last analysis this power rests on the right of self-preservation, "the ultimate value of any society," *Dennis* v. *United States*, 341 U.S. 494, 509. Justification for its exercise in turn rests on the long and widely accepted view that the tenets of the Communist Party include the ultimate overthrow of the Government of the United States by force and violence, a view which has been given formal expression by the Congress.

On these premises, this Court in its constitutional adjudications has consistently refused to view the Communist Party as an ordinary political party, and has upheld federal legislation aimed at the Communist problem which in a different context would certainly have raised constitutional issues of the gravest character . . . To suggest that because the Communist Party may also sponsor peaceable political reforms the constitutional issues before us should now be judged as if that Party were just an ordinary political party from the standpoint of national security, is to ask this Court to blind itself to world affairs which have determined the whole course of our national policy since the close of World War II, affairs to which Judge Learned Hand gave vivid expression in his opinion in *United States* v. *Dennis*, 183 F.2d 201, 213, and to the vast burdens which these conditions have entailed for the entire Nation.

We think that investigatory power in this domain is not to be denied Congress solely because the field of education is involved . . . Indeed we do not understand petitioner here to suggest that Congress in no circumstances may inquire into Communist activity in the field of education. Rather, his position is in effect that this particular investigation was aimed not at the revolutionary aspects but at the theoretical classroom discussion of communism.

In our opinion this position rests on a too constricted view of the nature of the investigatory process, and is not supported by a fair assessment of the record before us. An investigation of advocacy of or preparation for overthrow certainly embraces the right to identify a witness as a member of the Communist Party, and to inquire into the various manifestations of the Party's tenets. The strict requirements of a prosecution under the Smith Act are not the measure of the permissible scope of a congressional investigation into "overthrow," for of necessity the investigatory process must proceed step by step. Nor can it fairly be concluded that this investigation was directed at controlling what is being taught at our universities rather than at overthrow. The statement of the Subcommittee Chairman at the opening of the investigation evinces no such intention,[4] and so far as this record reveals nothing thereafter transpired which would justify our holding that the thrust of the investigation later changed. The record discloses considerable testimony concerning the foreign domination and revolutionary purposes and efforts of the Communist Party. That there was also testimony on the abstract philosophical level does not detract from the dominant theme of this investigation—Communist infiltration furthering the alleged ultimate purpose of overthrow. And certainly the conclusion would not be justified that the questioning of petitioner would have exceeded permissible bounds had he not shut off the Subcommittee at the threshold.

Nor can we accept the further contention that this investigation should not be deemed to have been in furtherance of a legislative purpose because the true objective of the Committee and of the Congress was purely "exposure." So long as Congress acts in pursuance of its constitutional power, the Judiciary lacks authority to intervene on the basis of the motives which spurred the exercise of that power. "It is, of course, true," as was said in *McCray* v. *United States*, 195 U.S. 27, 55, "that if there be no authority in the

---

[4] The following are excerpts from that statement:

". . . In opening this hearing, it is well to make clear to you and others just what the nature of this investigation is.

"From time to time, the committee has investigated Communists and Communist activities within the entertainment, newspaper, and labor fields, and also within the professions and the Government. In no instance has the work of the committee taken on the character of an investigation of entertainment organizations, newspapers, labor unions, the professions, or the Government, as such, and it is not now the purpose of this committee to investigate education or educational institutions, as such . . .

"The purpose of the committee in investigating Communists and Communist activities within the field of education is no greater and no less than its purpose in investigating Communists and Communist activities within the field of labor or any other field.

"The committee is charged by the Congress with the responsibility of investigating the extent, character, and objects of un-American propaganda activities in the United States, the diffusion within the United States of subversive and un-American propaganda that is instigated from foreign countries or of a domestic origin and attacks the principle of the form of government as guaranteed by our Constitution and all other questions in relation thereto that would aid Congress in any necessary remedial legislation . . ."

judiciary to restrain a lawful exercise of power by another department of the government, where a wrong motive or purpose has impelled to the exertion of the power, that abuses of a power conferred may be temporarily effectual. The remedy of this, however, lies, not in the abuse by the judicial authority of its functions, but in the people, upon whom, after all, under our institutions, reliance must be placed for the correction of abuses committed in the exercise of a lawful power." These principles of course apply as well to committee investigations into the need for legislation as to the enactments which such investigations may produce . . . The constitutional legislative power of Congress in this instance is beyond question.

Finally, the record is barren of other factors which in themselves might sometimes lead to the conclusion that the individual interests at stake were not subordinate to those of the state. There is no indication in this record that the Subcommittee was attempting to pillory witnesses. Nor did petitioner's appearance as a witness follow from indiscriminate dragnet procedures, lacking in probable cause for belief that he possessed information which might be helpful to the Subcommittee. And the relevancy of the questions put to him by the Subcommittee is not open to doubt.

We conclude that the balance between the individual and the governmental interests here at stake must be struck in favor of the latter, and that therefore the provisions of the First Amendment have not been offended.

We hold that petitioner's conviction for contempt of Congress discloses no infirmity, and that the judgment of the Court of Appeals must be

Affirmed.[5]

---

[5] Justice Brennan filed a brief dissent on the ground that no purpose had been shown for the investigation other than exposure for its own sake. Justice Black, joined by the Chief Justice and Justice Douglas in dissent, took issue with the Court at almost every point. He argued that Rule XI was unconstitutionally vague, that the committee's attempt to inquire into ideas and associations violated First Amendment freedoms in an area where "balancing" was not permitted, that society itself had a substantial interest in Barenblatt's right to remain silent, and that the committee's purpose of exposure and punishment rendered its action a bill of attainder. In an impassioned summation, he said: "Ultimately all the questions in this case really boil down to one—whether we as a people will try fearfully and futilely to preserve democracy by adopting totalitarian methods, or whether in accordance with our traditions and our Constitution we will have the confidence and courage to be free." This warning bears a striking similarity to the tenor of Justice Harlan's remarks delivered at Brandeis in 1955 (Part VI, below). [Ed.]

Lathrop v. *Donohue*

367 U.S. 820, 848 (1961)

Wisconsin is one of the states with an "integrated bar"; a rule promulgated by the state's Supreme Court[1] required all lawyers practicing in the state to be members of the "State Bar of Wisconsin" and to pay annual dues of $15. Trayton Lathrop, a Wisconsin attorney, paid his dues under protest and then sued for a refund alleging that his coerced support of this organization violated his rights of free speech and association under the Fourteenth Amendment. The state courts rejected his contention and on appeal the United States Supreme Court affirmed, 7–2. There was no opinion for the Court. Justice Brennan, for himself and three other justices, concluded that Lathrop could constitutionally be compelled to be a member of the State Bar and to pay reasonable annual dues. He relied heavily on the Court's earlier holding that the Railway Labor Act did not abridge protected rights of association in authorizing union shop agreements between railroads and unions.[2] But he refused to reach the question whether Lathrop's rights of free speech were infringed if his dues money were used to support political causes he opposed. The record, in his view, provided an inadequate basis for deciding such a claim.

The remaining five members of the Court all reached the merits of Lathrop's free speech claim, and three—Justices Harlan, Frankfurter, and Whittaker—concluded that it should be rejected. In his opinion concurring in the affirmance, Justice Harlan demonstrated an impatience with the refusal to reach the merits not unlike his dissent that same day in *Poe* v. *Ullman* (see above). On the "free speech" question itself—a question the Justice thought could not properly be separated from the free association claim as Justice Brennan had sought to do—the opinion attempts a point-by-point refutation of the arguments made on Lathrop's behalf. This refutation is a paradigm of the Justice's approach to these problems and must be counted among the most effective of his judicial briefs.

Mr. Justice Harlan, with whom Mr. Justice Frankfurter joins, concurring in the judgment.

I think it most unfortunate that the right of the Wisconsin Integrated Bar to use, in whole or in part, the dues of dissident members

---

[1] In re Integration of the Bar, 273 Wis. 281, 77 N.W.2d 602; 5 Wis.2d 618, 93 N.W.2d 601.

[2] Railway Employees' Dept. v. Hanson, 351 U.S. 225.

154

to carry on legislative and other programs of law reform—doubtless among the most useful and significant branches of its authorized activities—should be left in such disquieting Constitutional uncertainty. The effect of that uncertainty is compounded by the circumstance that it will doubtless also reach into the Integrated Bars of twenty-five other States.

I must say, with all respect, that the reasons stated in the plurality opinion for avoiding decision of this Constitutional issue can hardly be regarded as anything but trivial. For, given the unquestioned fact that the Wisconsin Bar uses or threatens to use, over appellant's protest, some part of its receipts to further or oppose legislation on matters of law reform and the administration of justice, I am at a loss to understand how it can be thought that this record affords "no sound basis" for adjudicating the issue simply because we are not "clearly apprised as to the views of the appellant on any particular legislative issues on which the State Bar has taken a position, or as to the way in which and the degree to which funds compulsorily exacted from its members are used to support the organization's political activities." I agree with my Brother Black that the Constitutional issue is inescapably before us.

Unless one is ready to fall prey to what are at best but alluring abstractions on rights of free speech and association, I think he will be hard put to it to find any solid basis for the Constitutional qualms which, though unexpressed, so obviously underlie the plurality opinion, or for the views of my two dissenting Brothers, one of whom finds unconstitutional the entire Integrated Bar concept, and the other of whom holds the operations of such a Bar unconstitutional to the extent that they involve taking "the money of protesting lawyers" and using "it to support causes they are against."

For me, there is a short and simple answer to all of this. The *Hanson* case, 351 U.S. 225, decided by a unanimous Court, surely lays at rest all doubt that a State may Constitutionally condition the right to practice law upon membership in an integrated bar association, a condition fully as justified by state needs as the union shop is by federal needs. Indeed the conclusion reached in *Hanson* with respect to compulsory union membership seems to me *a fortiori* true here, in light of the supervisory powers which the State, through its courts, has traditionally exercised over admission to the practice of law, and over the conduct of lawyers after admission. The Integrated Bar was in fact treated as such an *a fortiori* case in the *Hanson* opinion itself. So much, indeed, is recognized by the plurality opinion which rejects the contention that Wisconsin could not Constitutionally require appellant, a lawyer, to become and remain a dues-paying member of the State Bar.

That being so, I do not understand why it should become unconstitutional for the State Bar to use appellant's dues to fulfill some of the very purposes for which it was established. I am wholly unable to follow the force of reasoning which, on the one hand, denies that compulsory dues-paying membership in an Integrated Bar infringes "freedom of association," and, on the other, in effect affirms that such membership, to the extent it entails the use of a dissident member's dues for legitimate Bar purposes, infringes "freedom of speech." This is a refinement between two aspects of what, in circumstances like these, is essentially but a single facet of the "liberty" assured by the Fourteenth Amendment that is too subtle for me to grasp.

Nevertheless, since a majority of the Court here has deemed the "free speech" issue to be distinct from that of "free association," I shall also treat the case on that basis . . .

I

To avoid the pitfall of disarming, and usually obscuring, generalization which too often characterizes discussions in this Constitutional field, I see no alternative (even at the risk of being thought to labor the obvious) but to deal in turn with each of the various specific impingements on "free speech" which have been suggested or intimated to flow from the State Bar's use of an objecting member's dues for the purposes involved in this case. As I understand things, it is said that the operation of the Integrated Bar tends (1) to reduce a dissident member's "economic capacity" to espouse causes in which he believes; (2) to further governmental "establishment" of political views; (3) to threaten development of a "guild system" of closed, self-regulating professions and businesses; (4) to "drown out" the voice of dissent by requiring all members of the Bar to lend financial support to the views of the majority; and (5) to interfere with freedom of belief by causing "compelled affirmation" of majority-held views. With deference, I am bound to say that, in my view, all of these arguments border on the chimerical.

156

1. Reduction in "Economic Capacity" to Espouse Views

This argument which, if indeed suggested at all, is intimated only obliquely, is that the mere exaction of dues money works a Constitutionally cognizable inhibition of speech by reducing the resources otherwise available to a dissident member for the espousal of causes in which he believes. The untenability of such a proposition becomes immediately apparent when it is recognized that this rationale would make every governmental exaction the material of a "free speech" issue. Even the federal income tax would be suspect. And certainly this source of inhibition is as great if the Integrated Bar wastes its dues on dinners as if it spends them on recommendations to the legislature. Yet I suppose that no one would be willing to contend that every waste of money exacted by some form of compulsion is an abridgment of free speech.

2. "Establishment" of Political Views

The suggestion that a state-created Integrated Bar amounts to a governmental "establishment" of political belief is hardly worthy of more serious consideration. Even those who would treat the Fourteenth Amendment as embracing the identical protections afforded by the First would have to recognize the clear distinction in the wording of the First Amendment between the protections of speech and religion, only the latter providing a protection against "establishment." And as to the Fourteenth, viewed independently of the First, one can surely agree that a State could not "create a fund to be used in helping certain political parties or groups favored" by it "to elect their candidates or promote their controversial causes" any more than could Congress do so, without agreeing that this is in any way analogous to what Wisconsin has done in creating its Integrated Bar . . .

In establishing the Integrated Bar Wisconsin has, I assume all would agree, shown no interest at all in favoring particular candidates for judicial or legal office or particular types of legislation. Even if Wisconsin had such an interest, the Integrated Bar does not provide a fixed, predictable conduit for governmental encouragement of particular views, for the Bar makes its own decisions on legislative recommendations and appears to take no action at all with regard to candidates. By the same token the weight lent to one side of a controversial issue by the prestige of government is wholly lacking here.

In short, it seems to me fanciful in the extreme to find in the limited functions of the Wisconsin State Bar those risks of governmental self-perpetuation that might justify the recognition of a Constitutional protection against the "establishment" of political beliefs. A contrary conclusion would, it seems to me, as well embrace within its rationale the operations of the Judicial Conference of the United States, and the legislative recommendations of independent agencies such as the Interstate Commerce Commission and the Bureau of the Budget.

3. Development of a "Guild System"

It is said that the Integrated Bar concept tends toward the development of some sort of a "guild system." But there are no requirements of action or inaction connected with the Wisconsin Integrated Bar, as contrasted with any unintegrated bar, except for the requirement of payment of $15 annual dues. I would agree that the requirement of payment of dues could not be made the basis of limiting the profession of law to the comparatively wealthy. Nor, doubtless, could admission to the profession be restricted to relatives of those already admitted. But there is no such "guild" threat presented in this situation . . .

4. "Drowning Out" the Voice of Dissent

This objection can be stated in either of two ways. First: The requirement of dues payments to be spent to further views to which the payor is opposed tends to increase the volume of the arguments he opposes and thereby to drown out his own voice in opposition, in violation of his Constitutional right to be heard. Second: The United States Constitution creates a scheme of federal and state governments each of which is to be elected on a one-man-one-vote basis and on a one-man-one-political-voice basis. Of course several persons may voluntarily cumulate their political voices, but no governmental force can require a single individual to contribute money to support views to be adopted by a democratically organized group even if the individual is also free to say what he pleases separately.

It seems to me these arguments have little force. In the first place, their supposition is that the voice of a dissenter is less effective if

he speaks it first in an attempt to influence the action of a democratically organized group and then, if necessary, in dissent to the
recommendations of that group. This is not at all convincing. The
dissenter is not being made to contribute funds to the furtherance
of views he opposes but is rather being made to contribute funds
to a group expenditure about which he will have something to say.
To the extent that his voice of dissent can convince his lawyer
associates, it will later be heard by the State Legislature with a
magnified voice. In short, I think it begs the question to approach
the Constitutional issue with the assumption that the majority of
the Bar has a permanently formulated position which the dissenting
dues payor is being required to support, thus increasing the difficulty
of effective opposition to it.

Moreover, I do not think it can be said with any assurance that
being required to contribute to the dispersion of views one opposes
has a substantial limiting effect on one's right to speak and be
heard . . .

Beyond all this, the argument under discussion is contradicted
in the everyday operation of our society. Of course it is disagreeable
to see a group, to which one has been required to contribute, decide
to spend its money for purposes the contributor opposes. But the
Constitution does not protect against the mere play of personal
emotions. We recognized in *Hanson* that an employee can be
required to contribute to the propagation of personally repugnant
views on working conditions or retirement benefits that are expressed on union picket signs or in union handbills. A federal
taxpayer obtains no refund if he is offended by what is put out by
the United States Information Agency. Such examples could be
multiplied.

For me, this "drowning out" argument falls apart upon analysis.

5. "Compelled Affirmation" of Belief

It is argued that the requirement of Bar dues payments which
may be spent for legislative recommendations which the payor
opposes amounts to a compelled affirmation of belief of the sort
this Court struck down in *West Virginia Board of Education* v.
Barnette, 319 U.S. 624. While I agree that the rationale of *Barnette*
is relevant, I do not think that it is in any sense controlling in the
present case.

Mr. Justice Jackson, writing for the Court in *Barnette*, did not view the issue as turning merely "on one's possession of particular religious views or the sincerity with which they are held." 319 U.S. at 634. The holding of *Barnette* was that, no matter how strong or weak such beliefs might be, the Legislature of West Virginia was not free to require as concrete and intimate an expression of belief in any cause as that involved in a compulsory pledge of allegiance. It is in this light that one must assess the contention that, "Compelling a man by law to pay his money to elect candidates or advocate laws or doctrines he is against differs only in degree, if at all, from compelling him by law to speak for a candidate, a party, or a cause he is against." One could as well say that the same mere difference in degree distinguishes the *Barnette* flag salute situation from a taxpayer's objections to the views a government agency presents, at public expense, to Congress. What seems to me obvious is the large difference in degree between, on the one hand, being compelled to raise one's hand and recite a belief as one's own, and, on the other, being compelled to contribute dues to a bar association fund which is to be used in part to promote the expression of views in the name of the organization (not in the name of the dues payor), which views when adopted may turn out to be contrary to the views of the dues payor. I think this is a situation where the difference in degree is so great as to amount to a difference in substance . . .

It seems to me evident that the actual core of appellant's complaint as to "compelled affirmation" is not the identification with causes to which he objects that might arise from some conceivable tracing of the use of his dues in their support, but is his forced association with the Integrated Bar. That, however, is a bridge which, beyond all doubt and any protestations now made to the contrary, we crossed in the *Hanson* case. I can see no way to uncross it without overruling *Hanson*. Certainly it cannot be done by declaring as a rule of law that lawyers feel more strongly about the identification of their names with proposals for law reform than union members feel about the identification of their names with collective bargaining demands declared on the radio, in picket signs, and on handbills.

II

While I think that what has been said might well dispose of this case without more, in that Wisconsin lawyers retain "full freedom

160

to think their own thoughts, speak their own minds, support their own causes and wholeheartedly fight whatever they are against," I shall pass on to consider the state interest involved in the establishment of the Integrated Bar, the other ingredient of adjudication which arises whenever incidental impingement upon such freedoms may fairly be said to draw in question governmental action.

In this instance it can hardly be doubted that it was Constitutionally permissible for Wisconsin to regard the functions of an Integrated Bar as sufficiently important to justify whatever incursions on these individual freedoms may be thought to arise from the operations of the organization. The Wisconsin Supreme Court has described the fields of the State Bar's legislative activities . . . , has asserted its readiness to restrict legislative recommendations to those fields . . . [and] has declared its belief that the lawyers of the State possess an expertise useful to the public interest within these fields:

> We are of the opinion that the public welfare will be promoted by securing and publicizing the composite judgment of the members of the bar of the state on measures directly affecting the administration of justice and the practice of law. The general public and the legislature are entitled to know how the profession as a whole stands on such type of proposed legislation. This is a function an integrated bar, which is as democratically governed and administered as the State Bar, can perform much more effectively than can a voluntary bar association. [10 Wis.2d 230, 239–240, 102 N.W.2d 404, 409–410.]

I do not think that the State Court's view in this respect can be considered in any way unreasonable . . .

In this light I can only regard as entirely gratuitous a contention that there is anything less than a most substantial state interest in Wisconsin having the views of the members of its Bar "on measures directly affecting the administration of justice and the practice of law." Nor can I take seriously a suggestion that the lawyers of Wisconsin are merely being polled on matters of their own personal belief or predilection, any more than Congress had in mind such a poll when it made it the duty of federal circuit judges summoned to attend the Judicial Conference of the United States "to advise . . . as to any matters in respect of which the administration of justice in the courts of the United States may be improved." 42 Stat. 837, 838.

III

Beyond this conjunction of a highly significant state need and the chimerical nature of the claims of abridgment of individual freedom, there is still a further approach to the entire problem that combines both of these aspects and reinforces my belief in the Constitutionality of the Integrated Bar.

I had supposed it beyond doubt that a state legislature could set up a staff or commission to recommend changes in the more or less technical areas of the law into which no well-advised laymen would venture without the assistance of counsel. A state legislature could certainly appoint a commission to make recommendations to it on the desirability of passing or modifying any of the countless uniform laws dealing with all kinds of legal subjects, running all the way from the Uniform Commercial Code to the Uniform Simultaneous Death Law. It seems no less clear to me that a reasonable license tax can be imposed on the profession of being a lawyer, doctor, dentist, etc. In these circumstances, wherein lies the unconstitutionality of what Wisconsin has done? Does the Constitution forbid the payment of some part of the Constitutional license fee directly to the equally Constitutional state law revision commission? Or is it that such a commission cannot be chosen by a majority vote of all the members of the state bar? Or could it be that the Federal Constitution requires a separation of state powers according to which a state legislature can tax and set up commissions but a state judiciary cannot do these things?

I end as I began. It is exceedingly regrettable that such specious contentions as appellant makes in this case should have resulted in putting the Integrated Bar under this cloud of partial unconstitutionality.

162

NAACP v. *Button*

371 U.S. 415, 448 (1963)

The National Association for the Advancement of Colored People (NAACP) brought suit in a Virginia state court seeking to have certain statutory provisions declared inapplicable to the Association's activities[1] or, if applicable, unconstitutional. The Association prevailed on a number of its challenges at the state level, but the state supreme court did hold that Chapter 33 of the state's laws was applicable to the NAACP's activities and was a valid law. (That chapter, enacted in 1956, amended the provisions of the Virginia Code forbidding solicitation of legal business by a "runner" or "capper" to include, in the definition of those terms, an agent for an individual or organization which retains a lawyer in connection with an action to which it is not a party and in which it has no pecuniary right or liability.) The state supreme court also held that the activities of the NAACP which were prohibited by the statute were, in addition, in violation of Canons 35 and 47 of the American Bar Association's canons of ethics, adopted by the state court in 1938.

On review, the United States Supreme Court reversed, 6–3. Justice Brennan, speaking for five members of the Court, held that application of the statute and the canons of ethics to the activities of the NAACP violated the First Amendment rights of the Association and of its members to associate for the purpose of assisting those seeking legal redress.[2] He found no sufficient overriding state interest in the need to regulate the legal profession, in view of the absence from this case of any element of use of the legal process for "purely private gain."

Justice Douglas joined the opinion but added that in his view the statute, as a part of the state's program of massive resistance to desegregation, was intended to and did discriminate against the NAACP. Justice White concurred in the result on the ground of the statute's undue breadth but voiced concern that the majority would strike down a more narrowly drawn statute. Justice Harlan in his dissent was plainly willing to read the statute more narrowly than the majority and thus to avoid some troublesome

[1] These activities, many of which are summarized in Justice Harlan's dissenting opinion, related to the initiation and conduct of litigation aimed at securing the constitutional rights of Negro citizens. The NAACP Legal Defense and Educational Fund, Inc., was also a complainant, but did not seek direct review of the state court decision in the Supreme Court.

[2] The Court relied in part on a determination that the statute was constitutionally vulnerable on grounds of vagueness, a point dealt with by Justice Harlan in his dissent but omitted in the excerpt that follows.

constitutional issues. But, as the following excerpt shows, his disagreement was more fundamental; he argued strongly that the majority had slighted, or overlooked entirely, substantial state interests that need not and should not have been sacrificed despite the worthiness of the Association's cause.

Mr. Justice Harlan, whom Mr. Justice Clark and Mr. Justice Stewart join, dissenting.

No member of this Court would disagree that the validity of state action claimed to infringe rights assured by the Fourteenth Amendment is to be judged by the same basic constitutional standards whether or not racial problems are involved. No worse setback could befall the great principles established by *Brown* v. *Board of Education*, 347 U.S. 483, than to give fair-minded persons reason to think otherwise. With all respect, I believe that the striking down of this Virginia statute cannot be squared with accepted constitutional doctrine in the domain of state regulatory power over the legal profession.

I

At the outset the factual premises on which the Virginia Supreme Court of Appeals upheld the application of Chapter 33 to the activities of the NAACP in the area of litigation, as well as the scope of that court's holding, should be delineated.

First, the lawyers who participate in litigation sponsored by petitioner are, almost without exception, members of the legal staff of the NAACP Virginia State Conference. (It is, in fact, against Conference policy to give financial support to litigation not handled by a staff lawyer.) As such, they are selected by petitioner, are compensated by it for work in litigation (whether or not petitioner is a party thereto), and so long as they remain on the staff, are necessarily subject to its directions. As the Court recognizes, it is incumbent on staff members to agree to abide by NAACP policies.

Second, it is equally clear that the NAACP's directions, or those of its officers and divisions, to staff lawyers cover many subjects relating to the form and substance of litigation . . .

Third, . . . the present record establishes that the petitioner does a great deal more than to advocate litigation and to wait for prospective litigants to come forward. In several instances, especially in litigation touching racial discrimination in public schools, specific directions were given as to the types of prospective plaintiffs to be sought, and staff lawyers brought blank forms to meetings for the purpose of obtaining signatures authorizing the prosecution of litigation in the name of the signer.

Fourth, there is substantial evidence indicating that the normal incidents of the attorney-client relationship were often absent in litigation handled by staff lawyers and financed by petitioner. Forms signed by prospective litigants have on occasion not contained the name of the attorney authorized to act. In many cases, whether or not the form contained specific authorization to that effect, additional counsel have been brought into the action by staff counsel. There were several litigants who testified that at no time did they have any personal dealings with the lawyers handling their cases nor were they aware until long after the event that suits had been filed in their names. This is not to suggest that the petitioner has been shown to have sought plaintiffs under false pretenses or by inaccurate statements. But there is no basis for concluding that these were isolated incidents, or that petitioner's methods of operation have been such as to render these happenings out of the ordinary.

On these factual premises, amply supported by the evidence, the Virginia Supreme Court of Appeals held that petitioner and those associated with it

> solicit prospective litigants to authorize the filing of suits by NAACP and Fund [Educational Defense Fund] lawyers, who are paid by the conference and controlled by NAACP policies . . . (202 Va. at 159; 116 S.E.2d at 68–69),

and concluded that this conduct violated Chapter 33 as well as Canons 35 and 47 of the Canons of Professional Ethics of the American Bar Association, which had been adopted by the Virginia courts more than 20 years ago.

At the same time the Virginia court demonstrated a responsible awareness of two important limitations on the State's power to regulate such conduct. The first of these is the long-standing recognition, incorporated in the Canons, of the different treatment to be accorded to those aiding the indigent in prosecuting or defending against legal proceedings. The second, which coupled with the first led the court to strike down Chapter 36, is the constitutional right of any person to express his views, to disseminate those views to others, and to advocate action designed to achieve lawful objectives, which in the present case are also constitutionally due. Mindful of these limitations, the state court construed Chapter 33 not to prohibit petitioner and those associated with it from acquainting colored persons with what it believes to be their rights, or from advising them to assert those rights in legal proceedings, but only from "solicit[ing] legal business for their attorneys or any particular attorneys." Further, the court determined that Chapter 33 did not preclude petitioner from contributing money to persons to assist them in prosecuting suits, if the suits "have not been solicited by the appellants [the NAACP and Defense Fund] or those associated with them, and channeled by them to their attorneys or any other attorneys."

In my opinion the litigation program of the NAACP, as shown by this record, falls within an area of activity which a State may constitutionally regulate . . .

II

Freedom of expression embraces more than the right of an individual to speak his mind. It includes also his right to advocate and his right to join with his fellows in an effort to make that advocacy effective. And just as it includes the right jointly to petition the legislature for redress of grievances, so it must include the right to join together for purposes of obtaining judicial redress. We have passed the point where litigation is regarded as an evil that must be avoided if some accommodation short of a lawsuit can possibly be worked out. Litigation is often the desirable and orderly way of resolving disputes of broad public significance, and of obtaining vindication of fundamental rights. This is particularly so in the sensitive area of racial relationships.

But to declare that litigation is a form of conduct that may be associated with political expression does not resolve this case. Neither the First Amendment nor the Fourteenth constitutes an absolute bar to government regulation in the fields of free expression and association. This Court has repeatedly held that certain forms of speech are outside the scope of the protection of those Amendments, and that, in addition, "general regulatory statutes, not intended to control the content of speech but incidentally limiting its unfettered exercise," are permissible "when they have been found justified by subordinating valid governmental interests." [*Konigsberg v. State Bar*, 366 U.S. 36, 50–51.] The problem in each such case is to weigh the legitimate interest of the State against the effect of the regulation on individual rights . . .

[In] the present case, I think it evident that the basic rights in issue are those of the petitioner's members to associate, to discuss, and to advocate. Absent the gravest danger to the community, these rights must remain free from frontal attack or suppression, and the state court has recognized this in striking down Chapter 36 and in carefully limiting the impact of Chapter 33. But litigation, whether or not associated with the attempt to vindicate constitutional rights, is *conduct;* it is speech *plus.* Although the State surely may not broadly prohibit individuals with a common interest from joining together to petition a court for redress of their grievances, it is equally certain that the State may impose reasonable regulations limiting the permissible form of litigation and the manner of legal representation within its borders. Thus the State may, without violating protected rights, restrict those undertaking to represent others in legal proceedings to properly qualified practitioners. And it may determine that a corporation or association does not itself have standing to litigate the interests of its shareholders or members—that only individuals with a direct interest of their own may join to press their claims in its courts. Both kinds of regulation are undeniably matters of legitimate concern to the State and their possible impact on the rights of expression and association is far too remote to cause any doubt as to their validity.

So here, the question is whether the particular regulation of conduct concerning litigation has a reasonable relation to the furtherance of a proper state interest, and whether that interest outweighs any foreseeable harm to the furtherance of protected freedoms.

III

The interest which Virginia has here asserted is that of maintaining high professional standards among those who practice law within its borders. This Court has consistently recognized the broad range of judgments that a State may properly make in regulating any profession. But the regulation of professional standards for members of the bar comes to us with even deeper roots in history and policy, since courts for centuries have possessed disciplinary powers incident to the administration of justice.

The regulation before us has its origins in the long-standing common-law prohibitions of champerty, barratry, and maintenance, the closely related prohibitions in the Canons of Ethics against solicitation and intervention by a lay intermediary, and statutory provisions forbidding the unauthorized practice of law. The Court recognizes this formidable history, but puts it aside in the present case on the grounds that there is here no element of malice or of pecuniary gain, that the interests of the NAACP are not to be regarded as substantially different from those of its members, and that we are said to be dealing here with a matter that transcends mere legal ethics—the securing of federally guaranteed rights. But these distinctions are too facile. They do not account for the full scope of the State's legitimate interest in regulating professional conduct. For although these professional standards may have been born in a desire to curb malice and self-aggrandizement by those who would use clients and the courts for their own pecuniary ends, they have acquired a far broader significance during their long development.

First, with regard to the claimed absence of the pecuniary element, it cannot well be suggested that the attorneys here are donating their services, since they are in fact compensated for their work. Nor can it tenably be argued that petitioner's litigating activities fall into the accepted category of aid to indigent litigants. The reference is presumably to the fact that petitioner itself is a nonprofit organization not motivated by desire for financial gain but by public interest and to the fact that no monetary stakes are involved in the litigation.

But a State's felt need for regulation of professional conduct may reasonably extend beyond mere "ambulance chasing" . . .[3]

Underlying this impressive array of relevant precedent is the widely shared conviction that avoidance of improper pecuniary gain is not the only relevant factor in determining standards of professional conduct. Running perhaps even deeper is the desire of the profession, of courts, and of legislatures to prevent any interference

[3]There is omitted discussion of a number of cases dealing with state prohibition of the unauthorized practice of law and with the bans against "lay solicitation" of legal business. Considerable doubt has been cast on at least some of these decisions, it should be noted, by the evolution of constitutional doctrine since the *Button* case was handed down. See, e.g., UMW v. State Bar of Illinois, 389 U.S. 217. [Ed.]

with the uniquely personal relationship between lawyer and client and to maintain untrammeled by outside influences the responsibility which the lawyer owes to the courts he serves.

When an attorney is employed by an association or corporation to represent individual litigants, two problems arise, whether or not the association is organized for profit and no matter how unimpeachable its motives. The lawyer becomes subject to the control of a body that is not itself a litigant and that, unlike the lawyers it employs, is not subject to strict professional discipline as an officer of the court. In addition, the lawyer necessarily finds himself with a divided allegiance—to his employer and to his client—which may prevent full compliance with his basic professional obligations. The matter was well stated, in a different but related context, by the New York Court of Appeals in *In re Co-operative Law Co.*, 198 N.Y. 479, 483–484, 92 N.E. 15, 16:

> The relation of attorney and client is that of master and servant in a limited and dignified sense, and it involves the highest trust and confidence. It cannot be delegated without consent and it cannot exist between an attorney employed by a corporation to practice law for it, and a client of the corporation, for he would be subject to the directions of the corporation and not to the directions of the client.

There has, to be sure, been professional criticism of certain applications of these policies. But the continued vitality of the principles involved is beyond dispute, and at this writing it is hazardous at best to predict the direction of the future. For us, however, any such debate is without relevance, since it raises questions of social policy which have not been delegated to this Court for decision. Our responsibility is simply to determine the extent of the State's legitimate interest and to decide whether the course adopted bears a sufficient relation to that interest to fall within the bounds set by the Constitution.

Second, it is claimed that the interests of petitioner and its members are sufficiently identical to eliminate any "serious danger" of "professionally reprehensible conflicts of interest" . . .

The NAACP may be no more than the sum of the efforts and views infused in it by its members; but the totality of the separate interests of the members and others whose causes the petitioner champions, even in the field of race relations, may far exceed in

169

scope and variety that body's views of policy, as embodied in litigating strategy and tactics. Thus it may be in the interest of the Association in every case to make a frontal attack on segregation, to press for an immediate breaking down of racial barriers, and to sacrifice minor points that may win a given case for the major points that may win other cases too. But in a particular litigation, it is not impossible that after authorizing action in his behalf, a Negro parent, concerned that a continued frontal attack could result in schools closed for years, might prefer to wait with his fellows a longer time for good-faith efforts by the local school board than is permitted by the centrally determined policy of the NAACP. Or he might see a greater prospect of success through discussions with local school authorities than through the litigation deemed necessary by the Association. The parent, of course, is free to withdraw his authorization, but is his lawyer, retained and paid by petitioner and subject to its directions on matters of policy, able to advise the parent with that undivided allegiance that is the hallmark of the attorney-client relation? I am afraid not.

Indeed, the potential conflict in the present situation is perhaps greater than those in the union, automobile club, and some of the other cases discussed above. For here, the interests of the NAACP go well beyond the providing of competent counsel for the prosecution or defense of individual claims; they embrace broadly fixed substantive policies that may well often deviate from the immediate, or even long-range, desires of those who choose to accept its offers of legal representations. This serves to underscore the close interdependence between the State's condemnation of solicitation and its prohibition of the unauthorized practice of law by a lay organization.

Third, it is said that the practices involved here must stand on a different footing because the litigation that petitioner supports concerns the vindication of constitutionally guaranteed rights.[4]

But surely state law is still the source of basic regulation of the

---

[4] It is interesting to note the Court's reliance on Opinion 148, Opinions of the Committee on Professional Ethics and Grievances, American Bar Assn. This opinion, issued in 1935 at the height of the resentment in certain quarters against the New Deal, approved the practice of the National Lawyers Committee of the Liberty League in publicly offering free legal services (without compensation from any source) to anyone who was *unable to afford* to challenge the constitutionality of legislation which he believed was violating his rights. The opinion may well be debatable as a matter of interpretation of the Canons. But in any event I think it wholly untenable to suggest (as the Court does in its holding today) that a contrary opinion regarding *paid* legal services to *nonindigent* litigants would be unconstitutional.

legal profession, whether an attorney is pressing a federal or a state claim within its borders. The true question is whether the State has taken action which unreasonably obstructs the assertion of federal rights. Here, it cannot be said that the underlying state policy is inevitably inconsistent with federal interests. The State has sought to prohibit the solicitation and sponsoring of litigation by those who have no standing to initiate that litigation themselves and who are not simply coming to the assistance of indigent litigants. Thus the state policy is not unrelated to the federal rules of standing—the insistence that federal court litigants be confined to those who can demonstrate a pressing personal need for relief. This is a requirement of substance as well as form. It recognizes that, although litigation is not something to be avoided at all costs, it should not be resorted to in undue haste, without any effort at extrajudicial resolution, and that those lacking immediate private need may make unnecessary broad attacks based on inadequate records. Nor is the federal interest in impeding precipitate resort to litigation diminished when that litigation concerns constitutional issues; if anything, it is intensified.

There remains to be considered on this branch of the argument the question whether this particular exercise of state regulatory power bears a sufficient relation to the established and substantial interest of the State to overcome whatever indirect impact this statute may have on rights of free expression and association.

Chapter 33 as construed does no more than prohibit petitioner and those associated with it from soliciting legal business for its staff attorneys or, under a fair reading of the state court's opinion and amounting to the same thing, for "outside" attorneys who are subject to the Association's control in the handling of litigation which it refers to them. Such prohibitions bear a strong and direct relation to the area of legitimate state concern. In matters of policy, involving the form, timing, and substance of litigation, such attorneys are subject to the directions of petitioner and not of those nominally their clients. Further, the methods used to obtain litigants are not conducive to encouraging the kind of attorney-client relationships which the State reasonably may demand. There inheres in these arrangements, then, the potentialities of divided allegiance and diluted responsibility which the State may properly undertake to prevent.

The impact of such a prohibition on the rights of petitioner and its members to free expression and association cannot well be deemed so great as to require that it be struck down in the face of this substantial state interest. The important function of organizations like petitioner in vindicating constitutional rights is not of course to be minimized, but that function is not, in my opinion, substantially impaired by this statute. Of cardinal importance, this regulatory enactment as construed does not in any way suppress assembly, or advocacy of litigation in general or in particular. Moreover, contrary to the majority's suggestion, it does not, in my view, prevent petitioner from recommending the services of attorneys who are not subject to its directions and control. And since petitioner may contribute to those who need assistance, the prohibition should not significantly discourage anyone with sufficient interest from pressing his claims in litigation or from joining with others similarly situated to press those claims. It prevents only the solicitation of business for attorneys subject to petitioner's control, and as so limited, should be sustained . . .

The Process of
Statutory Construction

Yates v. United States

354 U.S. 298 (1957)

One of the principal responsibilities of the Supreme Court has been to construe acts of Congress with respect for the objectives sought to be achieved by the legislation but at the same time with a sensitive regard for the constitutional questions that might be raised by that legislation. No area has caused more difficulty for the Court in striving to attain this balance than that posed by the potential conflict between the Smith Act[1] and the protections of the First Amendment. The *Yates* and *Scales* decisions, included in this section, provide dramatic illustrations of that conflict.

The Court's initial struggle with the Smith Act occurred in *Dennis* v. *United States*,[2] decided four years before Justice Harlan's appointment to the bench, in which the conviction of a number of top officials of the Communist Party of the United States was sustained and a challenge to the constitutionality of the Smith Act rejected.

[1] 18 U.S.C. § 2385, originally enacted in 1940 and amended since *Yates* to include a definition of the word "organize." See also the general conspiracy statute, 18 U.S.C. § 371. Section 2385 declares, among other things, that: "Whoever knowingly or willfully advocates . . . or teaches the duty . . . or propriety of overthrowing or destroying the government of the United States . . . by force or violence" shall be guilty of an offense. A subsequent paragraph declares it to be a crime to organize any society or group for this purpose.
[2] 341 U.S. 494.

173

Many problems were left unresolved in *Dennis*, and these were raised in subsequent cases. The first to come to the Court was *Yates*, in which fourteen leaders of the Communist Party in California had been convicted for conspiring (1) to advocate and teach the duty and necessity of overthrowing the government of the United States by force and violence, and (2) to organize, as the Communist Party of the United States, a society of persons who so advocate and teach. Serious questions of defining "organize" and "advocate" in a way that would avoid infringing First Amendment rights were presented. In answering those questions the Court, speaking through Justice Harlan, rejected some of the broad implications of *Dennis* and narrowed the channel the prosecution must follow to obtain a conviction. In a 6–1 decision, the convictions were reversed. Four members of the majority held that while nine of the defendants could be retried, the other five could not be, in view of the insufficiency of the evidence against them.[3]

Mr. Justice Harlan delivered the opinion of the Court.

We brought these cases here to consider certain questions arising under the Smith Act which have not heretofore been passed upon by this Court, and otherwise to review the convictions of these petitioners for conspiracy to violate that Act . . .

In the view we take of this case, it is necessary for us to consider only the following of petitioners' contentions: (1) that the term "organize" as used in the Smith Act was erroneously construed by the two lower courts; (2) that the trial court's instructions to the jury erroneously excluded from the case the issue of "incitement to action"; (3) that the evidence was so insufficient as to require this Court to direct the acquittal of these petitioners; and (4) that petitioner Schneiderman's conviction was precluded by this Court's judgment in *Schneiderman* v. *United States*, 320 U.S. 118, under the doctrine of collateral estoppel.[4] For reasons given hereafter, we conclude that these convictions must be reversed and the case remanded to the District Court with instructions to enter judgments of acquittal as to certain of the petitioners, and to grant a new trial as to the rest.

[3] Justices Brennan and Whittaker did not participate. Justices Black and Douglas would have directed that all fourteen defendants be acquitted. Justice Clark dissented.

[4] In this excerpt, discussion of points (1), (2), and (3) has been abridged, and the discussion of point (4), rejecting Schneiderman's contention, has been omitted. [Ed.]

I. *The Term "Organize"*

One object of the conspiracy charged was to violate the third paragraph of 18 U.S.C. § 2385, which provides:

> Whoever organizes or helps or attempts to organize any society, group, or assembly of persons who teach, advocate, or encourage the overthrow or destruction of any [government in the United States] by force or violence . . . shall be fined not more than $10,000 or imprisoned not more than ten years, or both . . .

Petitioners claim that "organize" means to "establish," "found," or "bring into existence," and that in this sense the Communist Party was organized by 1945 at the latest. On this basis petitioners contend that this part of the indictment, returned in 1951, was barred by the three-year statute of limitations. The Government, on the other hand, says that "organize" connotes a continuing process which goes on throughout the life of an organization, and that, in the words of the trial court's instructions to the jury, the term includes such things as "the recruiting of new members and the forming of new units, and the regrouping or expansion of existing clubs, classes and other units of any society, party, group or other organization." The two courts below accepted the Government's position. We think, however, that petitioners' position must prevail, upon principles stated by Chief Justice Marshall more than a century ago in *United States* v. *Wiltberger*, 5 Wheat. 76, 95–96, as follows:

> The rule that penal laws are to be construed strictly, is perhaps not much less old than construction itself. It is founded on the tenderness of the law for the rights of individuals; and on the plain principle that the power of punishment is vested in the legislative, not in the judicial department. It is the legislature, not the Court, which is to define a crime, and ordain its punishment . . .

II. *Instructions to the Jury*

Petitioners contend that the instructions to the jury were fatally defective in that the trial court refused to charge that, in order to convict, the jury must find that the advocacy which the defendants conspired to promote was of a kind calculated to "incite" persons to action for the forcible overthrow of the Government. It is argued that advocacy of forcible overthrow as mere *abstract doctrine* is within the free speech protection of the First Amendment; that the Smith Act, consistently with that constitutional provision, must be taken as proscribing only the sort of advocacy which incites to illegal *action;* and that the trial court's charge, by permitting conviction for mere advocacy, unrelated to its tendency to produce forcible action, resulted in an unconstitutional application of the Smith Act. The Government, which at the trial also requested the court to charge in terms of "incitement," now takes the position, however, that the true constitutional dividing line is not between inciting and abstract advocacy of forcible overthrow, but rather between advocacy as such, irrespective of its inciting qualities, and the mere discussion or exposition of violent overthrow as an abstract theory . . .

There can be no doubt from the record that in . . . instructing the jury the court regarded as immaterial, and intended to withdraw from the jury's consideration, any issue as to the character of the advocacy in terms of its capacity to stir listeners to forcible action. Both the petitioners and the Government submitted proposed instructions which would have required the jury to find that the proscribed advocacy was not of a mere abstract doctrine of forcible overthrow, but of action to that end, by the use of language reasonably and ordinarily calculated to incite persons to such action. The trial court rejected these proposed instructions on the ground that any necessity for giving them which may have existed at the time the *Dennis* case [*Dennis* v. *United States*, 341 U.S. 494] was tried was removed by this Court's subsequent decision in that case. The court made it clear in colloquy with counsel that in its view the illegal advocacy was made out simply by showing that what was said dealt with forcible overthrow and that it was uttered with a specific intent to accomplish that purpose, insisting that all such advocacy was punishable "whether it is language of incitement or not." The Court of Appeals affirmed on a different theory, as we shall see later on.

We are thus faced with the question whether the Smith Act prohibits advocacy and teaching of forcible overthrow as an abstract principle, divorced from any effort to instigate action to that end, so long as such advocacy or teaching is engaged in with evil intent. We hold that it does not.

The distinction between advocacy of abstract doctrine and advocacy directed at promoting unlawful action is one that has been consistently recognized in the opinions of this Court. This distinction was heavily underscored in *Gitlow* v. *New York*, 268 U.S. 652, in which the statute involved was nearly identical with the one now before us, and where the Court, despite the narrow view there taken of the First Amendment, said:

> The statute does not penalize the utterance or publication of abstract "doctrine" or academic discussion having no quality of incitement to any concrete action . . . It is not the abstract "doctrine" of overthrowing organized government by unlawful means which is denounced by the statute, but the advocacy of action for the accomplishment of that purpose . . . This [Manifesto] . . . is [in] the language of direct incitement . . . That the jury were warranted in finding that the Manifesto advocated not merely the abstract doctrine of overthrowing organized government by force, violence and unlawful means, but action to that end, is clear . . . That utterances inciting to the overthrow of organized government by unlawful means, present a sufficient danger of substantive evil to bring their punishment within the range of legislative discretion, is clear. *Id.* at 664–669.

We need not, however, decide the issue before us in terms of constitutional compulsion, for our first duty is to construe this statute. In doing so we should not assume that Congress chose to disregard a constitutional danger zone so clearly marked, or that it used the words "advocate" and "teach" in their ordinary dictionary meanings when they had already been construed as terms of art carrying a special and limited connotation . . . The legislative history of the Smith Act and related bills shows beyond all question that Congress was aware of the distinction between the advocacy or teaching of abstract doctrine and the advocacy or teaching of action, and that it did not intend to disregard it. The statute was aimed at the advocacy and teaching of concrete action for the forcible overthrow of the Government, and not of principles divorced from action.

The Government's reliance on this Court's decision in *Dennis* is misplaced. The jury instructions which were refused here were given there, and were referred to by this Court as requiring "the jury to find the facts *essential* to establish the substantive crime."

341 U.S. at 512 (emphasis added). It is true that at one point in the late Chief Justice's opinion it is stated that the Smith Act "is directed at advocacy, not discussion," *id.* at 502, but it is clear that the reference was to advocacy of action, not ideas, for in the very next sentence the opinion emphasizes that the jury was properly instructed that there could be no conviction for "advocacy in the realm of ideas." The two concurring opinions in that case likewise emphasize the distinction with which we are concerned . . .

The Court of Appeals took a different view from that of the District Court. While seemingly recognizing that the proscribed advocacy must be associated in some way with action, and that the instructions given the jury here fell short in that respect, it considered that the instructions which the trial court refused were unnecessary in this instance because establishment of the conspiracy, here charged under the general conspiracy statute, required proof of an overt act, whereas in *Dennis,* where the conspiracy was charged under the Smith Act, no overt act was required. In other words, the Court of Appeals thought that the requirement of proving an overt act was an adequate substitute for the linking of the advocacy to action which would otherwise have been necessary. This, of course, is a mistaken notion, for the overt act will not necessarily evidence the character of the advocacy engaged in, nor, indeed, is an agreement to advocate forcible overthrow itself an unlawful conspiracy if it does not call for advocacy of action. The statement in *Dennis* that "it is the existence of the conspiracy which creates the danger," 341 U.S. at 511, does not support the Court of Appeals . . . The reference of the term "conspiracy," in context, was to an agreement to *accomplish* overthrow at some future time, implicit in the jury's findings under the instructions given, rather than to an agreement to speak. *Dennis* was thus not concerned with a conspiracy to engage at some future time in seditious advocacy, but rather with a conspiracy to advocate presently the taking of forcible action in the future. It was action, not advocacy, that was to be postponed until "circumstances" would "permit." We intimate no views as to whether a conspiracy to engage in advocacy in the future, where speech would thus be separated from action by one further remove, is punishable under the Smith Act.

We think, thus, that both of the lower courts here misconceived *Dennis.*

In light of the foregoing we are unable to regard the District Court's charge upon this aspect of the case as adequate. The jury was never told that the Smith Act does not denounce advocacy in the sense of preaching abstractly the forcible overthrow of the Government. We think that the trial court's statement that the proscribed advocacy must include the "urging," "necessity," and "duty" of forcible overthrow, and not merely its "desirability" and "propriety," may not be regarded as a sufficient substitute for charging that the Smith Act reaches only advocacy of action for the overthrow of government by force and violence. The essential distinction is that those to whom the advocacy is addressed must be urged to *do* something, now or in the future, rather than merely to *believe* in something. At best the expressions used by the trial court were equivocal, since in the absence of any instructions differentiating advocacy of abstract doctrine from advocacy of action, they were as consistent with the former as they were with the latter. Nor do we regard their ambiguity as lessened by what the trial court had to say as to the right of the defendants to announce their beliefs as to the inevitability of violent revolution, or to advocate other unpopular opinions. Especially when it is unmistakable that the court did not consider the urging of action for forcible overthrow as being a necessary element of the proscribed advocacy, but rather considered the crucial question to be whether the advocacy was uttered with a specific intent to accomplish such overthrow, we would not be warranted in assuming that the jury drew from these instructions more than the court itself intended them to convey . . .

III. *The Evidence*

The determinations already made require a reversal of these convictions. Nevertheless, in the exercise of our power under 28 U.S.C. § 2106 to "direct the entry of such appropriate judgment . . . as may be just under the circumstances," we have conceived it to be our duty to scrutinize this lengthy record with care, in order to determine whether the way should be left open for a new trial of all or some of these petitioners. Such a judgment, we think, should, on the one hand, foreclose further proceedings against those of the petitioners as to whom the evidence in this record would be palpably insufficient upon a new trial, and should, on the other

179

hand, leave the Government free to retry the other petitioners under proper legal standards, especially since it is by no means clear that certain aspects of the evidence against them could not have been clarified to the advantage of the Government had it not been under a misapprehension as to the burden cast upon it by the Smith Act . . .

As to the petitioners Connelly, Kusnitz, Richmond, Spector, and Steinberg we find no adequate evidence in the record which would permit a jury to find that they were members of such a conspiracy. For all purposes relevant here, the sole evidence as to them was that they had long been members, officers or functionaries of the Communist Party of California; and that standing alone, as Congress has enacted in § 4(f) of the Internal Security Act of 1950,[5] makes out no case against them. So far as this record shows, none of them has engaged in or been associated with any but what appear to have been wholly lawful activities, or has ever made a single remark or been present when someone else made a remark, which would tend to prove the charges against them. Connelly and Richmond were, to be sure, the Los Angeles and Executive Editors, respectively, of the Daily People's World, the West Coast Party organ, but we can find nothing in the material introduced into evidence from that newspaper which advances the Government's case.

Moreover, apart from the inadequacy of the evidence to show, at best, more than the abstract advocacy and teaching of forcible overthrow by the Party, it is difficult to perceive how the requisite specific intent to accomplish such overthrow could be deemed proved by a showing of mere membership or the holding of office in the Communist Party. We therefore think that as to these petitioners the evidence was entirely too meagre to justify putting them to a new trial, and that their acquittal should be ordered.

As to the nine remaining petitioners, we consider that a different conclusion should be reached. There was testimony from the witness Foard, and other evidence, tying Fox, Healey, Lambert, Lima, Schneiderman, Stack, and Yates to Party classes conducted in the San Francisco area during the year 1946, where there occurred what might be considered to be the systematic teaching and advocacy

---

[5] 64 Stat. 987, 50 U.S.C. § 783(f): "Neither the holding of office nor membership in any Communist organization by any person shall constitute per se a violation of subsection (a) or subsection (c) of this section or of any other criminal statute."

of illegal action which is condemned by the statute. It might be found that one of the purposes of such classes was to develop in the members of the group a readiness to engage at the crucial time, perhaps during war or during attack upon the United States from without, in such activities as sabotage and street fighting, in order to divert and diffuse the resistance of the authorities and if possible to seize local vantage points. There was also testimony as to activities in the Los Angeles area, during the period covered by the indictment, which might be considered to amount to "advocacy of action," and with which petitioners Carlson and Dobbs were linked. From the testimony of the witness Scarletto, it might be found that individuals considered to be particularly trustworthy were taken into an "underground" apparatus and there instructed in tasks which would be useful when the time for violent action arrived. Scarletto was surreptitiously indoctrinated in methods, as he said, of moving "masses of people in time of crisis." It might be found, under all the circumstances, that the purpose of this teaching was to prepare the members of the underground apparatus to engage in, to facilitate, and to cooperate with violent action directed against government when the time was ripe. In short, while the record contains evidence of little more than a general program of educational activity by the Communist Party which included advocacy of violence as a theoretical matter, we are not prepared to say, at this stage of the case, that it would be impossible for a jury, resolving all conflicts in favor of the Government and giving the evidence as to these San Francisco and Los Angeles episodes its utmost sweep, to find that advocacy of action was also engaged in when the group involved was thought particularly trustworthy, dedicated, and suited for violent tasks . . .

As to these nine petitioners, then, we shall not order an acquittal . . .

The judgment of the Court of Appeals [affirming the convictions] is reversed, and the case remanded to the District Court for further proceedings consistent with this opinion.

It is so ordered.

181

Scales v. United States

367 U.S. 203 (1961)

The Smith Act also proscribes knowing *membership* in any society that advocates the overthrow of the government by force or violence, and in two cases arising in the 1960 Term the Court was confronted with the question whether this prohibition could be reconciled with the protections of the First and Fifth Amendments.

In one of the cases, *Scales*, the Court affirmed a conviction of a Communist Party member for violation of this prohibition and upheld its constitutionality. It did so, however, only after confining application of the prohibition to "active" members who had knowledge of the Party's illegal advocacy and a specific intent to bring about violent overthrow "as speedily as circumstances would permit." Speaking for the majority in a 5–4 decision, Justice Harlan also insisted that the evidence in such a case must be carefully considered by the reviewing court "to make sure that substantive constitutional standards have not been thwarted." This insistence resulted in the reversal of a similar conviction on the ground of insufficient evidence in *Noto* v. *United States*,[1] a case decided on the same day as *Scales* in an opinion written by Justice Harlan.

The Justice's full opinion in *Scales* is the longest of those represented in this volume, running over fifty pages in the official report. Substantial editing was therefore required to bring it within the compass of the present work.

Mr. Justice Harlan delivered the opinion of the Court.

Our writ issued in this case to review a judgment of the Court of Appeals affirming petitioner's conviction under the so-called membership clause of the Smith Act. 18 U.S.C. § 2385. The Act, among other things, makes a felony the acquisition or holding of knowing membership in any organization which advocates the overthrow of the Government of the United States by force or violence.[2] The indictment charged that from January 1946 to the date

---

[1] 367 U.S. 290.

[2] Section 2385 (whose membership clause we place in italics) reads: . . .

"Whoever organizes or helps or attempts to organize any society, group, or assembly of persons who teach, advocate, or encourage the overthrow or destruction of any such government by force or violence; *or becomes or is a member of*, or affiliates with, *any such society, group, or assembly of persons, knowing the purposes thereof—*

182

of its filing (November 18, 1954) the Communist Party of the United States was such an organization, and that petitioner throughout that period was a member thereof, with knowledge of the Party's illegal purpose and a specific intent to accomplish overthrow "as speedily as circumstances would permit."

The validity of this conviction is challenged on statutory, constitutional, and evidentiary grounds, and further on the basis of certain alleged trial and procedural errors. We decide the issues raised upon the fullest consideration, the case having had an unusually long history in this Court. For reasons given in this opinion we affirm the Court of Appeals . . .

Constitutional Challenge to the Membership Clause on Its Face

Petitioner's constitutional attack goes both to the statute on its face and as applied. At this point we deal with the first aspect of the challenge and with one part of its second aspect. The balance of the latter, which essentially concerns the sufficiency of the evidence, is discussed in the next section of this opinion.

It will bring the constitutional issues into clearer focus to notice first the premises on which the case was submitted to the jury. The jury was instructed that in order to convict it must find that within the three-year limitations period (1) the Communist Party advocated the violent overthrow of the Government, in the sense of present "advocacy of action" to accomplish that end as soon as circumstances were propitious; and (2) petitioner was an "active" member of the Party, and not merely "a nominal, passive, inactive or purely technical" member, with knowledge of the Party's illegal advocacy and a specific intent to bring about violent overthrow "as speedily as circumstances would permit."

The constitutional attack upon the membership clause, as thus construed, is that the statute offends (1) the Fifth Amendment, in that it impermissibly imputes guilt to an individual merely on the basis of his associations and sympathies, rather than because of some concrete personal involvement in criminal conduct; and (2) the First Amendment, in that it infringes on free political expression and association . . .

"Shall be fined not more than $20,000 or imprisoned not more than twenty years, or both, and shall be ineligible for employment by the United States or any department or agency thereof, for the five years next following his conviction . . ."

1. *Statutory Construction*

Before reaching petitioner's constitutional claims, we should first ascertain whether the membership clause permissibly bears the construction put upon it below. We think it does.

The trial court's definition of the kind of organizational advocacy that is proscribed was fully in accord with what was held in *Yates* v. *United States*, 354 U.S. 298. And the statute itself requires that a defendant must have knowledge of the organization's illegal advocacy.

The only two elements of the crime, as defined below, about which there is controversy are therefore "specific intent" and "active" membership. As to the former, this Court held in *Dennis* v. *United States*, 341 U.S. 494, 499–500, that even though the "advocacy" and "organizing" provisions of the Smith Act, unlike the "literature" section, did not expressly contain such a specific intent element, such a requirement was fairly to be implied. We think that the reasoning of *Dennis* applies equally to the membership clause, and are left unpersuaded by the distinctions petitioner seeks to draw between this clause and the advocacy and organizing provisions of the Smith Act.

We find hardly greater difficulty in interpreting the membership clause to reach only "active" members. We decline to attribute to Congress a purpose to punish nominal membership, even though accompanied by "knowledge" and "intent," not merely because of the close constitutional questions that such a purpose would raise, but also for two other reasons: It is not to be lightly inferred that Congress intended to visit upon mere passive members the heavy penalties imposed by the Smith Act. Nor can we assume that it was Congress' purpose to allow the quality of the punishable membership to be measured solely by the varying standards of that relationship as subjectively viewed by different organizations. It is more reasonable to believe that Congress contemplated an objective standard fixed by the law itself, thereby assuring an evenhanded application of the statute . . .

We find no substance in the further suggestion that petitioner could not be expected to anticipate a construction of the statute that included within its elements activity and specific intent, and hence that he was not duly warned of what the statute made

184

criminal. It is, of course, clear that the lower courts' construction was narrower, not broader, than the one for which petitioner argues in defining the character of the forbidden conduct and that therefore, according to petitioner's own construction, his actions were forbidden by the statute. The contention must then be that petitioner had a right to rely on the statute's, as *he* construed it, being held unconstitutional. Assuming, *arguendo,* that petitioner's construction was not unreasonable, no more can be said than that—in light of the courts' traditional avoidance of constructions of dubious constitutionality and in light of their role in construing the purpose of a statute—there were two ways one could reasonably anticipate this statute's being construed, and that petitioner had clear warning that his actions were in violation of both constructions. There is no additional constitutional requirement that petitioner should be entitled to rely upon the statute's being construed in such a way as possibly to render it unconstitutional. In sum, this argument of a "right" to a literal construction simply boils down to a claim that the view of the statute taken below did violence to the congressional purpose. Of course a litigant is always prejudiced when a court errs, but whether or not the lower courts erred in their construction is an issue which can only be met on its merits, and not by reference to a "right" to a particular interpretation.

We hold that the statute was correctly interpreted by the two lower courts, and now turn to petitioner's basic constitutional challenge.

2. *Fifth Amendment*

In our jurisprudence guilt is personal, and when the imposition of punishment on a status or on conduct can only be justified by reference to the relationship of that status or conduct to other concededly criminal activity (here advocacy of violent overthrow), that relationship must be sufficiently substantial to satisfy the concept of personal guilt in order to withstand attack under the Due Process Clause of the Fifth Amendment. Membership, without more, in an organization engaged in illegal advocacy, it is now said, has not heretofore been recognized by this Court to be such a relationship. This claim stands, and we shall examine it, independently of the claim made under the First Amendment . . .

What must be met . . . is the argument that membership, even

185

when accompanied by the elements of knowledge and specific intent, affords an insufficient quantum of participation in the organization's alleged criminal activity, that is, an insufficiently significant form of aid and encouragement to permit the imposition of criminal sanctions on that basis. It must indeed be recognized that a person who merely becomes a member of an illegal organization, by that "act" alone need be doing nothing more than signifying his assent to its purposes and activities on one hand, and providing, on the other, only the sort of moral encouragement which comes from the knowledge that others believe in what the organization is doing. It may indeed be argued that such assent and encouragement do fall short of the concrete, practical impetus given to a criminal enterprise which is lent for instance by a commitment on the part of a conspirator to act in furtherance of that enterprise. A member, as distinguished from a conspirator, may indicate his approval of a criminal enterprise by the very fact of his membership without thereby necessarily committing himself to further it by any act or course of conduct whatever.

In an area of the criminal law which this Court has indicated more than once demands its watchful scrutiny, these factors have weight and must be found to be overborne in a total constitutional assessment of the statute. We think, however, they are duly met when the statute is found to reach only "active" members having also a guilty knowledge and intent, and which therefore prevents a conviction on what otherwise might be regarded as merely an expression of sympathy with the alleged criminal enterprise, unaccompanied by any significant action in its support or any commitment to undertake such action.

Thus, given the construction of the membership clause already discussed, we think the factors called for in rendering members criminally responsible for the illegal advocacy of the organization fall within established, and therefore presumably constitutional, standards of criminal imputability.

3. First Amendment

Little remains to be said concerning the claim that the statute infringes First Amendment freedoms. It was settled in *Dennis* that the advocacy with which we are here concerned is not constitutionally protected speech, and it was further established that a combination to promote such advocacy, albeit under the aegis of what purports to be a political party, is not such association as is protected by the First Amendment. We can discern no reason why membership, when it constitutes a purposeful form of complicity in a group engaging in this same forbidden advocacy, should receive any greater degree of protection from the guarantees of that Amendment.

If it is said that the mere existence of such an enactment tends to inhibit the exercise of constitutionally protected rights, in that it engenders an unhealthy fear that one may find himself unwittingly embroiled in criminal liability, the answer surely is that the statute provides that a defendant must be proven to have knowledge of the proscribed advocacy before he may be convicted. It is, of course, true that quasi-political parties or other groups that may embrace both legal and illegal aims differ from a technical conspiracy, which is defined by its criminal purpose, so that *all* knowing association with the conspiracy is a proper subject for criminal proscription as far as First Amendment liberties are concerned. If there were a similar blanket prohibition of association with a group having both legal and illegal aims, there would indeed be a real danger that legitimate political expression or association would be impaired, but the membership clause, as here construed, does not cut deeper into the freedom of association than is necessary to deal with "the substantive evils that Congress has a right to prevent." *Schenck* v. *United States*, 249 U.S. 47, 52. The clause does not make criminal all association with an organization which has been shown to engage in illegal advocacy. There must be clear proof that a defendant "specifically intend[s] to accomplish [the aims of the organization] by resort to violence." *Noto* v. *United States* [367 U.S. 290] at p. 299. Thus the member for whom the organization is a vehicle for the advancement of legitimate aims and policies does not fall within the ban of the statute: he lacks the requisite specific intent "to bring about the overthrow of the government as speedily as circumstances would permit." Such a person may be foolish, deluded, or perhaps merely optimistic, but he is not by this statute made a criminal.

We conclude that petitioner's constitutional challenge must be overruled.

Evidentiary Challenge

Only in rare instances will this Court review the general sufficiency of the evidence to support a criminal conviction, for ordinarily that is a function which properly belongs to and ends with the Court of Appeals. We do so in this case and in No. 9, *Noto v. United States* [367 U.S.] 290—our first review of convictions under the membership clause of the Smith Act—not only to make sure that substantive constitutional standards have not been thwarted, but also to provide guidance for the future to the lower courts in an area which borders so closely upon constitutionally protected rights . . .

We agree with petitioner that the evidentiary question here is controlled in large part by *Yates*. The decision in *Yates* rested on the view (not articulated in the opinion, though perhaps it should have been) that the Smith Act offenses, involving as they do subtler elements than are present in most other crimes, call for strict standards in assessing the adequacy of the proof needed to make out a case of illegal advocacy. This premise is as applicable to prosecutions under the membership clause of the Smith Act as it is to conspiracy prosecutions under that statute as we had in *Yates*.

The impact of *Yates* with respect to this petitioner's evidentiary challenge is not limited, however, to that decision's requirement of strict standards of proof. *Yates* also articulates general criteria for the evaluation of evidence in determining whether this requirement is met. The *Yates* opinion, through its characterizations of large portions of the evidence which were either described in detail or referred to by reference to the record, indicates what type of evidence is needed to permit a jury to find that (a) there was "advocacy of action" and (b) the Party was responsible for such advocacy . . .[3]

We conclude that this evidence sufficed to make a case for the jury on the issue of illegal Party advocacy. *Dennis* and *Yates* have definitely laid at rest any doubt that present advocacy of *future* action for violent overthrow satisfies statutory and constitutional requirements equally with advocacy of *immediate* action to that end.

---

[3] Detailed discussion of the evidence in the case, covering almost 20 pages in the official report, is here omitted. [Ed.]

Hence this record cannot be considered deficient because it contains no evidence of advocacy for immediate overthrow.

Since the evidence amply showed that Party leaders were continuously preaching during the indictment period the inevitability of eventual forcible overthrow, the first and basic question is a narrow one: whether the jury could permissibly infer that such preaching, in whole or in part, "was aimed at building up a seditious group and maintaining it in readiness for action at a propitious time . . . the kind of indoctrination preparatory to action which was condemned in *Dennis*." *Yates, supra* at 321–322. On this score, we think that the jury, under instructions which fully satisfied the requirements of *Yates*, was entitled to infer from this systematic preaching that where the explicitness and concreteness, of the sort described previously, seemed necessary and prudent, the doctrine of violent revolution—elsewhere more a theory of historical predictability than a rule of conduct—was put forward as a guide to future action, in whatever tone, be it emotional or calculating, that the audience and occasion required; in short, that "advocacy of action" was engaged in . . .

The sufficiency of the evidence as to other elements of the crime requires no exposition. Scales's "active" membership in the Party is indisputable, and that issue was properly submitted to the jury under instructions that were entirely adequate. The elements of petitioner's "knowledge" and "specific intent" require no further discussion of the evidence beyond that already given as to Scales's utterances and activities. Compare *Noto* v. *United States* [367 U.S.] at 299–300. They bear little resemblance to the fragmentary and equivocal utterances and conduct which were found insufficient in *Nowak* v. *United States*, 356 U.S. 660, 666–667, and in *Maisenberg* v. *United States*, 356 U.S. 670, 673.

We hold that this prosecution does not fail for insufficiency of the proof . . .

The judgment of the Court of Appeals must be

Affirmed.[4]

---

[4]For Justice Black, in dissent, the narrowing construction of the membership clause adopted by the majority was so far from the language of the statute that "neither petitioner [Scales] nor anyone else could ever have guessed that this law would be held to mean what this Court now holds it does mean. For that reason, it appears that petitioner has been convicted under a law that is, at best, unconstitutionally vague and, at worst, *ex post facto*." [Ed.]

III

The Individual
and the Administration
of Federal Justice

The cases in Part III, each of which was decided with an opinion for the Court by Justice Harlan, attest to his concern that the highest standards be maintained in the administration of justice by the federal government. In the first two of these cases, the Justice found the sources of judicial control in the Bill of Rights itself. In the last three, the approach followed was to construe the governing rule or statute in a way that made it unnecessary to face the difficult issues of due process that lay close to the surface. In all five, it is significant that the questions arose in a context unaffected by problems of interference with state policies and processes; in the Justice's view, the institutional role of the Court is very different when that added dimension is not present.[1]

Several of the cases in this Part are also of interest because they reveal the Justice's particular sensitivity to issues of fairness in the conduct of litigation, a sensitivity that may arise in part from his long experience as a trial attorney in civil and criminal cases.

---

[1] With the cases in this Part, compare, for example, the Justice's opinion for the Court in Spencer v. Texas, 385 U.S. 554. Of course, to the extent that the Court rests a proscription against the federal government on a provision of the Bill of Rights, rather than on its general supervisory powers or on its construction of a statute or rule, that proscription may, *ipso facto*, apply to the states under the "selective incorporation" approach. See, for example, Duncan v. Louisiana, above. But such an approach has been consistently opposed by the Justice.

The Fourth and
Fifth Amendments

Simmons v. United States

390 U.S. 377 (1968)

Justice Harlan's concern that the individual's right of privacy be protected from governmental interference[1] has been manifested in a number of decisions applying the Fourth Amendment prohibition of unreasonable search and seizure.[2] Though considerations of federalism led him to dissent from the extension of the exclusionary rule to state courts in *Mapp* v. *Ohio*,[3] he has also expressed apprehension that application of that rule to the states in all its aspects might result in dilution of the protections accorded under the Fourth Amendment to defendants in federal proceedings.[4]

[1] Cf. Poe v. Ullman, 367 U.S. 497, 522 (dissenting opinion).

[2] E.g., Jones v. United States, 357 U.S. 493; Giordenello v. United States, 357 U.S. 480; Katz v. United States, 389 U.S. 347 (concurring opinion); Spinelli v. United States, 89 S. Ct. 584; cf. Mancusi v. De Forte, 392 U.S. 364.

[3] 367 U.S. 643, 672. This case, decided in 1961, held that evidence seized in violation of the defendant's constitutional rights may not be used against him in a state criminal proceeding.

[4] In Ker v. California, 374 U.S. 23, 44, 45–46 (concurring opinion), decided in 1963, the Justice said: "If the Court is prepared to relax Fourth Amendment standards in order to avoid unduly fettering the States, this would be in derogation of law enforcement standards in the federal system."

The *Simmons* case is of particular interest because it involves the interplay between the Fourth and Fifth Amendments. Thomas Simmons, Robert Garrett, and William Andrews were convicted in a federal court of armed robbery. Prior to trial, Garrett moved to suppress certain incriminating evidence (consisting of a suitcase and its contents) which had been found by FBI agents in the basement of Andrews' mother's house and which allegedly had been seized in violation of the Fourth Amendment. In order to establish his standing to make the motion, Garrett testified that the suitcase looked like one belonging to him and that he was the owner of clothing found inside it. The motion to suppress was denied, and Garrett's testimony at the suppression hearing was used against him at the trial to establish guilt. Garrett argued that even if the motion to suppress was properly denied, use of this testimony at trial violated his constitutional rights. After rejecting other arguments made by Simmons and Garrett, the Court sustained this contention in a 6–2 decision.

Mr. Justice Harlan delivered the opinion of the Court . . .

It is contended that it was reversible error to allow the Government to use against Garrett on the issue of guilt the testimony given by him upon his unsuccessful motion to suppress as evidence the suitcase seized from Mrs. Mahon's basement and its contents. That testimony established that Garrett was the owner of the suitcase.

In order to effectuate the Fourth Amendment's guarantee of freedom from unreasonable searches and seizures, this Court long ago conferred upon defendants in federal prosecutions the right, upon motion and proof, to have excluded from trial evidence which had been secured by means of an unlawful search and seizure . . .

However, we have also held that rights assured by the Fourth Amendment are personal rights, and that they may be enforced by exclusion of evidence only at the instance of one whose own protection was infringed by the search and seizure. See, e.g., *Jones* v. *United States*, 362 U.S. 257, 260–261. At one time, a defendant who wished to assert a Fourth Amendment objection was required to show that he was the owner or possessor of the seized property or that he had a possessory interest in the searched premises. In part to avoid having to resolve the issue presented by this case, we relaxed those standing requirements in two alternative ways in *Jones* v. *United States*, *supra*. First, we held that when, as in *Jones*, possession of the seized evidence is itself an essential element of

193

the offense with which the defendant is charged, the Government is precluded from denying that the defendant has the requisite possessory interest to challenge the admission of the evidence. Second, we held alternatively that the defendant need have no possessory interest in the searched premises in order to have standing; it is sufficient that he be legitimately on those premises when the search occurs. Throughout this case, petitioner Garrett has justifiably, and without challenge from the Government, proceeded on the assumption that the standing requirements must be satisfied. On that premise, he contends that testimony given by a defendant to meet such requirements should not be admissible against him at trial on the question of guilt or innocence. We agree.

Under the standing rules set out in *Jones,* there will be occasions, even in prosecutions for nonpossessory offenses, when a defendant's testimony will be needed to establish standing. This case serves as an example. Garrett evidently was not in Mrs. Mahon's house at the time his suitcase was seized from her basement. The only, or at least the most natural, way in which he could found standing to object to the admission of the suitcase was to testify that he was its owner. Thus, his testimony is to be regarded as an integral part of his Fourth Amendment exclusion claim. Under the rule laid down by the courts below, he could give that testimony only by assuming the risk that the testimony would later be admitted against him at trial. Testimony of this kind, which links a defendant to evidence which the Government considers important enough to seize and to seek to have admitted at trial, must often be highly prejudicial to a defendant. This case again serves as an example, for Garrett's admitted ownership of a suitcase which only a few hours after the robbery was found to contain money wrappers taken from the victimized bank was undoubtedly a strong piece of evidence against him. Without his testimony, the Government might have found it hard to prove that he was the owner of the suitcase.

The dilemma faced by defendants like Garrett is most extreme in prosecutions for possessory crimes, for then the testimony required for standing itself proves an element of the offense. We eliminated that Hobson's choice in *Jones* v. *United States, supra,* by relaxing the standing requirements. This Court has never considered squarely the question whether defendants charged with nonpossessory crimes, like Garrett, are entitled to be relieved of their dilemma entirely. The lower courts which have considered the matter, both before and after *Jones*, have with two exceptions agreed with the holdings of the courts below that the defendant's testimony may be admitted when, as here, the motion to suppress has failed. The reasoning of some of these courts would seem to suggest that the testimony would be admissible even if the motion to suppress had succeeded, but the only court which has actually decided that question held that when the motion to suppress succeeds the testimony given in support of it is excludable as a "fruit" of the unlawful search. The rationale for admitting the testimony when the motion fails has been that the testimony is voluntarily given and relevant, and that it is therefore entitled to admission on the same basis as any other prior testimony or admission of a party.

It seems obvious that a defendant who knows that his testimony may be admissible against him at trial will sometimes be deterred from presenting the testimonial proof of standing necessary to assert a Fourth Amendment claim. The likelihood of inhibition is greatest when the testimony is known to be admissible regardless of the outcome of the motion to suppress. But even in jurisdictions where the admissibility of the testimony depends upon the outcome of the motion, there will be a deterrent effect in those marginal cases in which it cannot be estimated with confidence whether the motion will succeed. Since search-and-seizure claims depend heavily upon their individual facts, and since the law of search and seizure is in a state of flux, the incidence of such marginal cases cannot be said to be negligible. In such circumstances, a defendant with a substantial claim for the exclusion of evidence may conclude that the admission of the evidence, together with the Government's proof linking it to him, is preferable to risking the admission of his own testimony connecting himself with the seized evidence.

The rule adopted by the courts below does not merely impose upon a defendant a condition which may deter him from asserting a Fourth Amendment objection—it imposes a condition of a kind to which this Court has always been peculiarly sensitive. For a defendant who wishes to establish standing must do so at the risk that the words which he utters may later be used to incriminate him. Those courts which have allowed the admission of testimony given to establish standing have reasoned that there is no violation of the Fifth Amendment's Self-Incrimination Clause because the testimony was voluntary. As an abstract matter, this may well be true. A defendant is "compelled" to testify in support of a motion to suppress only in the sense that if he refrains from testifying he will have to forgo a benefit, and testimony is not always involuntary as a matter of law simply because it is given to obtain a benefit. However, the assumption which underlies this reasoning is that the defendant has a choice: he may refuse to testify and give up the benefit. When this assumption is applied to a situation in which the "benefit" to be gained is that afforded by another provision of the Bill of Rights, an undeniable tension is created. Thus, in this case Garrett was obliged either to give up what he believed, with advice of counsel, to be a valid Fourth Amendment claim or, in legal effect, to waive his Fifth Amendment privilege against self-incrimination. In these circumstances, we find it intolerable that one constitutional right should have to be surrendered in order to assert another. We therefore hold that when a defendant testifies in support of a motion to suppress evidence on Fourth Amendment grounds, his testimony may not thereafter be admitted against him at trial on the issue of guilt unless he makes no objection . . .[5]

Marchetti v. *United States*

390 U.S. 38 (1968)

Marchetti is one of three closely related decisions, all handed down on the same day, which added a new and important dimension to the protections afforded by the Fifth Amendment's privilege against self-incrimination.[1]

---

[5] In his dissent, Justice Black argued that there had been an effective waiver and said: "Highly probative evidence such as that involved here should not lightly be held inadmissible. For me the importance of bringing guilty criminals to book is a far more crucial consideration than the desirability of giving defendants every possible assistance in their attempts to invoke an evidentiary rule which itself can result in the exclusion of highly relevant evidence." [Ed.]

[1] As in other areas involving the provisions of the first eight amendments to the Constitution, Justice Harlan has strongly dissented from the across-the-board application of the privilege against self-incrimination to the states. Malloy v. Hogan, 378 U.S. 1, 14 (dissenting opinion). In his view the test of the constitutionality of state action under the Fourteenth Amendment should remain whether the demands of fundamental fairness have been satisfied. See Part I above.

In *Marchetti*, the petitioner argued that in view of that privilege he could not constitutionally be convicted for failure to register and to pay the occupational tax imposed by federal law on persons engaged in the business of accepting wagers. In the related cases, similar attacks were made on federal statutes imposing an excise tax on wagering[2] and prohibiting the knowing possession of certain types of firearms if they had not been duly registered with federal authorities.[3] In each case the Court, in an opinion by Justice Harlan, reversed the conviction and upheld the contentions of the petitioner based on the Fifth Amendment. The *Marchetti* opinion contains a painstaking explanation of the Court's reasons for overruling two earlier decisions rejecting similar contentions.

Mr. Justice Harlan delivered the opinion of the Court.

Petitioner was convicted in the United States District Court for the District of Connecticut under two indictments which charged violations of the federal wagering tax statutes. The first indictment averred that petitioner and others conspired to evade payment of the annual occupational tax imposed by 26 U.S.C. § 4411. The second indictment included two counts: the first alleged a willful failure to pay the occupational tax, and the second a willful failure to register, as required by 26 U.S.C. § 4412, before engaging in the business of accepting wagers.

After verdict, petitioner unsuccessfully sought to arrest judgment, in part on the basis that the statutory obligations to register and to pay the occupational tax violated his Fifth Amendment privilege against self-incrimination. The Court of Appeals for the Second Circuit affirmed, on the authority of *United States* v. *Kahriger*, 345 U.S. 22, and *Lewis* v. *United States*, 348 U.S. 419.

We granted certiorari to re-examine the constitutionality under the Fifth Amendment of the pertinent provisions of the wagering tax statutes, and more particularly to consider whether *Kahriger* and *Lewis* still have vitality. For reasons which follow, we have concluded that these provisions may not be employed to punish criminally those persons who have defended a failure to comply with their requirements with a proper assertion of the privilege against self-incrimination. The judgment below is accordingly reversed.

[2] Grosso v. United States, 390 U.S. 62.
[3] Haynes v. United States, 390 U.S. 85.

197

The provisions in issue here are part of an interrelated statutory system for taxing wagers. The system is broadly as follows. Section 4401 of Title 26 imposes upon those engaged in the business of accepting wagers an excise tax of 10% on the gross amount of all wagers they accept, including the value of chances purchased in lotteries conducted for profit. Parimutuel wagering enterprises, coin-operated devices, and state-conducted sweepstakes are expressly excluded from taxation. 26 U.S.C. § 4402 (1964 ed., Supp. II). Section 4411 imposes in addition an occupational tax of $50 annually, both upon those subject to taxation under § 4401 and upon those who receive wagers on their behalf.

The taxes are supplemented by ancillary provisions calculated to assure their collection. In particular, § 4412 requires those liable for the occupational tax to register each year with the director of their local internal revenue district . . .

Each principal internal revenue office is instructed to maintain for public inspection a listing of all who had paid the occupational tax, and to provide certified copies of the listing upon request to any state or local prosecuting officer. 26 U.S.C. § 6107. Finally, payment of the wagering taxes is declared not to "exempt any person from any penalty provided by a law of the United States or of any State for engaging" in any taxable activity. 26 U.S.C. § 4422.

The issue before us is *not* whether the United States may tax activities which a State or Congress has declared unlawful. The Court has repeatedly indicated that the unlawfulness of an activity does not prevent its taxation, and nothing that follows is intended to limit or diminish the vitality of those cases. The issue is instead whether the methods employed by Congress in the federal wagering tax statutes are, in this situation, consistent with the limitations created by the privilege against self-incrimination guaranteed by the Fifth Amendment. We must for this purpose first examine the implications of these statutory provisions.

Wagering and its ancillary activities are very widely prohibited under both federal and state law . . .

Connecticut, in which petitioner allegedly conducted his activities, has adopted a variety of measures for the punishment of gambling and wagering . . . By any standard, in Connecticut and throughout the United States, wagering is "an area permeated with criminal statutes," and those engaged in wagering are a group "inherently suspect of criminal activities." *Albertson* v. *SACB*, 382 U.S. 70, 79.

Information obtained as a consequence of the federal wagering tax laws is readily available to assist the efforts of state and federal authorities to enforce these penalties . . .

In these circumstances, it can scarcely be denied that the obligations to register and to pay the occupational tax created for petitioner "real and appreciable," and not merely "imaginary and unsubstantial," hazards of self-incrimination. *Reg.* v. *Boyes*, 1 B. & S. 311, 330; *Brown* v. *Walker*, 161 U.S. 591, 599–600; *Rogers* v. *United States*, 340 U.S. 367, 374. Petitioner was confronted by a comprehensive system of federal and state prohibitions against wagering activities; he was required, on pain of criminal prosecution, to provide information which he might reasonably suppose would be available to prosecuting authorities, and which would surely prove a significant "link in a chain"[4] of evidence tending to establish his guilt. Unlike the income tax return in question in *United States* v. *Sullivan*, 274 U.S. 259, every portion of these requirements had the direct and unmistakable consequence of incriminating petitioner; the application of the constitutional privilege to the entire registration procedure was in this instance neither "extreme" nor "extravagant." See *id.* at 263. It would appear to follow that petitioner's assertion of the privilege as a defense to this prosecution was entirely proper, and accordingly should have sufficed to prevent his conviction.

Nonetheless, this Court has twice concluded that the privilege against self-incrimination may not appropriately be asserted by those in petitioner's circumstances. *United States* v. *Kahriger, supra; Lewis* v. *United States, supra.* We must therefore consider whether those cases have continuing force in light of our more recent decisions . . .

The Court held in *Lewis* that the registration and occupational tax requirements do not infringe the constitutional privilege because they do not compel self-incrimination, but merely impose on the

---

[4] The metaphor is to be found in the opinions both of Lord Eldon in Paxton v. Douglas, 19 Ves. Jr. 225, 227, and of Chief Justice Marshall in United States v. Burr, In re Willie, 25 Fed. Cas. 38, 40 (No. 14,692e).

gambler the initial choice of whether he wishes, at the cost of his constitutional privilege, to commence wagering activities. The Court reasoned that even if the required disclosures might prove incriminating, the gambler need not register or pay the occupational tax if only he elects to cease, or never to begin, gambling. There is, the Court said, "no constitutional right to gamble." 348 U.S. at 423.

We find this reasoning no longer persuasive. The question is not whether petitioner holds a "right" to violate state law, but whether, having done so, he may be compelled to give evidence against himself. The constitutional privilege was intended to shield the guilty and imprudent as well as the innocent and foresighted; if such an inference of antecedent choice were alone enough to abrogate the privilege's protection, it would be excluded from the situations in which it has historically been guaranteed, and withheld from those who most require it. Such inferences, bottomed on what must ordinarily be a fiction, have precisely the infirmities which the Court has found in other circumstances in which implied or uninformed waivers of the privilege have been said to have occurred. To give credence to such "waivers" without the most deliberate examination of the circumstances surrounding them would ultimately license widespread erosion of the privilege through "ingeniously drawn legislation." Morgan, "The Privilege against Self-Incrimination," 34 *Minn. L. Rev.* 1, 37. We cannot agree that the constitutional privilege is meaningfully waived merely because those "inherently suspect of criminal activities" have been commanded either to cease wagering or to provide information incriminating to themselves, and have ultimately elected to do neither.

. . . The Court held in both *Kahriger* and *Lewis* that the registration and occupational tax requirements are entirely prospective in their application, and that the constitutional privilege, since it offers protection only as to past and present acts, is accordingly unavailable. This reasoning appears to us twice deficient: first, it overlooks the hazards here of incrimination as to past or present acts; and second, it is hinged upon an excessively narrow view of the scope of the constitutional privilege . . .

[The linchpin of the reasoning of *Kahriger* and *Lewis*] is plainly the premise that the privilege is entirely inapplicable to prospective acts; for this the Court in *Kahriger* could vouch as authority only a generalization at 8 Wigmore, Evidence § 2259c (3d ed. 1940). We see no warrant for so rigorous a constraint upon the constitutional privilege. History, to be sure, offers no ready illustrations of the privilege's application to prospective acts, but the occasions on which such claims might appropriately have been made must necessarily have been very infrequent. We are, in any event, bid to view the constitutional commands as "organic living institutions," whose significance is "vital not formal." *Gompers* v. *United States*, 233 U.S. 604, 610.

The central standard for the privilege's application has been whether the claimant is confronted by substantial and "real," and not merely trifling or imaginary, hazards of incrimination. *Rogers* v. *United States*, 340 U.S. 367, 374; *Brown* v. *Walker*, 161 U.S. 591, 600. This principle does not permit the rigid chronological distinction adopted in *Kahriger* and *Lewis*. We see no reason to suppose that the force of the constitutional prohibition is diminished merely because confession of a guilty purpose precedes the act which it is subsequently employed to evidence. Yet, if the factual situations in which the privilege may be claimed were inflexibly defined by a chronological formula, the policies which the constitutional privilege is intended to serve could easily be evaded. Moreover, although prospective acts will doubtless ordinarily involve only speculative and insubstantial risks of incrimination, this will scarcely always prove true. As we shall show, it is not true here. We conclude that it is not mere time to which the law must look, but the substantiality of the risks of incrimination.

The hazards of incrimination created by §§ 4411 and 4412 as to future acts are not trifling or imaginary. Prospective registrants can reasonably expect that registration and payment of the occupational tax will significantly enhance the likelihood of their prosecution for future acts, and that it will readily provide evidence which will facilitate their convictions. Indeed, they can reasonably fear that registration, and acquisition of a wagering tax stamp, may serve as decisive evidence that they have in fact subsequently violated state gambling prohibitions. Insubstantial claims of the privilege as to entirely prospective acts may certainly be asserted, but such claims are not here, and they need only be considered when a litigant has the temerity to pursue them.

We conclude that nothing in the Court's opinions in *Kahriger* and *Lewis* now suffices to preclude petitioner's assertion of the constitutional privilege as a defense to the indictments under which he was convicted. To this extent *Kahriger* and *Lewis* are overruled . . .

We have been urged by the United States to permit continued enforcement of the registration and occupational tax provisions, despite the demands of the constitutional privilege, by shielding the privilege's claimants through the imposition of restrictions upon the use by federal and state authorities of information obtained as a consequence of compliance with the wagering tax requirements . . .

The Constitution of course obliges this Court to give full recognition to the taxing powers and to measures reasonably incidental to their exercise. But we are equally obliged to give full effect to the constitutional restrictions which attend the exercise of those powers. We do not, as we have said, doubt Congress' power to tax activities which are, wholly or in part, unlawful. Nor can it be doubted that the privilege against self-incrimination may not properly be asserted if other protection is granted which "is so broad as to have the same extent in scope and effect" as the privilege itself. *Counselman* v. *Hitchcock*, 142 U.S. 547, 585. The Government's suggestion is thus in principle an attractive and apparently practical resolution of the difficult problem before us. Nonetheless, we think that it would be entirely inappropriate in the circumstances here for the Court to impose such restrictions.

The terms of the wagering tax system make quite plain that Congress intended information obtained as a consequence of registration and payment of the occupational tax to be provided to interested prosecuting authorities. This has evidently been the consistent practice of the Revenue Service. We must therefore assume that the imposition of use-restrictions would directly preclude effectuation of a significant element of Congress' purposes in adopting the wagering taxes. Moreover, the imposition of such restrictions would necessarily oblige state prosecuting authorities to establish in each case that their evidence was untainted by any connection with information obtained as a consequence of the wagering taxes; the federal requirements would thus be protected only at the cost of hampering, perhaps seriously, enforcement of state prohibitions against gambling. We cannot know how Congress would assess the competing demands of the federal treasury and of state gambling prohibitions; we are, however, entirely certain that the Constitution has entrusted to Congress, and not to this Court, the task of striking an appropriate balance among such values. We therefore must decide that it would be improper for the Court to impose restrictions of the kind urged by the United States . . .

Reversed.[5]

[5] The Chief Justice dissented in each of the three related cases. He argued that all three differed from Albertson v. Subversive Activities Control Board, 382 U.S. 70, in which a unanimous Court had invalidated on Fifth Amendment grounds the federal requirement that Communist Party members must register with the Board, in that the present statutes served legitimate purposes and did not clash with First Amendment rights.

In a recent opinion for the Court by Justice Harlan, the principles developed in *Marchetti* were applied in reversing a conviction under the federal narcotics laws. Leary v. United States, 37 *U.S.L. Week* 4397, decided May 19, 1969. [Ed.]

B

The Process of
Interpretation

Societe Internationale v. Rogers

357 U.S. 197 (1958)

Acting pursuant to the Trading with the Enemy Act,[1] the U.S. government during World War II seized more than $100,000 of assets that were allegedly owned or held for the benefit of I. G. Farben, a German firm. The assets included approximately 90 percent of the capital stock of General Aniline & Film Corp., a Delaware corporation. In 1948 the petitioner, a Swiss company, brought suit in a federal district court to recover these assets on the ground that it was the true owner and was a national of a neutral power. The government denied the petitioner's claim of ownership and asserted that in any event the petitioner was so intimately connected with I. G. Farben as to be affected with "enemy taint." To obtain evidence in support of this assertion, the government moved under Rule 34 of the Federal Rules of Civil Procedure for a court order requiring the petitioner to make available a large number of the records of Sturzenegger & Cie, a Swiss banking firm. The trial court granted the motion, holding that the petitioner had "control" over the records in question.

The petitioner then made several motions to be relieved of this requirement on the ground that production of the records would violate Swiss

[1] 50 U.S.C. App. § 5(b).

penal law. While the matter was pending, the Swiss Federal Attorney took action amounting to an interdiction against Sturzenegger's transmission of the records. As matters approached an impasse, the trial court referred the case to a master, who found that the petitioner had acted in good faith in trying to comply with the production order and that there was no evidence of collusion between petitioner and the Swiss government.

Despite these findings, the trial court in 1953 granted the government's motion to dismiss the complaint, stating that Rule 37(b) of the Federal Rules,[2] as well as its inherent power, enabled it to dismiss the action for failure to produce. The petitioner was afforded two subsequent grace periods, however, to permit further efforts at compliance through negotiations with the Swiss government. By July 1956, over 190,000 documents had been released, but certain records had still not been produced. The trial court, refusing to consider whether there had been substantial compliance with the production order or to entertain a plan for a "neutral" expert to look at additional documents, directed final dismissal, and the Court of Appeals affirmed.[3]

Speaking for the Supreme Court in its unanimous reversal of the decision below, Justice Harlan stated, first, that petitioner had been shown to have "control" of the documents despite the ban on disclosure imposed by Swiss law, and, second, that the matter was governed exclusively by Rule 37(b), "which addresses itself with particularity to the consequences of a failure to make discovery." This brought him, in the excerpt included here, to the question of the meaning of the rule.

Mr. Justice Harlan delivered the opinion of the Court . . .

We turn to the remaining question, whether the District Court properly exercised its powers under Rule 37(b) by dismissing this complaint despite the findings that petitioner had not been in collusion with the Swiss authorities to block inspection of the Sturzenegger records, and had in good faith made diligent efforts to execute the production order.

We must discard at the outset the strongly urged contention of the Government that dismissal of this action was justified because petitioner conspired with I. G. Farben, Sturzenegger & Cie, and

---

[2] This rule provided, in pertinent part: "If any party . . . refuses to obey . . . an order made under Rule 34 to produce any document or thing for inspection, . . . the court may make such orders in regard to the refusal as are just . . . [including an order] dismissing the action or proceeding or any part thereof."

[3] The Court of Appeals did not rely on Rule 37(b) but rather on the broader provisions of Rule 41 and on the inherent power of the trial court.

others to transfer ownership of General Aniline to it prior to 1941 so that seizure would be avoided and advantage taken of Swiss secrecy laws. In other words, the Government suggests that petitioner stands in the position of one who deliberately courted legal impediments to production of the Sturzenegger records, and who thus cannot now be heard to assert its good faith after this expectation was realized. Certainly these contentions, if supported by the facts, would have a vital bearing on justification for dismissal of the action, but they are not open to the Government here. The findings below reach no such conclusions; indeed, it is not even apparent from them whether this particular charge was ever passed upon below. Although we do not mean to preclude the Government from seeking to establish such facts before the District Court upon remand, or any other facts relevant to justification for dismissal of the complaint, we must dispose of this case on the basis of the findings of good faith made by the Special Master, adopted by the District Court, and approved by the Court of Appeals.

The provisions of Rule 37 which are here involved must be read in light of the provisions of the Fifth Amendment that no person shall be deprived of property without due process of law, and more particularly against the opinions of this Court in *Hovey* v. *Elliott*, 167 U.S. 409, and *Hammond Packing Co.* v. *Arkansas*, 212 U.S. 322. These decisions establish that there are constitutional limitations upon the power of courts, even in aid of their own valid processes, to dismiss an action without affording a party the opportunity for a hearing on the merits of his cause . . .

These two decisions leave open the question whether Fifth Amendment due process is violated by the striking of a complaint because of a plaintiff's inability, despite good-faith efforts, to comply with a pretrial production order . . . Certainly substantial constitutional questions are provoked by such action. Their gravity is accented in the present case where petitioner, though cast in the role of *plaintiff*, cannot be deemed to be in the customary role of a party invoking the aid of a court to vindicate rights asserted against another. Rather petitioner's position is more analogous to that of a *defendant*, for it belatedly challenges the Government's action by now protesting against a seizure and seeking the recovery of assets which were summarily possessed by the Alien Property Custodian without the opportunity for protest by any party claiming that seizure was unjustified under the Trading with the Enemy Act. Past decisions of this Court emphasize that this summary power to seize property which is believed to be enemy-owned is rescued from constitutional invalidity under the Due Process and Just Compensation Clauses of the Fifth Amendment only by those provisions of the Act which afford a nonenemy claimant a later judicial hearing as to the propriety of the seizure.

The findings below, and what has been shown as to petitioner's extensive efforts at compliance, compel the conclusion on this record that petitioner's failure to satisfy fully the requirements of this production order was due to inability fostered neither by its own conduct nor by circumstances within its control. It is hardly debatable that fear of criminal prosecution constitutes a weighty excuse for nonproduction, and this excuse is not weakened because the laws preventing compliance are those of a foreign sovereign. Of course this situation should be distinguished from one where a party claims that compliance with a court's order will reveal facts which may provide the basis for criminal prosecution of that party under the penal laws of a foreign sovereign thereby shown to have been violated. Here the findings below establish that the very fact of compliance by disclosure of banking records will itself constitute the initial violation of Swiss laws. In our view, petitioner stands in the position of an American plaintiff subject to criminal sanctions in Switzerland because production of documents in Switzerland pursuant to the order of a United States court might violate Swiss laws. Petitioner has sought no privileges because of its foreign citizenship which are not accorded domestic litigants in United States courts. It does not claim that Swiss laws protecting banking records should here be enforced. It explicitly recognizes that it is subject to procedural rules of United States courts in this litigation and has made full efforts to follow these rules. It asserts no immunity from them. It asserts only its *inability* to comply because of foreign law.

In view of the findings in this case, the position in which petitioner stands in this litigation, and the serious constitutional questions we have noted, we think that Rule 37 should not be construed to authorize dismissal of this complaint because of petitioner's noncompliance with a pretrial production order when it has been established that failure to comply has been due to inability, and not to willfulness, bad faith, or any fault of petitioner.

This is not to say that petitioner will profit through its inability to tender the records called for. In seeking recovery of the General Aniline stock and other assets, petitioner recognizes that it carries the ultimate burden of proof of showing itself not to be an "enemy" within the meaning of the Trading with the Enemy Act. The Government already has disputed its right to recovery by relying on information obtained through seized records of I. G. Farben, documents obtained through petitioner, and depositions taken of persons affiliated with petitioner. It may be that in a trial on the merits, petitioner's inability to produce specific information will prove a serious handicap in dispelling doubt the Government might be able to inject into the case. It may be that in the absence of complete disclosure by petitioner, the District Court would be justified in drawing inferences unfavorable to petitioner as to particular events. So much indeed petitioner concedes. But these problems go to the adequacy of petitioner's proof and should not on this record preclude petitioner from being able to contest on the merits.

On remand, the District Court possesses wide discretion to proceed in whatever manner it deems most effective. It may desire to afford the Government additional opportunity to challenge petitioner's good faith. It may wish to explore plans looking toward fuller compliance. Or it may decide to commence at once trial on the merits. We decide only that on this record dismissal of the complaint with prejudice was not justified.

The judgment of the Court of Appeals is reversed and the case is remanded to the District Court for further proceedings in conformity with this opinion.

It is so ordered.

Vitarelli v. *Seaton*

359 U.S. 535 (1959)

Like the cases involving congressional investigations, those actions in which employees of government and industry complained of their dismissals as "security risks" arose in part out of the excesses of the McCarthy era. Along with other members of the Court, Justice Harlan was most reluctant to reach the underlying constitutional questions presented by such dismissals, so long as they could be avoided by narrow construction of the controlling statute or by requiring the agency involved to adhere closely to its own established procedures in reaching a decision.[1]

The latter technique was employed in upholding the petitioner's attack on his discharge in the *Vitarelli* case. The case is of special interest because it illustrates so sharply the depths to which some agencies sank in their handling of security matters in the early 1950's. Also, the case confronted the Court with the difficult question of how to respond to a belated government effort to right all its wrongs by "redischarging" Vitarelli while the case was pending on appeal—this time without giving *any* reason for its action.

Mr. Justice Harlan delivered the opinion of the Court.

This case concerns the legality of petitioner's discharge as an employee of the Department of the Interior. Vitarelli, an educator holding a doctor's degree from Columbia University, was appointed in 1952 by the Department of the Interior as an Education and Training Specialist in the Education Department of the Trust Territory of the Pacific Islands, at Koror in the Palau District, a mandated area for which this country has responsibility.

By a letter dated March 30, 1954, respondent Secretary's predecessor in office notified petitioner of his suspension from duty without pay, effective April 2, 1954, assigning as ground therefor various charges. Essentially, the charges were that petitioner from 1941 to 1945 had been in "sympathetic association" with three named persons alleged to have been members of or in sympathetic association with the Communist Party, and had concealed from the Government the true extent of these associations at the time of a previous inquiry into them; that he had registered as a supporter of the American Labor Party in New York City in 1945, had subscribed to the USSR Information Bulletin, and had purchased copies of the Daily Worker and New Masses; and that because such associations and activities tended to show that petitioner was "not reliable or trustworthy" his continued employment might be "contrary to the best interests of national security."

[1] See, e.g., the Justice's opinions for the Court in Cole v. Young, 351 U.S. 536 (discussed in the excerpt that follows), and Service v. Dulles, 354 U.S. 363, as well as his special concurrence in Greene v. McElroy, 360 U.S. 474, 509. Some of the constitutional issues were passed upon in 1961 in Cafeteria & Restaurant Workers Union v. McElroy, 367 U.S. 886.

Petitioner filed a written answer to the statement of charges, and appeared before a security hearing board on June 22 and July 1, 1954. At this hearing no evidence was adduced by the Department in support of the charges, nor did any witness testify against petitioner. Petitioner testified at length, and presented four witnesses, and he and the witnesses were extensively cross-examined by the security officer and the members of the hearing board. On September 2, 1954, a notice of dismissal effective September 10, 1954, was sent petitioner over the signature of the Secretary, reciting that the dismissal was "in the interest of national security for the reasons specifically set forth in the letter of charges dated March 30, 1954." This was followed on September 21, 1954, with the filing of a "Notification of Personnel Action" setting forth the Secretary's action. The record does not show that a copy of this document was ever sent to petitioner.

After having failed to obtain reinstatement by a demand upon the Secretary, petitioner filed suit in the United States District Court for the District of Columbia seeking a declaration that his dismissal had been illegal and ineffective and an injunction requiring his reinstatement. On October 10, 1956, while the case was pending in the District Court, a copy of a new "Notification of Personnel Action," dated September 21, 1954, and reciting that it was "a revision of and replaces the original bearing the same date," was filed in the District Court, and another copy of this document was delivered to petitioner shortly thereafter. This notification was identical with the one already mentioned, except that it omitted any reference to the reason for petitioner's discharge and to the authority under which it was carried out. Thereafter the District Court granted summary judgment for the respondent. That judgment was affirmed by the Court of Appeals, one judge dissenting. We granted certiorari to consider the validity of petitioner's discharge.

The Secretary's letter of March 30, 1954, and notice of dismissal of September 2, 1954, both relied upon Exec. Order No. 10450, 18 Fed. Reg. 2489 (1953), the Act of August 26, 1950, 64 Stat. 476, 5 U.S.C. § 22–21 *et seq.*, and Department of the Interior Order No. 2738, all relating to discharges of government employees on security or loyalty grounds, as the authority for petitioner's dismissal. In *Cole* v. *Young*, 351 U.S. 536, this Court held that the statute referred to did not apply to government employees in positions not desig-

210

nated as "sensitive." Respondent takes the position that since petitioner's position in government service has at no time been designated as sensitive the effect of *Cole*, which was decided after the 1954 dismissal of petitioner, was to render also inapplicable to petitioner Department of the Interior Order No. 2738, under which the proceedings relating to petitioner's dismissal were had. It is urged that in this state of affairs petitioner, who concededly was at no time within the protection of the Civil Service Act, Veterans' Preference Act, or any other statute relating to employment rights of government employees, and who, as a "Schedule A" employee, could have been summarily discharged by the Secretary at any time without the giving of a reason, under no circumstances could be entitled to more than that which he has already received—namely, an "expunging" from the record of his 1954 discharge of any reference to the authority or reasons therefor.

Respondent misconceives the effect of our decision in *Cole*. It is true that the Act of August 26, 1950, and the Executive Order did not alter the power of the Secretary to discharge summarily an employee in petitioner's status, without the giving of any reason. Nor did the Department's own regulations preclude such a course. Since, however, the Secretary gratuitously decided to give a reason, and that reason was national security, he was obligated to conform to the procedural standards he had formulated in Order No. 2738 for the dismissal of employees on security grounds . . . Having chosen to proceed against petitioner on security grounds, the Secretary here, as in *Service* [v. *Dulles*, 354 U.S. 363], was bound by the regulations which he himself had promulgated for dealing with such cases, even though without such regulations he could have discharged petitioner summarily.

Petitioner makes various contentions as to the constitutional invalidity of the procedures provided by Order No. 2738. He further urges that even assuming the validity of the governing procedures, his dismissal cannot stand because the notice of suspension and hearing given him did not comply with the Order. We find it unnecessary to reach the constitutional issues, for we think that petitioner's second position is well taken and must be sustained.

Preliminarily, it should be said that departures from departmental regulations in matters of this kind involve more than mere consideration of procedural irregularities. For in proceedings of this nature, in which the ordinary rules of evidence do not apply, in which matters involving the disclosure of confidential information are withheld, and where it must be recognized that counsel is under practical constraints in the making of objections and in the tactical handling of his case which would not obtain in a cause being tried in a court of law before trained judges, scrupulous observance of departmental procedural safeguards is clearly of particular importance. In this instance an examination of the record, and of the transcript of the hearing before the departmental security board, discloses that petitioner's procedural rights under the applicable regulations were violated in at least three material respects in the proceedings which terminated in the final notice of his dismissal.

First, § 15(a) of Order No. 2738 requires that the statement of charges served upon an employee at the time of his suspension on security grounds "shall be as specific and detailed as security considerations, including the need for protection of confidential sources of information, permit . . . and shall be subject to amendment within 30 days of issuance." Although the statement of charges furnished petitioner appears on its face to be reasonably specific, the transcript of hearing establishes that the statement, which was never amended, cannot conceivably be said in fact to be as specific and detailed as "security considerations . . . permit." For petitioner was questioned by the security officer and by the hearing board in great detail concerning his association with and knowledge of various persons and organizations nowhere mentioned in the statement of charges, and at length concerning his activities in Bucks County, Pennsylvania, and elsewhere after 1945, activities as to which the charges are also completely silent. These questions were presumably asked because they were deemed relevant to the inquiry before the board, and the very fact that they were asked and thus spread on the record is conclusive indication that "security considerations" could not have justified the omission of any statement concerning them in the charges furnished petitioner.

Second, §§ 21(a) and (e) require that hearings before security hearing boards shall be "orderly" and that "reasonable restrictions shall be imposed as to relevancy, competency, and materiality of matters considered." The material set forth in the margin, taken from the transcript, and illustrative rather than exhaustive, shows that these indispensable indicia of a meaningful hearing were not observed.[2] It is not an overcharacterization to say that as the hearing proceeded it developed into a wide-ranging inquisition into this man's educational, social, and political beliefs, encompassing even a question as to whether he was "a religious man."

Third, § 21(c) (4) gives the employee the right "to cross-examine any witness offered in support of the charges." It is apparent from an over-all reading of the regulations that it was not contemplated that this provision should require the Department to call witnesses to testify in support of any or all of the charges, because it was

[2] "Mr. Armstrong [the departmental security officer, inquiring about petitioner's activities as a teacher in a Georgia college]: Were these activities designed to be put into effect by both the white and the colored races? . . . What were your feelings at that time concerning race equality? . . . How about civil rights? Did that enter into a discussion in your seminar groups?"

"Mr. Armstrong: Do I interpret your statement correctly that maybe Negroes and Jews are denied some of their constitutional rights at present?

"Mr. Vitarelli: Yes.

"Mr. Armstrong: In what way?

"Mr. Vitarelli: I saw it in the South where certain jobs were open to white people and not open to Negroes because they were Negroes . . . In our own university, there was a quota at Columbia College for the medical students. Because they were Jewish, they would permit only so many. I thought that was wrong.

"Chairman Towson: Doctor, isn't it also true that Columbia College had quotas by states and other classifications as well?

"Mr. Vitarelli: I don't remember that. It may be true.

"Mr. Armstrong: In other words, wasn't there a quota on Gentiles as well as Jews?

"Mr. Vitarelli: . . . I had remembered that some Jews seemed to feel, and I felt, too, at the time, that they were being persecuted somewhat . . .

Petitioner was also asked the following questions by the security officer during the course of the hearing:

"Mr. Armstrong: I think you indicated in an answer or a reply to an interrogatory that you at times voted for and sponsored the principles of Franklin Delano Roosevelt, Norman A. Thomas, and Henry Wallace? . . . How many times did you vote for . . . [Thomas] if you care to say? . . . How about Henry Wallace? . . . How about Norman Thomas? Did his platform coincide more nearly with your ideas of democracy? . . . At one time, or two, you were a strong advocate of the United Nations. Are you still? . . . The file indicates, too, that you were quite hepped up over the one world idea at one time; is that right?"

Witnesses presented by petitioner were asked by the security officer and board members such questions as:

"The Doctor indicated that he was acquainted with and talked to Norman Thomas on occasions. Did you know about that? . . . How about Dr. Vitarelli? Is he scholarly? . . . A good administrator? . . . Was he careless with his language around the students or careful? . . . Did you consider Dr. Vitarelli as a religious man? . . . Was he an extremist on equality of races? . . . In connection with the activities that Dr. Vitarelli worked on that you know about, either in the form of projects or in connection with the educational activities that you have mentioned, did they extend to the Negro population of the country? In other words, were they contacts with Negro groups, with Negro instructors, with Negro students, and so on?"

It is not apparent how any of the above matters could be material to a consideration of the question whether petitioner's retention in government service would be consistent with national security.

expected that charges might rest on information gathered from or by "confidential informants." We think, however, that § 21(c) (4) did contemplate the calling by the Department of any informant not properly classifiable as "confidential," if information furnished by that informant was to be used by the board in assessing an employee's status. The transcript shows that this provision was violated on at least one occasion at petitioner's hearing, for the security officer identified by name a person who had given information apparently considered detrimental to petitioner, thus negating any possible inference that that person was considered a "confidential informant" whose identity it was necessary to keep secret, and questioned petitioner at some length concerning the information supplied from this source without calling the informant and affording petitioner the right to cross-examine.[3]

Because the proceedings attendant upon petitioner's dismissal from government service on grounds of national security fell substantially short of the requirements of the applicable departmental regulations, we hold that such dismissal was illegal and of no effect.

Respondent urges that even if the dismissal of September 10, 1954, was invalid, petitioner is not entitled to reinstatement by reason of the fact that he was at all events validly dismissed in October 1956, when a copy of the second "Notification of Personnel Action," omitting all reference to any statute, order, or regulation relating to security discharges, was delivered to him. Granting that the Secretary could at any time after September 10, 1954, have validly dismissed petitioner without any statement of reasons, and independently of the proceedings taken against him under Order No. 2738, we cannot view the delivery of the new notification to petitioner as an exercise of that summary dismissal power. Rather, the fact that it was dated "9–21–54," contained a termination of employment date of "9–10–54," was designated as "a revision" of the 1954 notification, and was evidently filed in the District Court before its delivery to petitioner indicates that its sole purpose was an attempt to moot petitioner's suit in the District Court by an "expunging" of the grounds for the dismissal which brought Order No. 2738 into play. In these circumstances, we would not be justified

---

[3]The information was to the effect that petitioner had criticized as "bourgeois" the purchase of a house by a woman associate in Georgia. Petitioner flatly denied that he had made the remark attributed to him, and said that he could never have made such a statement except in a spirit of levity.

in now treating the 1956 action, plainly intended by the Secretary as a grant of relief to petitioner in connection with the form of the 1954 discharge, as an exercise of the Secretary's summary removal power as of the date of its delivery to petitioner.[4]

It follows from what we have said that petitioner is entitled to the reinstatement which he seeks, subject, of course to any lawful exercise of the Secretary's authority hereafter to dismiss him from employment in the Department of the Interior.

Reversed.

Lynch v. *Overholser*

369 U.S. 705 (1962)

The confinement of the mentally ill—or of those alleged to be mentally ill—is one of the many low-visibility problems that in recent years have attracted increasing concern. Among the practices that have come under fire is the not uncommon one of confining a man in a mental institution for an indefinite period because he has been found "not guilty by reason of insanity" of an offense that carries a maximum jail sentence of only a few years or less.[1] Such confinement is worrisome enough when the criminal defendant has chosen to assert the defense of insanity, but what if he wanted to plead guilty and the court would not permit it? That was the issue in *Lynch*, a habeas corpus proceeding brought by an inmate of Saint Elizabeth's Hospital in the District of Columbia. In a 6–1 decision the Court avoided the constitutional questions presented by holding that the statutory provision for mandatory commitment of a person acquitted on the ground of insanity did not apply in such a case. The task of statutory construction that fell to Justice Harlan in this case was not an easy one.

Mr. Justice Harlan delivered the opinion of the Court . . .

Two informations filed in the Municipal Court for the District of Columbia on November 6, 1959, charged petitioner with having violated D.C. Code § 22–1410 by drawing and negotiating checks

---

[4]On the effect of the government's 1956 action, there were four dissents. Justice Frankfurter argued for these dissenters that this action was an effective discharge as of the date it was taken and that the Court's conclusion "attributes to governmental action the empty meaning of confetti throwing." [Ed.]

[1]See, e.g., Comment, "Commitment Following Acquittal by Reason of Insanity and the Equal Protection of the Laws," 116 *U. Pa. L. Rev.* 924 (1968).

in the amount of $50 each with knowledge that he did not have sufficient funds or credit with the drawee bank for payment. On the same day, petitioner appeared in Municipal Court to answer these charges and a plea of not guilty was recorded. He was thereupon committed under D.C. Code § 24–301(a) to the District of Columbia General Hospital for a mental examination to determine his competence to stand trial. On December 4, 1959, the Assistant Chief Psychiatrist of the Hospital reported that petitioner's mental condition was such that he was then "of unsound mind, unable to adequately understand the charges and incapable of assisting counsel in his own defense." The case was continued while petitioner was given treatment at the General Hospital.

On December 28, 1959, the Assistant Chief Psychiatrist sent a letter to the court advising that petitioner had "shown some improvement and at this time appears able to understand the charges against him, and to assist counsel in his own defense." This communication also noted that it was the psychiatrist's opinion that petitioner "was suffering from a mental disease, i.e., a manic depressive psychosis, at the time of the crime charged," such that the crime "would be a product of this mental disease." As for petitioner's current condition, the psychiatrist added that petitioner "appears to be in an early stage of recovery from manic depressive psychosis," but that it was "possible that he may have further lapses of judgment in the near future." He stated that it "would be advisable for him to have a period of further treatment in a psychiatric hospital."

Petitioner was brought to trial the following day in the Municipal Court before a judge without a jury. The record before us contains no transcript of the proceedings, but it is undisputed that petitioner, represented by counsel, sought at that time to withdraw the earlier plea of not guilty and to plead guilty to both informations. The trial judge refused to allow the change of plea, apparently on the basis of the Hospital's report that petitioner's commission of the alleged offenses was the product of mental illness.

At the trial one of the prosecution's witnesses, a physician representing the General Hospital's Psychiatric Division, testified, over petitioner's objection, that petitioner's crimes had been committed as a result of mental illness. Although petitioner never claimed that he had not been mentally responsible when the offenses were committed and presented no evidence to support an acquittal by reason of insanity, the trial judge concluded that petitioner was "not guilty on the ground that he was insane at the time of the commission of the offense." The court then ordered that petitioner be committed to Saint Elizabeth's Hospital as prescribed by D.C. Code § 24–301(d), which reads:

> (d) If any person tried upon an indictment or information for an offense, or tried in the juvenile court of the District of Columbia for an offense, is acquitted solely on the ground that he was insane at the time of its commission, the court shall order such person to be confined in a hospital for the mentally ill.

There can be no doubt as to the effect of this provision with respect to a defendant who has asserted a defense of insanity at some point during the trial . . .

Petitioner maintains, however, that his confinement is illegal for a variety of other reasons, among which is the assertion that the "mandatory commitment" provision, as applied to an accused who protests that he is presently sane and that the crime he committed was not the product of mental illness, deprives one so situated of liberty without due process of law.[2] We find it unnecessary to consider this and other constitutional claims concerning the fairness of the Municipal Court proceeding, since we read § 24–301(d) as applicable only to a defendant acquitted on the ground of insanity who has affirmatively relied upon a defense of insanity, and not to one, like the petitioner, who has maintained that he was mentally responsible when the alleged offense was committed.

The decisions of this Court have repeatedly warned against the dangers of an approach to statutory construction which confines itself to the bare words of a statute, for "literalness may strangle meaning," *Utah Junk Co.* v. *Porter,* 328 U.S. 39, 44. Heeding that principle we conclude that to construe § 24–301(d) as applying only to criminal defendants who have interposed a defense of insanity is more consistent with the general pattern of laws governing the confinement of the mentally ill in the District of Columbia, and

[2] In essence the claim is that § 24-301(d) compels the indeterminate commitment of such a person without any inquiry as to his present sanity, and solely on evidence sufficient to warrant a reasonable doubt as to his mental responsibility as of the time he committed the offense charged . . .

with the congressional policy that impelled the enactment of this mandatory commitment provision, than would be a literal reading of the section. That construction finds further support in the rule that a statute should be interpreted, if fairly possible, in such a way as to free it from not insubstantial constitutional doubts. Such doubts might arise in this case were the Government's construction of § 24–301(d) to be accepted.

I

To construe § 24–301(d) as requiring a court, without further proceedings, automatically to commit a defendant who, as in the present case, has competently and advisedly not tendered a defense of insanity to the crime charged and has not been found incompetent at the time of commitment is out of harmony with the awareness that Congress has otherwise shown for safeguarding those suspected of mental incapacity against improvident confinement.

Thus, a civil commitment must commence with the filing of a verified petition and supporting affidavits. D.C. Code § 21–310. This is followed by a preliminary examination by the staff of Saint Elizabeth's Hospital, a hearing before the Commission on Mental Health, and then another hearing in the District Court, which must be before a jury if the person being committed demands one. D.C. Code § 21–311. At both of these hearings representation by counsel or by a guardian *ad litem* is necessary. The burden of proof is on the party seeking commitment, and it is only if the trier of fact is "satisfied that the alleged insane person is insane," that he may be committed "for the best interest of the public and of the insane person." D.C. Code § 21–315 . . .

Considering the present case against this background, we should be slow in our reading of § 24–301(d) to attribute to Congress a purpose to compel commitment of an accused who never throughout the criminal proceedings suggests that he is, or ever was, mentally irresponsible. This is the more so when there is kept in mind the contrast between the nature of an acquittal by reason of insanity and the finding of insanity required in other kinds of commitment proceedings. In the District of Columbia, as in all federal courts, an accused "is entitled to an acquittal of the specific crime charged if upon all the evidence there is reasonable doubt whether he was capable in law of committing crime." *Davis* v. *United States*, 160

U.S. 469, 484. Consequently, the trial judge or jury must reach a judgment or verdict of not guilty by reason of insanity even if the evidence as to mental responsibility at the time the offense was committed raises no more than a reasonable doubt of sanity. If § 24–301(d) were taken to apply to petitioner's situation, there would be an anomalous disparity between what § 24–301(d) commands and what § 24–301(a) forbids. On the one hand, § 24–301(d) would *compel* posttrial commitment upon the suggestion of the Government and over the objection of the accused merely on evidence introduced by the Government that raises a reasonable doubt of the accused's sanity as of the time at which the offense was committed. On the other hand, § 24–301(a) would *prohibit* pretrial commitment upon the suggestion of the Government and over the objection of the accused, although the record contained an affirmative medical finding of present insanity, unless the Government is able to prove, by a preponderance of the evidence, that the accused is presently of unsound mind.

Of course the posttrial commitment of § 24-301(d) presupposes a determination that the accused has committed the criminal act with which he is charged, whereas pretrial commitment antedates any such finding of guilt. But the fact that the accused has pleaded guilty or that, overcoming some defense other than insanity, the Government has established that he committed a criminal act constitutes only strong evidence that his continued liberty could imperil "the preservation of public peace." It no more rationally justifies his indeterminate commitment to a mental institution on a bare reasonable doubt as to past sanity than would any other cogent proof of possible jeopardy to "the rights of persons and of property" in any civil commitment.

Moreover, the literal construction urged here by the Government is quite out of keeping with the congressional policy that underlies the elaborate procedural precautions included in the civil commitment provisions. It seems to have been Congress' intention to insure that only those who need treatment and may be dangerous are confined; committing a criminal defendant who denies the existence of any mental abnormality merely on the basis of a reasonable doubt as to his condition at some earlier time is surely at odds with this policy.

The criminal defendant who chooses to claim that he was

mentally irresponsible when his offense was committed is in quite a different position. It is true that he may avoid the ordinary criminal penalty merely by submitting enough evidence of an abnormal mental condition to raise a reasonable doubt of his responsibility at the time of committing the offense. Congress might have thought, however, that having successfully claimed insanity to avoid punishment, the accused should then bear the burden of proving that he is no longer subject to the same mental abnormality which produced his criminal acts. Alternatively, Congress might have considered it appropriate to provide compulsory commitment for those who successfully invoke an insanity defense in order to discourage false pleas of insanity. We need go no further here than to say that such differentiating considerations are pertinent to ascertaining the intended reach of this statutory provision.

II

The enactment of § 24–301(d) in 1955 was the direct result of the change in the standard of criminal responsibility in the District of Columbia wrought by *Durham* v. *United States*, 94 U.S. App. D.C. 228, 214 F.2d 862. That decision provoked a congressional re-examination of the laws governing commitment of the criminally insane . . . A Committee on Mental Disorder as a Criminal Defense was established by the Council on Law Enforcement in the District of Columbia to inquire into "the substantive and procedural law of the District of Columbia bearing on mental disorder as a defense in a criminal prosecution." S.Rep. No. 1170, 84th Cong., 1st Sess. 1 (1955); H.R. Rep. No. 892, 84th Cong., 1st Sess. 1 (1955). Among its recommendations was a mandatory commitment provision, subsequently enacted as § 24–301(d) . . .

It is significant to note that in finding that mandatory commitment would not result in "impairing the rights of the accused" and that it was "just and reasonable . . . that the insanity, once established, should be presumed to continue . . . until it can be shown that . . . [the accused] has recovered," the Committee Report, which was embraced in the reports of the Senate and House committees on the bill, spoke entirely in terms of one who "has pleaded insanity as a defense to a crime." Certainly such confidence could hardly have been vouchsafed with respect to a defendant who, as in this case, had stoutly denied his mental incompetence at any time. And it is surely straining things to assume that any of the committees had in mind such cases as this, which are presumably rare.

Nor is it necessary to read § 24–301(d) as an assurance that an accused who requires medical treatment will be hospitalized rather than be confined in jail. Simultaneously with the mandatory commitment provision, Congress enacted the present § 24–302, which permits transfers of mentally ill convicts from penal institutions to hospitals. Consequently, if an accused who pleads guilty is found to be in need of psychiatric assistance, he may be transferred to a hospital following sentence.

Finally, it is not necessary to accept the Government's literal reading of § 24–301(d) in order to effectuate Congress' basic concern, in passing this legislation, of reassuring the public. Section 24–301(a) provides a procedure for confining an accused who, though found competent to stand trial, is nonetheless committable as a person of unsound mind. That section permits the trial judge to act "prior to the imposition of sentence or prior to the expiration of any period of probation," if he has reason to believe that the accused "is of unsound mind *or* is mentally incompetent so as to be unable to understand the proceedings against him." (Emphasis added). The statute provides for a preliminary examination by a hospital staff, and then "if the court shall find the accused to be then of unsound mind *or* mentally incompetent to stand trial, the court shall order the accused confined to a hospital for the mentally ill." (Emphasis added.) This inquiry, therefore, is not limited to the accused's competence to stand trial; the judge may consider, as well, whether the accused is presently committable as a person of unsound mind. Since this inquiry may be undertaken at any time "prior to the imposition of sentence," it appears to be as available after the jury returns a verdict of not guilty by reason of insanity as before trial.

In light of the foregoing considerations we conclude that it was not Congress' purpose to make commitment compulsory when, as here, an accused disclaims reliance on a defense of mental irresponsibility. This does not mean, of course, that a criminal defendant has an absolute right to have his guilty plea accepted by the court. As provided in Rule 11, Fed. Rules Crim. Proc., and Rule 9, D.C. Munic. Ct. Crim. Rules, the trial judge may refuse to accept such a plea and enter a plea of not guilty on behalf of the accused. We decide in this case only that if this is done and the defendant, despite his own assertions of sanity, is found not guilty by reason of insanity, § 24–301(d) does not apply. If commitment is then considered warranted, it must be accomplished either by resorting to § 24–301(a) or by recourse to the civil commitment provisions in Title 21 of the D.C. Code.

The judgment of the Court of Appeals is reversed and the case is remanded to the District Court for further proceedings consistent with this opinion.

It is so ordered.[3]

[3] In his dissent Justice Clark described the Court's failure to reach the constitutional issue as a "disingenuous evasion," since "petitioner has no constitutional right to choose jail confinement instead of hospitalization." [Ed.]

IV

Further Aspects of the Role of the Court

A body whose jurisdiction is as broad as that of the Supreme Court, and whose pronouncements are so far-reaching, must always be careful about the cases it selects for hearing and the way in which it decides them. As the ultimate arbiter of all questions in the federal courts, and all federal questions in the state courts, it cannot hope to correct every mistake or to see that "justice" is done in every case if it is to fulfill its function of guiding the lower courts in important matters. Having determined to accept a case for review, it should not dispose of any but the simplest questions without full consideration and articulation of the grounds of decision; summary, uninformative dispositions may often mislead and are always hard to follow. At the same time, any court—and perhaps most especially the Supreme Court in view of its awesome responsibility—should be reluctant to reach beyond the case at hand in formulating the principles of decision.

While the precepts just suggested, like those in the Boy Scout Manual, would doubtless be endorsed by all, or almost all, the consensus is bound to disintegrate when the time comes to apply them, and in each of the cases that follows, Justice Harlan found himself in dissent.

A

The Selection and Disposition of Cases— FELA and All That

Rogers v. Missouri Pacific Railroad Co.

352 U.S. 500, 559 (1957)

Several statutes enacted by Congress since 1891 have narrowed the area of the Supreme Court's obligatory jurisdiction and enlarged its "certiorari" jurisdiction—its discretion to determine which cases will be accepted for review.[1] The Court's policy in exercising this discretion has been that the affirmative vote of four justices will result in a grant of certiorari and a hearing on the merits. But agreement on that policy has not meant agreement on the kinds of cases that should be heard, and the discord has been loudest in cases involving the application of federal laws imposing liability for negligence.[2] This discord reached a crescendo in a series of cases decided in 1957, of which *Rogers* was one.

Whether motivated by sympathy for injured plaintiffs, by distaste for judicial interference with jury verdicts, or by a combination of these and other factors, the Court has over a number of years heard many cases in which the sole issue presented was whether the evidence was sufficient to support the jury's verdict. In most of these cases, the decision on the merits

---

[1]E.g., 26 Stat. 828 (1891); 39 Stat. 726 (1916); 43 Stat. 936 (1925). The principal provisions governing Supreme Court review today are contained in 28 U.S.C. §§ 1254, 1257.

[2]E.g., Federal Employers' Liability Act (FELA), 45 U.S.C. §§ 51–60; Jones Act, 46 U.S.C. § 688.

has been to sustain that verdict by reversing the judgment of the court below.

The *Rogers* series of four cases fit this pattern. Three, including *Rogers,* arose under the Federal Employers' Liability Act,[3] and the fourth under the Jones Act.[4] In all but one,[5] the Court disagreed with the courts below and held the evidence sufficient to warrant the jury's verdict for the plaintiff. Justice Brennan, writing for the majority, justified the decisions to review by stating:

> The kind of misconception evidenced in the opinion below, which fails to take into account the special features of this statutory negligence action that make it significantly different from the ordinary common-law negligence action, has required this Court to review a number of cases . . . Special and important reasons for the grant of certiorari in these cases are certainly present when lower federal and state courts persistently deprive litigants of their right to a jury determination.

Justice Frankfurter, in a thirty-five-page opinion, dissented in all four cases. He stated that his fundamental disagreement with the Court's certiorari policy compelled him to vote to dismiss the writs as improvidently granted. The reasons underlying his refusal to vote on the merits were, perhaps, best summarized in a passage discussing the facts of one of the four cases:

> For the Supreme Court of the United States to spend two hours of solemn argument, plus countless other hours reading the briefs and record and writing opinions, to determine whether there was evidence to support an allegation that it could reasonably be foreseen that an ice-cream server on a ship would use a butcher's knife to scoop out ice cream that was too hard to be scooped with a regular scoop, is surely to misconceive the discretion that was entrusted to the wisdom of the Court for the control of its calendar. The Court may or may not be "doing justice" in the four insignificant cases it decides today; it certainly is doing injustice to the significant and important cases on the calendar and to its own role as the supreme judicial body of the country.

Justice Harlan, concurring in the decision upholding the judgment of the court below and dissenting from the three reversals, found that despite his unhappiness with the presence of the cases in the Court, he was unable

[3]The other two cases were Webb v. Illinois C.R.R., 352 U.S. 512; Herdman v. Pennsylvania R.R., 352 U.S. 518.

[4]Ferguson v. Moore–McCormack Lines, Inc., 352 U.S. 521.

[5]In Herdman v. Pennsylvania R.R., 352 U.S. 518, the Court agreed with the courts below that the evidence of negligence was not sufficient to take the case to the jury. The plaintiff in the *Herdman* case had been injured while working on a train that had made a sudden stop to avoid hitting an automobile.

to agree with Justice Frankfurter's refusal to vote on the merits. His discussion raises the most pointed questions—questions that have relevance far beyond the confines of these cases—about the limits of the right of dissent.

Mr. Justice Harlan, concurring in No. 46 [*Herdman*] and dissenting in Nos. 28, 42, and 59 [*Rogers, Webb,* and *Ferguson*].

I

I am in full agreement with what my Brother Frankfurter has written in criticism of the Court's recurring willingness to grant certiorari in cases of this type. For the reasons he has given, I think the Court should not have heard any of these four cases. Nevertheless, the cases having been taken, I have conceived it to be my duty to consider them on their merits, because I cannot reconcile voting to dismiss the writs as "improvidently granted" with the Court's "rule of four." In my opinion due adherence to that rule requires that once certiorari has been granted a case should be disposed of on the premise that it is properly here, in the absence of considerations appearing which were not manifest or fully apprehended at the time certiorari was granted. In these instances I am unable to say that such considerations exist, even though I do think that the arguments on the merits underscored the views of those of us who originally felt that the cases should not be taken because they involved only issues of fact, and presented nothing of sufficient general importance to warrant this substantial expenditure of the Court's time.

I do not think that, in the absence of the considerations mentioned, voting to dismiss a writ after it has been granted can be justified on the basis of an inherent right of dissent. In the case of a petition for certiorari that right, it seems to me—again without the presence of intervening factors—is exhausted once the petition has been granted and the cause set for argument.[6] Otherwise the "rule of four" surely becomes a meaningless thing in more than one respect. *First,* notwithstanding the "rule of four," five objecting

---

[6] In some instances where the Court has granted certiorari and simultaneously summarily disposed of the case on the merits, individual Justices (including the writer) have merely noted their dissent to the grant without reaching the merits. Even here, I am bound to say, it would probably be better practice for a Justice, who has unsuccessfully opposed certiorari, to face the merits, and to dissent from the summary disposition rather than from the grant of certiorari if he is not prepared to reach the merits without full-dress argument.

Justices could undo the grant by voting, after the case has been heard, to dismiss the writ as improvidently granted—a course which would hardly be fair to litigants who have expended time, effort, and money on the assumption that their cases would be heard and decided on the merits. While in the nature of things litigants must assume the risk of "improvidently granted" dismissals because of factors not fully apprehended when the petition for certiorari was under consideration, short of that it seems to me that the Court would stultify its own rule if it were permissible for a writ of certiorari to be annulled by the later vote of five objecting Justices. Indeed, if that were proper, it would be preferable to have the vote of annulment come into play the moment after the petition for certiorari has been granted, since then at least the litigants would be spared useless effort in briefing and preparing for the argument of their cases. *Second,* permitting the grant of a writ to be thus undone would undermine the whole philosophy of the "rule of four," which is that any case warranting consideration in the opinion of such a substantial minority of the Court will be taken and disposed of. It appears to me that such a practice would accomplish just the contrary of what representatives of this Court stated to Congress as to the "rule of four" at the time the Court's certiorari jurisdiction was enlarged by the Judiciary Act of 1925. In effect the "rule of four" would, by indirection, become a "rule of five." *Third,* such a practice would, in my opinion, be inconsistent with the long-standing and desirable custom of not announcing the Conference vote on petitions for certiorari. For in the absence of the intervening circumstances which may cause a Justice to vote to dismiss a writ as improvidently granted, such a disposition of the case on his part is almost bound to be taken as reflecting his original Conference vote on the petition. And if such a practice is permissible, then by the same token I do not see how those who voted in favor of the petition can reasonably be expected to refrain from announcing their Conference votes at the time the petition is acted on.

My Brother Frankfurter states that the course he advocates will not result in making of the "rule of four" an empty thing, suggesting that in individual cases "a doubting Justice" will normally respect "the judgment of his brethren that the case does concern issues important enough for the Court's consideration and adjudication," and that it is only "when a class of cases is systematically taken for review" that such a Justice "cannot forego his duty to voice his dissent to the Court's action." However, it seems to me that it is precisely in that type of situation where the exercise of the right of dissent may well result in nullification of the "rule of four" by the action of five Justices. For differences of view as to the desirability of the Court's taking particular "classes" of cases—the situation we have here—are prone to lead to more or less definite lines of cleavage among the Justices, which past experience has shown may well involve an alignment of four Justices who favor granting certiorari in such cases and five who do not. If in such situations it becomes the duty of one Justice among the disagreeing five not to "forego" his right to dissent, then I do not see why it is not equally the duty of the remaining four, resulting in the "rule of four" being set at naught. I thus see no basis in the circumstance that a case is an "individual" one rather than one of a "class" for distinctions in what may be done by an individual Justice who disapproves of the Court's action in granting certiorari.

Although I feel strongly that cases of this kind do not belong in this Court, I can see no other course, consistent with the "rule of four," but to continue our Conference debates, with the hope that persuasion or the mounting calendars of the Court will eventually bring our differing brethren to another point of view.

II

Since I can find no intervening circumstances which would justify my voting now to dismiss the writs in these cases as improvidently granted, I turn to the merits of the four cases before us. I agree with, and join in, the Court's opinion in No. 46. I dissent in Nos. 28, 42, and 59. No doubt the evidence in the latter three cases can be viewed both as the three courts below did and as this Court does. So far as I can see all this Court has done is to substitute its views on the evidence for those of the Missouri Supreme Court and the two Courts of Appeals, and that is my first reason for dissenting. In my view we should not interfere with the decisions of these three courts in the absence of clear legal error, or some capricious or unreasonable action on their part. Nothing of that kind has been shown here . . .

I dissent also for another reason. No scientific or precise yardstick can be devised to test the sufficiency of the evidence in a negligence case. The problem has always been one of judgment, to be applied in view of the purposes of the statute. It has, however, been common ground that a verdict must be based on evidence—not on a scintilla of evidence but evidence sufficient to enable a *reasoning* man to infer both negligence and causation by *reasoning from the evidence.* And it has always been the function of the court to see to it that jury verdicts stay within that boundary, that they be arrived at by reason and not by will or sheer speculation. Neither the Seventh Amendment nor the Federal Employers' Liability Act lifted that duty from the courts. However, in judging these cases, the Court appears to me to have departed from these long-established standards, for, as I read these opinions, the implication seems to be that the question, at least as to the element of causation, is not whether the evidence is sufficient to convince a reasoning man, but whether there is any scintilla of evidence at all to justify the jury verdicts. I cannot agree with such a standard, for I consider it a departure from a wise rule of law, not justified either by the provision of the FELA making employers liable for injuries resulting "in whole or in part" from their negligence, or by anything else in the Act or its history, which evinces no purpose to depart in these respects from common-law rules.

For these reasons I think the judgments in Nos. 28, 42, and 59, as well as that in No. 46, should be affirmed.

Mr. Justice Burton concurs in Part I of this opinion.

The Chief Justice, Mr. Justice Black, Mr. Justice Douglas, Mr. Justice Clark, and Mr. Justice Brennan concur in Part I of this opinion except insofar as it disapproves of the grant of the writ of certiorari in these cases.

O'Keeffe v. *Smith, Hinchman & Grylls Associates, Inc.*

380 U.S. 359, 365 (1965)

O'Keeffe complements the FELA cases nicely, because it demonstrates that the enactment of a workman's compensation system will not solve all the problems of the Court or of injured employees.[1] Recovery under such a system ordinarily turns on whether injury or death arose "out of and in the course of employment,"[2] an issue to be decided in the first instance by an administrative official, subject to judicial review. The question of how much deference to an administrative determination must be given by the reviewing court is not too different from that of the sanctity of jury verdicts in FELA cases. Under *O'Keeffe*, the answer may be that, at least when benefits have been awarded at the administrative level, anything the administrator says goes.[3] In this case a five member majority of the Court, in a per curiam decision rendered without argument, summarily reversed a Court of Appeals determination setting aside the administrator's award. Justice Harlan's dissent notes the startling implications of the decision, criticizes the Court for its summary treatment of the case, and deftly exposes the weaknesses of the majority's position. The opinion displays a lightness of style that makes it eminently readable but at the same time does not detract from the force of the points made.

Mr. Justice Harlan, whom Mr. Justice Clark and Mr. Justice White join, dissenting.

Ecker was employed in Seoul, Korea, as an assistant administrative officer for Smith, Hinchman & Grylls Associates, Inc., an engineering management concern working under contracts with the United States and Korean Governments. His duties were restricted to Seoul where he was responsible for personnel in the stenographic and clerical departments. He was subject to call at the job site at any time, but the usual work week was 44 hours, and employees were accustomed to travel far from the job site on weekends and holidays for recreational purposes. Ecker did not live at the job site; he was given an allowance to live on the economy in Seoul. On his Memorial Day weekend he went to a lake 30 miles east of Seoul

---

[1] In Dennis v. Denver & R.G.W.R.R., 375 U.S. 208, 212, 213, an FELA case, Justice Harlan said in dissent: "The means for requiting industrial accidents of this sort should be found not in destroying the supervisory power of the courts over jury verdicts unsupported by evidence of employer fault, but in legislative expansion of the concepts of workmen's compensation laws, under which compensation is not dependent on a showing of employer negligence."

[2] The particular federal statute involved in *O'Keeffe*, which contained this language, was the Longshoremen's and Harbor Workers' Compensation Act, 33 U.S.C. §§ 901–950, as extended by the Defense Bases Act, 42 U.S.C. §§ 1651–1654.

[3] Compare Basham v. Pennsylvania R.R., 372 U.S. 699, 701, another FELA case, in which the Justice said in dissent: "The only premise on which this reversal can be justified is that anything a jury says goes."

where a friend of his (not a co-employee) had a house. Ecker intended to spend the holiday there with his friend and another visitor. Their Saturday afternoon project was to fill in the beach in front of the house with sand, but none was readily available. In order to obtain it the three crossed the lake in a small aluminum boat to a sandy part of the shore. There they filled the boat with a load of sand, intending to transport it back to the house. The return trip, however, put Archimedes' Principle to the test; in the middle of the lake the boat capsized and sank. Two of the three men drowned, including Ecker.

The Longshoremen's and Harbor Workers' Compensation Act, as extended by the Defense Bases Act, provides workmen's compensation for any

> accidental injury or death arising out of and in the course of employment, and such occupational disease or infection as arises naturally out of such employment or as naturally or unavoidably results from such accidental injury, and includes an injury caused by the willful act of a third person directed against an employee because of his employment. 33 U.S.C. § 902(2).

The Court holds, *per curiam,* that Ecker died in the course of his employment. I see no meaningful interpretation of the statute which will support this result except a rule that any decision made by a Deputy Commissioner must be upheld (compare *Rogers v. Missouri Pac. R. Co.,* 352 U.S. 500). That interpretation, although meaningful, is unsupportable . . .

I read [*O'Leary v. Brown-Pacific-Maxon, Inc.,* 340 U.S. 504, relied on by the majority] to mean that some questions of application of "arising out of and in the course of employment" to the facts of a case will be left to the discretion of the administrator, and review of his decision treated as review of a finding of fact. The cases in which this limited review of the administrator's decision is appropriate are those in which one application of the statute to the external facts of the case effectuates the judicially recognizable purpose of the statute as well as another. Dominion over the broad or clear purposes of the statute thus remains firmly in the courts' hands, while within the confines of such statutory purposes, administrators are left discretion to provide the intimate particularizations of statutory application. *Brown-Pacific-Maxon* is illustrative. The employee drowned in a particularly treacherous channel with which his job brought him into proximity. The danger was not great that circumstance would force him to swim in the channel, but the danger existed and was peculiar to the locality to which his job brought him; and it was out of this special danger that the employee's injury arose. This, taken together with the other elements of job connection which the administrator thought relevant, rendered an award in the case consistent with the broad purposes of the compensation statute. Yet had the Deputy Commissioner come out the other way, I think that his decision would have been equally supportable. Although it was true that the injury was related to an especially dangerous channel with which the employee's job brought him into proximity, the administrator could have ruled that the danger, although special, was so remote that the connection between the job and the injury was not sufficient to justify compensation. Either result would have been consistent with the statutory purpose of compensating all job-connected injuries on the actual job site and, additionally, those injuries off the job site which result from the "special" dangers of the employment. In the sense that both results would have been supportable, the review of the choice actually made by the Deputy Commissioner was treated as review of a finding of fact.

In the case before us, the Deputy Commissioner's ruling is not consistent with the statutory purpose. The injury did not take place on the actual job site, and it did not arise out of any special danger created by the job. In no sense can it be said that Ecker's job created any "special" danger of his drowning in a lake, or more particularly, of his loading a small boat with sand and capsizing it. Nothing indicates that the lake was rougher, the boat tippier, or the sand heavier than their counterparts in the United States. If there were "exacting and unconventional conditions" in Korea it does not appear that the lake, boat, or sand was one of them. There is nothing more than a "but for" relationship between the accident and the employment. To permit the award of compensation to stand reads the "job-connected" emphasis right out of the statute, an emphasis which is clearly there. Only injuries "arising out of" the employment are compensated. A disease or infection is covered if it arises "naturally out of such employment." Injuries willfully inflicted by third persons upon an employee are covered only if inflicted "because of his employment." A "but for" relationship between the injury and the employment should not in itself be sufficient to bring about coverage.

Whether the injury is compensable should depend to some degree on the cause of the injury as well as the time of day, location, and momentary activity of the employee at the time of the accident. I would distinguish between a case in which Ecker smashed his hand in a filing cabinet while at the office and one in which he tripped over a pebble while off on a weekend hike. In the first case Ecker's injury would have arisen out of and in the course of his employment, whereas the statute would not apply to the second case unless the injury were traceable to some special danger peculiar to the employment, which was clearly not the case. Thus, if while off on that same weekend hike Ecker stepped on a mine left over from the Korean conflict, a different result could follow.

This view of the statute makes far more sense to me than the view adopted by the Court as indicated by the result in this case and its approving citation of such cases as *Self* v. *Hanson,* 305 F.2d 699, and *Pan American World Airways, Inc.* v. *O'Hearne,* 335 F.2d 70, cert. denied today. It is difficult to determine just what such cases stand for. In *Self* v. *Hanson,* for instance, Miss Williams was in the company of a gentleman in a pick-up truck parked at the end of a breakwater on Guam Island at 11 o'clock in the evening. The gentleman said that he wanted to show her a ship in the harbor. Apparently they had been looking at it for over half an hour when the driver of another vehicle on the breakwater lost control and ran into the pick-up truck, causing Miss Williams spinal injuries. The Ninth Circuit upheld the Deputy Commissioner's ruling that she was injured in the course of her employment as a secretary on a Guam defense project.

To permit compensation for such injuries is to impose absolute liability upon the employer for any and all injuries, whatever their nature, whatever their cause, just so long as the Deputy Commissioner makes an award and the job location is one to which the reviewing judge would not choose to go if he had his choice of vacation spots. Before setting its stamp of approval on such an interpretation of the statute, the Court at the very least should hear argument and receive briefs on the merits. The Solicitor General has pointed out that "there are several thousands of injury cases reported annually" under this Act. He urged that this question be definitively resolved by this Court. Because of the importance placed by all parties upon resolution of the proper application of the Act to these cases, and because I do not believe *Brown-Pacific-Maxon, supra,* dictates the Court's result, I respectfully dissent from its decision to treat *O'Keeffe* v. *Smith, Hinchman & Grylls Associates, Inc.,* summarily, from its decision on the merits in that case, and from its denial of certiorari in *Pan-American World Airways, Inc.* v. *O'Hearne,* No. 474, and *Pan American World Airways, Inc.* v. *O'Keeffe,* No. 852.[4]

[4]Justice Douglas joined neither the majority nor the dissent. Describing his position as "dubitante," he said he "would not be inclined to reverse a Court of Appeals that disagreed with a Deputy Commissioner over findings as exotic as we have here." [Ed.]

B

"Guidelines" and the
Decisional Process

Sanders v. United States

373 U.S. 1, 23 (1963)

Prisoners held pursuant to a federal conviction may seek relief under 28 U.S.C. § 2255, which provides in relevant part:

> A prisoner in custody under sentence of a court established by Act of Congress claiming the right to be released upon the ground [among others] that the sentence was imposed in violation of the Constitution or laws of the United States . . . may move the court which imposed the sentence to vacate, set aside or correct the sentence . . . The sentencing court shall not be required to entertain a second or successive motion for similar relief on behalf of the same prisoner.

Sanders, serving a fifteen-year term for robbery of a federally insured bank, filed a motion under § 2255 on various grounds, including the invalidity of the indictment, denial of counsel, and coercion of his plea of guilty. After this motion was denied without a hearing, Sanders filed a second motion, alleging that at the time of his trial and sentence he was mentally incompetent as a result of the administration of narcotics by medical authorities at the jail where he was being held. This motion too was denied without a hearing on the grounds that there was no reason why the allegation could not have been raised in the first motion and in any event the

235

allegation was "without merit in fact." The Court of Appeals affirmed per curiam, but the Supreme Court reversed in a 7–2 decision, holding that Sanders was entitled to a hearing on the issues of fact raised in the second motion. Sanders' claim, the Court stated, was not conclusively shown by the records and files in the case to be without merit.

In the course of the opinion Justice Brennan, speaking for the Court, laid down some specific rules for district courts to follow under § 2255 and in other applications for federal collateral relief:

A. Successive Motions on Grounds Previously Heard and Determined

Controlling weight may be given to denial of a prior application for federal habeas corpus or § 2255 relief only if (1) the same ground presented in the subsequent application was determined adversely to the applicant on the prior application, (2) the prior determination was on the merits, and (3) the ends of justice would not be served by reaching the merits of the subsequent application . . .

B. The Successive Application Claimed to be an Abuse of Remedy

No matter how many prior applications for federal collateral relief a prisoner has made, the principle elaborated in Subpart A, *supra*, cannot apply if a different ground is presented by the new application. So too, it cannot apply if the same ground was earlier presented but not adjudicated on the merits. In either case, full consideration of the merits of the new application can be avoided only if there has been an abuse of the writ or motion remedy; and this the Government has the burden of pleading.

In his dissent Justice Harlan argued that the statute enacted by the Court—for that is what it appeared to be in form and substance—had no relation to the one enacted by Congress and that there had been no abuse of discretion by the district judge in this case. In a brief concluding paragraph, the Justice voiced a more basic objection: That such sweeping judicial pronouncements as that of the majority had no proper place within the confines of the adjudicatory process.

Mr. Justice Harlan, whom Mr. Justice Clark joins, dissenting.

This case, together with *Townsend* v. *Sain*, 372 U.S. 293, and *Fay* v. *Noia*, 372 U.S. 391 [*see above*] form a trilogy of "guideline" decisions in which the Court has undertaken to restate the responsibilities of the federal courts in federal post-conviction proceedings. *Sain* and *Noia* relate to federal habeas corpus proceedings arising out of state criminal convictions. The present case involves successive § 2255 applications (and similar habeas corpus proceedings under § 2244, which the Court finds sets the pattern for § 2255) arising out of federal convictions.

The over-all effect of this trilogy of pronouncements is to relegate to a back seat, as it affects state and federal criminal cases finding their way into federal post-conviction proceedings, the principle that there must be some end to litigation.

While, contrary to the Court, I think the District Court's denial without hearing of a second § 2255 application in this case was entirely proper in the circumstances shown by the record, the more serious aspect of the Court's opinion is the impact it is likely to have in curbing the ability of the Federal District Courts to cope efficiently, as well as fairly, with successive applications by federal prisoners, the number of which will doubtless increase as a result of what is said today. The net of it is that the Court has come forth with a new § 2255 of its own which bears little resemblance to the statute enacted by Congress. And in the process the Court has even gone so far as to suggest that any tampering with its new composition may run afoul of the Constitution.

I

At the outset, there is one straw man that should be removed from this case. The Court is at great pains to develop the theme that denial of a prisoner's application for collateral relief is not *res judicata*. But the Government recognizes, as indeed it must in view of the decisions, that strict doctrines of *res judicata* do not apply in this field. The consequences of injustice—loss of liberty and sometimes loss of life—are far too great to permit the automatic application of an entire body of technical rules whose primary relevance lies in the area of civil litigation.

This is not to suggest, however, that finality, as distinguished from the particular rules of *res judicata*, is without significance in the criminal law. Both the individual criminal defendant and society have an interest in insuring that there will at some point be the certainty that comes with an end to litigation, and that attention will ultimately be focused not on whether a conviction was free from error but rather on whether the prisoner can be restored to a useful place in the community. It is with this interest in mind, as well as the desire to avoid confinements contrary to fundamental justice, that

237

courts and legislatures have developed rules governing the availability of collateral relief . . .

Concern with existing and potential abuse of the remedy [of habeas corpus] by prisoners who made a pastime of filing collateral proceedings led to proposals that successive applications for habeas corpus on grounds previously available would be wholly barred, except in the form of petitions for rehearing to the same judge, and that applications under what became § 2255 would have to be submitted within one year after discovery of the facts or a change in the law. These proposals were rejected in favor of the traditional discretion exercised by courts with respect to successive applications, and it was made clear that this discretion extended to a case in which an applicant asserted for the first time a ground that could have been raised before. Thus the final wording of § 2244 [dealing with habeas corpus applications] provided that the court shall not be *required* to entertain a petition

> . . . if it appears that the legality of such detention has been determined . . . on a prior application . . . and the petition presents no *new* ground not theretofore presented and determined . . . (Emphasis added.)

The word "new," a word ignored by the Court in its discussion of this provision, is of cardinal importance. A memorandum by Circuit Judge Stone, adopted in a Senate Report (S. Rep. No. 1527, 80th Cong., 2d Sess.), noted that two of the purposes of an earlier version of this provision were "to compel petitioner to state in his petition all of the grounds for the writ then known to him" and "to afford unlimited opportunity to present any grounds which petitioner may *thereafter discover* at any time." (Emphasis added.) This latter purpose was "brought about by allowing presentation of a subsequent petition based upon 'new' grounds 'not theretofore presented and determined.'" Thus a "new ground," within the meaning of § 2244, is one that has not previously been asserted and had not previously been *known*. The Court is manifestly in error in its conclusion that the discretion provided for it § 2244 is limited to petitions relying on grounds previously heard and decided.

Although the wording of § 2255 is more general, it is clearly directed to the same end . . .

Further, it would appear from the language of § 2255—the

"sentencing court" is not "required to entertain" successive motions—that the court was given discretion to deny a second motion, on grounds of abuse, on its own initiative and without waiting for the Government to raise the point in its return. The provision, to this extent, departed from the rule of pleading declared in the year of its adoption in *Price* v. *Johnston* [334 U.S. 266] at 292—that in habeas corpus applications, "it rests with the Government to make that claim [of abuse] with clarity and particularity in its return to the order to show cause." Such a departure was amply justified by the fact that on a § 2255 motion, unlike a habeas corpus application, the prisoner's claim is presented to the sentencing court (usually the trial judge himself), which has ready access to the record of the original conviction and of the prior motions. Moreover, Congress could certainly have reasonably concluded, as did the dissenters in *Price,* that:

> It is not too much to ask the petitioner to state, however informally, that his . . . petition is based on newly discovered matter, or, in any event, on a claim that he could not fairly have been asked to bring to the court's attention in his . . . prior petitions. Such a requirement certainly does not narrow the broad protection which the writ . . . serves. 334 U.S. at 294.

The Court in *Price* held only that the burden is on the Government to *plead* abuse of the writ; the burden of *proving* an adequate excuse was explicitly placed on the prisoner:

> Once a particular abuse has been alleged, the prisoner has the burden of answering that allegation and of proving that he has not abused the writ. 334 U.S. at 292.

The Court today, however, leaves the crucial question of burden of proof up in the air. If it means to suggest that this burden also rests with the Government, then it is going far beyond the holding of the sharply divided Court in *Price.* The relevant facts on the question of abuse would almost always lie within the exclusive possession of the prisoner, and any evidentiary burden placed on the Government would therefore be one that it could seldom meet.

It is startling enough that the Government may now be required to *establish,* in a collateral attack on a prior conviction, that a

239

successive application is an abuse of the remedy. It is at least equally startling to learn that the question whether or not there has been abuse of the remedy may turn on whether the prisoner had "deliberately" withheld the ground now urged or had "deliberately" abandoned it at some earlier stage. The established concept of inexcusable neglect is apparently in the process of being entirely eliminated from the criminal law, cf. *Fay* v. *Noia,* 372 U.S. 391, and the standard that seems to be taking its place will, I am afraid, prove wholly inadequate and in the long run wholly unsatisfactory.

I must also protest the implication in the Court's opinion that every decison of this Court in the field of habeas corpus—even one like *Price* v. *Johnston,* dealing with a purely procedural question on which resonable men surely may differ—has become enshrined in the Constitution because of the guarantee in Article I against suspension of the writ. This matter may perhaps be brought back into proper perspective by noting again that at the time of the adoption of the Constitution, and for many years afterward, a claim of the kind asserted by Price, or asserted here by petitioner, was not cognizable in habeas corpus at all.

II

Section 2255, read against the background of this Court's decisions and the history of the related provision § 2244, is surely designed to vest in the District Court a sound discretion to deny a successive motion, on its own initiative, for abuse of the remedy. At the very least, this exercise of discretion should be upheld in a case in which there has been no adequate explanation of the earlier failure to make the claim *and* in which the whole record, including that of the prior motion, casts substantial doubts on the merit of that claim. This is such a case . . .

The motion before us now was filed some nine months after the initial application. In addition to commenting that he was "not required to entertain a second motion for similar relief," the trial judge said that he had "reviewed the entire file" and was "of the view that petitioner's complaints are without merit in fact." In support of this conclusion, in addition to whatever inferences the judge may properly have drawn from his own observation of Sanders at the trial, there is:

(1) the record of the original trial, which strongly indicates

that, contrary to his sworn allegation, petitioner did understand precisely what was going on and responded promptly and intelligently;

(2) an initial application under § 2255 which not only failed to mention the claim now urged—a lack of mental competence to understand—but indeed advanced a wholly inconsistent claim —that the court allowed him to be "intimidated and coerced" into pleading guilty; and

(3) a second application, not filed for another nine months, without any explanation why a point which was obviously known to petitioner before, and which would so clearly have been relevant, had not previously been raised.

In the light of the whole record, including the prior application, the second motion rested on an assertion of fact that was highly suspect, if not self-refuting. If the assertion had been made in the initial application, or if a valid excuse had been offered for the failure to do so, a hearing would doubtless have been necessary. But to require a hearing under the present circumstances, and to tell the trial court that it has abused its discretion, is to sanction manifest abuse of the remedy.

III

I seriously doubt the wisdom of these "guideline" decisions. They suffer the danger of pitfalls that usually go with judging in a vacuum. However carefully written, they are apt in their application to carry unintended consequences which once accomplished are not always easy to repair. Rules respecting matters daily arising in the federal courts are ultimately likely to find more solid formulation if left to focused adjudication on a case-by-case basis, or to the normal rule-making processes of the Judicial Conference, rather than to *ex cathedra* pronouncements by this Court, which is remote from the arena.

In dealing with cases of this type, I think we do better to confine ourselves to the particular issues presented, and on that basis I would affirm the judgment of the Court of Appeals.

V

The Art of Judging and the Exercise of Judicial Responsibility

"We are not final because we are infallible," Justice Jackson once said of the Supreme Court, "we are infallible only because we are final."[1] This aphorism concisely expresses the source of the Court's power and of its critics' apprehensions. Thus, short of a constitutional amendment, the Court is the final arbiter of the most basic issues of the separation and allocation of powers among all the branches of government. And even outside the constitutional arena, the Court is the ultimate judge of the scope and direction of acts of Congress—acts that may often do little more than express in general terms an ill-conceived or poorly defined legislative policy.[2]

Fulfillment of the responsibility imposed by the existence of such power demands all the skills in the judicial arsenal: craftsmanship, fairmindedness, sympathetic understanding of the objectives and problems of the other branches of government, and an awareness of the obligations and inherent limitations of the judiciary. Each of the opinions in Part V attests to the Justice's ability to meet these demands. Reasonable men, of course, can differ and have differed about the proper result in these cases, but it is hard to differ about the eloquence of the Justice's opinions, their professional competence, or their sensitivity to the place of the judiciary in a democratic society.

[1] Brown v. Allen, 344 U.S. 443, 540 (concurring opinion).

[2] "Of course, Congress can come back to say that what the Court said it had meant was not what it had meant at all. But that, too, requires legislation; and political forces not strong enough to enact legislation may yet be strong enough to prevent repeal of the Court's interpretation." Henkin, "Foreword [to the Supreme Court, 1967 Term]: On Drawing Lines," 82 *Harv. L. Rev.* 63, 84 (1968).

The Reach of the Antitrust Laws:
How Blank is the Check?

United States v. Continental Can Co.

378 U.S. 441, 467 (1964)

Few statutes are as broad in conception or in language as the antitrust laws, and thus few statutes place so heavy a burden on the courts. In recent years, the Supreme Court's response has been to expand the reach of those laws by holding against the antitrust defendant in almost every case.

Justice Harlan, who came to the Court with considerable experience in antitrust litigation, has often found himself in dissent in these cases, and when he has agreed with the judgment of the Court, has been unable to accept the majority's rationale. The opinions of the Justice in this area, although often necessarily technical, have much to teach about his approach to statutory construction and his view of the proper role of the Court.[1] Taken with his other opinions relating to federal regulation of business,[2]

---

[1] See, e.g., California v. FPC, 369 U.S. 482, 491 (dissenting opinion); Brown Shoe Co. v. United States, 370 U.S. 294, 357 (dissenting in part and concurring in part); United States v. Philadelphia National Bank, 374 U.S. 321, 373 (dissenting opinion); FTC v. Procter & Gamble Co., 386 U.S. 568, 581 (concurring opinion); FTC v. Fred Meyer, Inc., 390 U.S. 341, 359 (dissenting opinion).

[2] See, e.g., United Gas Pipe Line Co. v. Memphis Light, Gas and Water Div., 358 U.S. 103; San Diego Bldg. Trades Council v. Garmon, 359 U.S. 236, 249 (dissenting in part and concurring in part); Sunray Mid-Continent Oil Co. v. FPC, 364 U.S. 137, 159 (dissenting opinion); ICC v. New York, N.H. & H.R.R., 372 U.S. 744; Wisconsin v. FPC, 373 U.S. 294; Permian Basin Area Rate Cases, 390 U.S. 747.

they would in themselves make a most interesting volume, and selection among them for the present work was not an easy task. *Continental Can* was chosen because of the relatively narrow question involved and because of the vigor and directness of the Justice's dissent. Also, it is representative of the Justice's dismay at what he regards as the open-ended character of the Court's opinions in the field and at its failure to recognize economic realities.

In this case, the government brought a civil action attacking the acquisition of the assets of Hazel-Atlas Glass Company by the Continental Can Company. The statute claimed to be violated was section 7 of the Clayton Act, which prohibits corporations engaged in commerce from acquiring:

> the whole or any part of the assets of another corporation engaged also in commerce, where in any line of commerce in any section of the country, the effect of such acquisition may be substantially to lessen competition, or to tend to create a monopoly.[3]

The district court dismissed the complaint, holding that although Continental was the second largest metal container producer and Hazel-Atlas the third largest glass container producer in the United States, the government had failed to prove an adverse effect on any "line of commerce." On direct appeal, the Supreme Court reversed, 7–2, holding contrary to the district court that the evidence thus far revealed was "sufficient to warrant treating as a relevant product market [or line of commerce] the combined glass and metal container industries and all end uses for which they compete." The Court then stated that through the acquisition Continental had increased its share of this "market" from 21.9 percent to 25 percent and had reduced the most significant competitors from five to four. In terms of both the "static competitive situation" and the "dynamic long-run potential," the government had met its burden of proving "prima facie anticompetitive effect."

Justice Harlan in dissent accused the Court of exercising its "creative powers" to "invent a line of commerce the existence of which no one, not even the Government, has imagined."

Mr. Justice Harlan, whom Mr. Justice Stewart joins, dissenting.

Measured by any antitrust yardsticks with which I am familiar, the Court's conclusions are, to say the least, remarkable. Before the merger which is the subject of this case, Continental Can manufactured metal containers and Hazel-Atlas manufactured glass containers. The District Court found, with ample support in the record, that the Government had wholly failed to prove that the merger

[3] 15 U.S.C. § 18.

of these two companies would adversely affect competition in the metal container industry, in the glass container industry, or between the metal container industry and the glass container industry. Yet this Court manages to strike down the merger under § 7 of the Clayton Act, because, in the Court's view, it is anticompetitive. With all respect, the Court's conclusion is based on erroneous analysis, which makes an abrupt and unwise departure from established antitrust law.

I agree fully with the Court that "we must recognize meaningful competition where it is found," and that "inter-industry" competition, such as that involved in this case, no less than "intra-industry" competition is protected by § 7 from anticompetitive mergers. As this Court has, in effect, recognized in past cases, the concept of an "industry," or "line of commerce," is not susceptible of reduction to a precise formula. It would, therefore, be artificial and inconsistent with the broad protective purpose of § 7 to attempt to differentiate between permitted and prohibited mergers merely by asking whether a probable reduction in competition, if it is found, will be within a single "industry" or between two or more "industries."

Recognition that the purpose of § 7 is not to be thwarted by limiting its protection to intramural competition within strictly defined "industries," does not mean, however, that the concept of a "line of commerce" is no longer serviceable. More precisely, it does not, as the majority seems to think, entail the conclusion that wherever "meaningful competition" exists, a "line of commerce" is to be found. The Court declares the initial question of this case to be "whether the admitted competition between metal and glass containers for uses other than packaging beer was of the type and quality deserving of § 7 protection and *therefore* the basis for defining a relevant product market." (Emphasis added.) And the Court's answer is similarly phrased: ". . . We hold that *the inter-industry competition* between glass and metal containers *is sufficient to warrant treating as a relevant product market* the combined glass and metal container industries and all end uses for which they compete." (Emphasis added.) Quite obviously, such a conclusion simply reads the "line of commerce" element out of § 7, and destroys its usefulness as an aid to analysis.

The distortions to which this approach leads are evidenced by the Court's application of it in this case. Having found that there is "interindustry competition between glass and metal containers" the Court concludes that "the combined glass and metal container industries" is the relevant line of commerce or "product market" in which anticompetitive effects must be measured. Applying that premise, the Court then notes Continental's "dominant position" in the *metal can industry,* and finds that Continental has a "major position" in the "relevant product market—*the combined metal and glass container industries."* (Emphasis added.) Hazel-Atlas, being the third largest producer of *glass containers,* is found to rank sixth in the relevant product market—again, the combined metal and glass container industries. This "evidence," coupled with the market shares of Continental and Hazel-Atlas in the combined product market,[4] leads the Court to conclude that the merger violates § 7.

"The resulting percentage of the combined firms," the Court says, "approaches that held presumptively bad in *United States* v. *Philadelphia National Bank,* 374 U.S. 321." The *Philadelphia Bank* case, which involved the merger of two banks plainly engaged in the same line of commerce, is, however, entirely distinct from the present situation, which involves two separate industries. The bizarre result of the Court's approach is that market percentages of a nonexistent market enable the Court to dispense with "elaborate proof of market structure, market behavior and probable anticompetitive effects." As I shall show, the Court has "dispensed with" proof which, given heed, shows how completely fanciful its market-share analysis is.

In fairness to the District Court it should be said that it did not err in failing to consider the "line of commerce" on which this Court now relies. For the Government did not even suggest that such a line of commerce existed until it got to this Court. And it does not seriously suggest even now that such a line of commerce exists. The truth is that "glass and metal containers" form a distinct line of commerce only in the mind of this Court.

The District Court found, and this Court accepts the finding, that this case "deals with three separate and distinct industries manufacturing separate and distinct types of products": metal, glass, and plastic containers . . .

Each industry and each of the manufacturers within it was seeking to improve their products so that they would appeal to

---

[4] The Court confesses to some difficulty in determining market shares.

new customers or hold old ones. Hazel-Atlas and Continental were part of this overall industrial pattern, each in a recognized separate industry producing distinct products but engaged in inter-industry competition for the favor of various end users of their products. 217 F. Supp. at 780–781.

Only this Court will not be "concerned" that without support in reason or fact, it dips into this network of competition and establishes metal and glass containers as a separate "line of commerce," leaving entirely out of account all other kinds of containers: "plastic, paper, foil and any other materials competing for the same business."[5] [*Brown Shoe Co.* v. *United States,* 370 U.S. 294] on which the Court relies for this travesty of economics, spoke of "*well-defined submarkets*" within a broader market, and said that "the boundaries of such a submarket" were to be determined by "*practical indicia,*" 370 U.S. at 325. (Emphasis added.) Since the Court here provides its own definition of a market, unrelated to any market reality whatsoever, *Brown Shoe* must in this case be regarded as a bootstrap . . .

If attention is paid to the conclusions of the court below, it is obvious that this Court's analysis has led it to substitute a meaningless figure—the merged companies' share of a nonexistent "market"—for the sound, careful factual findings of the District Court.

The District Court found:

(1) With respect to the merger's effect on competition within the metal container industry, that "prior to its acquisition Hazel-Atlas did not manufacture or sell metal cans . . ." 217 F.Supp. at 770.

(2) With respect to the merger's effect on competition within the glass container industry, that "Continental did not, directly or through subsidiaries, manufacture or sell glass containers . . ." *Ibid.*

(3) With respect to the merger's effect on the metal container industry's efforts to compete with the glass container industry,

The Government fared no better on its claim that as a result of the merger Continental was likely to lose the incentive to push

[5] If the competition between metal and glass containers is sufficient to constitute them collectively a "line of commerce," why does their competition with plastic containers and "other materials competing for the same business" not require that all such containers be included in the same line of commerce? The Court apparently concedes that the competition is multilateral.

can sales at the expense of glass. The Government introduced no evidence showing either that there had been or was likely to be any slackening of effort to push can sales. On the contrary, as has been pointed out, the object of the merger was diversification, and Continental was actively promoting intra-company competition between its various product lines. Since by far the largest proportion of Continental's business was in metal cans, it scarcely seemed likely that cans would suffer at the expense of glass.

Moreover, subsequent to the merger Continental actively engaged in a vigorous research and promotion program in both its metal and glass container lines. *In the light of the record and of the competitive realities, the notion that it was likely to cease being an innovator in either line is patently absurd.* 217 F. Supp. at 790 (footnote omitted). (Emphasis added.)

(4) With respect to the merger's effect on the glass container industry's efforts to compete with the metal container industry,

In addition the Government advanced the converse of the proposition which it urged with respect to the metal can line— that as a result of the merger Continental was likely to lose the incentive to push glass container sales at the expense of cans. In view of what has been said concerning the purpose of Continental's diversification program and the course it pursued after the merger, it is no more likely that Continental would slacken its efforts to promote glass than that it would slacken its efforts to promote cans. Indeed, if it had planned to do so there would have been little, if any, point to acquiring Hazel-Atlas, a major glass container producer. 217 F.Supp. at 793.

It is clear from the foregoing that the District Court fully considered the possibility that merger of leading producers in two industries between which there was competition would dampen the inter-industry rivalry. The basis of the decision below was not, therefore, an erroneous belief that § 7 did not reach such competition but a careful study of the Government's proof, which led to the conclusion that "in the light of the record and of the competitive realities, the notion that . . . [the merged company] was likely to cease being an innovator in either line is patently absurd."

Surely this failure of the Court's mock-statistical analysis to reflect the facts as found on the record demonstrates what the Government concedes, and what one would in any event have thought to be obvious: When a merger is attacked on the ground that competition *between* two distinct industries, or lines of commerce, will be affected, the shortcut "market share" approach developed in the *Philadelphia Bank* case has no place. In such a case, the legality of the merger must surely depend, as it did below, on an inquiry into competitive effects in the actual lines of commerce which are involved. In this case, the result depends—or should depend—on the impact of the merger in the two lines of commerce here involved: the metal container industry and the glass container industry. As the findings of the District Court which are quoted above make plain, reference to these two actual lines of commerce does not preclude protection of inter-industry competition. Indeed, by placing the merged company in the setting of other companies in each of the respective lines of commerce which are also engaged in inter-industry competition, this approach is far more likely than the Court's to give § 7 full, but not artificial, scope.

The Court's spurious market-share analysis should not obscure the fact that the Court is, in effect, laying down a *"per se"* rule that mergers between two large companies in related industries are presumptively unlawful under § 7. Had the Court based this new rule on a conclusion that such mergers are inherently likely to dampen inter-industry competition or that so few mergers of this kind would fail to have that effect that a *"per se"* rule is justified, I could at least understand the thought process which lay behind its decision. It would, of course, be inappropriate to prescribe *per se* rules in the first case to present a problem, let alone a case in which the facts suggest that a *per se* rule is unsound. And to lay down a rule on either of the bases suggested would require a much more careful look at the nature of competition between industries than the Court's casual glance in that direction.

In any event, the Court does not take this tack. It chooses instead to invent a line of commerce the existence of which no one, not even the Government, has imagined; for which businessmen and economists will look in vain; a line of commerce which sprang into existence only when the merger took place and will cease to exist when the merger is undone. I have no idea where § 7 goes from here, nor will businessmen or the antitrust bar. Hitherto, it has been thought that the validity of a merger was to be tested by examining its effect in identifiable, "well-defined" (*Brown Shoe, supra* at 325) markets. Hereafter, however slight (or even nonexistent) the competitive impact of a merger on any actual market, businessmen must rest uneasy lest the Court create some "market," in which the merger presumptively dampens competition, out of bits and pieces of real ones. No one could say that such a fear is unfounded, since the Court's creative powers in this respect are declared to be as extensive as the competitive relationships between industries. This is said to be recognizing "meaningful competition where it is found to exist." It is in fact imagining effects on competition where none has been shown.

I would affirm the judgment of the District Court.

B

Separation and
Allocation of the Powers
of the Federal Government

Reid v. Covert

354 U.S. 1, 65 (1957)

This case and a companion case, *Kinsella* v. *Krueger*, each involved the wife of an American serviceman who had been tried by military court-martial for the murder of her husband. In each case the alleged murder had been committed while the husband was stationed overseas, and court-martial jurisdiction had rested on Article 2(11) of the Uniform Code of Military Justice.[1] While imprisoned in the United States,[2] each wife sought habeas corpus, claiming the constitutional right to be tried by a jury in a civilian court, with all of the constitutional protections applicable in those courts.

In the first decisions in these cases, five members of the Court held that Article 2(11) was constitutional and that the courts-martial therefore had jurisdiction.[3] Subsequently the Court granted rehearing, and after further argument, six members of the Court agreed that the courts-martial lacked

[1] Then in 50 U.S.C. § 552(11), now in 10 U.S.C. § 802(11).

[2] One of the women had been convicted and was serving a life sentence in a federal penitentiary in West Virginia. The other had also been convicted, but the judgment had been reversed by the Court of Military Appeals, and she was imprisoned in the District of Columbia jail pending retrial by court-martial.

[3] Kinsella v. Krueger, 351 U.S. 470; Reid v. Covert, 351 U.S. 487.

jurisdiction. Four of the six based their conclusion on the view that a civilian dependent could not constitutionally be tried by a court-martial in time of peace, while the remaining two, Justices Frankfurter and Harlan, limited their holding to civilian dependents charged with capital offenses.

As he states in his opinion, Justice Harlan was the only member of the majority who had also joined the majority in the original decisions. His opinion is noteworthy both because of its candid admission of error and because of its searching analysis of the extent of Congress's power to make rules "for the Government and Regulation of the land and naval Forces."[4] In the tentative balance struck between the needs of government and the requirements of procedural fairness, the opinion was a harbinger of the Justice's approach in *In re Gault* (see above).

Mr. Justice Harlan, concurring in the result.

I concur in the result, on the narrow ground that where the offense is capital, Article 2(11) cannot constitutionally be applied to the trial of civilian dependents of members of the armed forces overseas in times of peace.

Since I am the only one among today's majority who joined in the Court's opinions of June 11, 1956, which sustained the court-martial jurisdiction in these cases, I think it appropriate to state the reasons which led to my voting, first, to rehear these cases, and, now, to strike down that jurisdiction.

I

The petitions for rehearing which were filed last summer afforded an opportunity for a greater degree of reflection upon the difficult issues involved in these cases than, at least for me, was possible in the short interval between the argument and decision of the cases in the closing days of last Term. As a result I became satisfied that this court-martial jurisdiction could in any event not be sustained upon the reasoning of our prior opinion. In essence, that reasoning was this: (1) Under *In re Ross*, 140 U.S. 453, and the *Insular Cases*,[5] the requirement of a trial by an Article III court and the other specific safeguards of Article III and the Fifth and Sixth Amendments are not applicable to the trial of American citizens outside

---

[4] U.S. Const., Art. I, § 8, cl. 14.

[5] Downes v. Bidwell, 182 U.S. 244; Hawaii v. Mankichi, 190 U.S. 197; Dorr v. United States, 195 U.S. 138; Balzac v. Porto Rico, 258 U.S. 298.

the United States; (2) there is thus no express consitutional prohibi-tion against the use of courts-martial for such trials abroad; (3) the choice of a court-martial in cases such as these was "reasonable," because of these women's connection with the military, and there-fore satisfied due process; (4) the court-martial jurisdiction was thus constitutional. I have since concluded that this analysis was not sound, for two reasons:

(1) The underlying premise of the prior opinion, it seems to me, is that under the Constitution the mere absence of a prohibition against an asserted power, plus the abstract reasonableness of its use, is enough to establish the existence of the power. I think this is erroneous. The powers of Congress, unlike those of the English Parliament, are constitutionally circumscribed. Under the Constitu-tion Congress has only such powers as are expressly granted or those that are implied as reasonably necessary and proper to carry out the granted powers. Hence the constitutionality of the statute here in question must be tested, not by abstract notions of what is reasonable "in the large," so to speak, but by whether the statute, as applied in these instances, is a reasonably necessary and proper means of implementing a power granted to Congress by the Consti-tution. To say that the validity of the statute may be rested upon the inherent "sovereign powers" of this country in its dealings with foreign nations seems to me to be no more than begging the ques-tion. As I now see it, the validity of this court-martial jurisdiction must depend upon whether the statute, as applied to these women, can be justified as an exercise of the power, granted to Congress by Art. I, § 8, cl. 14 of the Constitution, "To make Rules for the Government and Regulation of the land and naval Forces." I can find no other constitutional power to which this statute can properly be related. I therefore think that we were wrong last Term in considering that we need not decide the case in terms of the Article I power. In my opinion that question squarely confronts us.

(2) I also think that we were mistaken in interpreting *Ross* and the *Insular Cases* as standing for the sweeping proposition that the safeguards of Article III and the Fifth and Sixth Amendments automatically have no application to the trial of American citizens outside the United States, no matter what the circumstances. Aside from the questionable wisdom of mortgaging the future by such a broad pronouncement, I am satisfied that our prior holding swept

too lightly over the historical context in which this Court upheld the jurisdiction of the old consular and territorial courts in those cases . . .

II

I come then to the question whether this court-martial jurisdiction can be justified as an exercise of Congress' Article I power to regulate the armed forces.

At the outset, I cannot accept the implication of my brother Black's opinion that this Article I power was intended to be unmodified by the Necessary and Proper Clause of the Constitution, and that therefore this power is incapable of expansion under changing circumstances. The historical evidence, in fact, shows quite the opposite. True, the records of the time indicate that the Founders shared a deep fear of an unchecked military branch. But what they feared was a military branch unchecked by the *legislature,* and susceptible to use by an arbitrary *executive* power. So far as I know, there is no evidence at all that the Founders intended to limit the power of the *people,* as embodied in the legislature, to make such laws in the regulation of the land and naval forces as are necessary to the proper functioning of those forces. In other words, there is no indication that any special limitation on the power of Congress, as opposed to the power of the executive, was subsumed in the grant of power to govern the land and naval forces . . .

No less an authority than Chief Justice Marshall, in *McCulloch* v. *Maryland,* 4 Wheat. 316, has taught us that the Necessary and Proper Clause is to be read with *all* the powers of Congress, so that "where the law is not prohibited, and is really calculated to effect any of the objects entrusted to the government, to undertake here to inquire into the degree of its necessity, would be to pass the line which circumscribes the judicial department, and to tread on legislative ground." *Id.* at 423.

I think it no answer to say, as my brother Black does, that "having run up against the steadfast bulwark of the Bill of Rights, the Necessary and Proper Clause cannot extend the scope of [Art. I] Clause 14." For that simply begs the question as to whether there is such a collision, an issue to which I address myself below.

For analytical purposes, I think it useful to break down the issue before us into two questions: First, is there a rational connection between the trial of these army wives by court-martial and the power of Congress to make rules for the governance of the land and naval forces; in other words, is there any initial power here at all? Second, if there is such a rational connection, to what extent does this statute, though reasonably calculated to subserve an enum-erater power, collide with other express limitations on congressional power . . . ?

A

I assume, for the moment, therefore, that we may disregard other limiting provisions of the Constitution, and examine the Article I power in isolation. So viewed, I do not think the courts-martial of these army wives can be said to be an arbitrary extension of congres-sional power.

It is suggested that historically the Article I power was intended to embody a rigid and unchangeable self-limitation, namely, that it could apply only to those in the actual service of the armed forces. I cannot agree that this power has any such rigid content. First of all, the historical evidence presented by the Government convinces me that, at the time of the adoption of the Constitution, military jurisdiction was not thought to be rigidly limited to uniformed personnel. The fact is that it was traditional for "retainers to the camp" to be subjected to military discipline, that civilian de-pendents encamped with the armies were traditionally regarded as being in that class, and that the concept was not strictly limited to times of war. Indeed, the British, who are no less sensitive than we to maintaining the supremacy of civil justice, have recently enacted a law comparable to the statute involved here.

Thinking, as I do, that Article I, still taking it in isolation, must be viewed as supplemented by the Necessary and Proper Clause, I cannot say that the court-martial jurisdiction here involved has no rational connection with the stated power. The Government, it seems to me, has made a strong showing that the court-martial of civilian dependents abroad has a close connection to the proper and effective functioning of our overseas military contingents. There is no need to detail here the various aspects of this connection, which have been well dealt with in the dissenting opinion of my brother Clark. Suffice it to say that to all intents and purposes these civilian dependents are part of the military community overseas, are so regarded by the host country, and must be subjected to the same discipline if the military commander is to have the power to prevent activities which would jeopardize the security and effectiveness of his command[6] . . .

B

I turn now to the other side of the coin. For no matter how practical and how reasonable this jurisdiction might be, it still cannot be sustained if the Constitution guarantees to these army wives a trial in an Article III court, with indictment by grand jury and trial as provided by the Fifth and Sixth Amendments.

We return, therefore, to the *Ross* question: to what extent do these provisions of the Constitution apply outside the United States?

As I have already stated, I do not think that it can be said that these safeguards of the Constitution are never operative without the United States, regardless of the particular circumstances. On the other hand, I cannot agree with the suggestion that every provision of the Constitution must always be deemed automatically applicable to American citizens in every part of the world. For *Ross* and the *Insular Cases* do stand for an important proposition, one which seems to me a wise and necessary gloss on our Constitution. The proposition is, of course, not that the Constitution "does not apply" overseas, but that there are provisions in the Constitution which do not *necessarily* apply in all circumstances in every foreign place. In other words, it seems to me that the basic teaching of *Ross* and the *Insular Cases* is that there is no rigid and abstract rule that Congress, as a condition precedent to exercising power over Americans overseas, must exercise it subject to all the guarantees of the Constitution, no matter what the conditions and considerations are that would make adherence to a specific guarantee altogether impracticable and anomalous. To take but one example: *Balzac* v. *Porto Rico*, 258 U.S. 298, is not good authority for the proposition that jury trials need never be provided for American citizens tried by the United States abroad; but the case *is* good authority for the proposition that there is no rigid rule that jury

[6] This necessity is particularly acute with regard to peculiarly "military" and "local" offenses which must be dealt with swiftly and effectively. Thus security regulations at these military installations must be enforced against civilian dependents as well as servicemen; the same is true of base traffic violations, black marketeering, and misuse of military customs and post-exchange privileges.

trial must *always* be provided in the trial of an American overseas, if the circumstances are such that trial by jury would be impractical and anomalous. In other words, what *Ross* and the *Insular Cases* hold is that the particular local setting, the practical necessities, and the possible alternatives are relevant to a question of judgment, namely, whether jury trial *should* be deemed a necessary condition of the exercise of Congress' power to provide for the trial of Americans overseas.

I think the above thought is crucial in approaching the cases before us. Decision is easy if one adopts the constricting view that these constitutional guarantees as a totality do or do not "apply" overseas. But, for me, the question is *which* guarantees of the Constitution *should* apply in view of the particular circumstances, the practical necessities, and the possible alternatives which Congress had before it. The question is one of judgment, not of compulsion. And so I agree with my brother Frankfurter that, in view of *Ross* and the *Insular Cases*, we have before us a question analogous, ultimately, to issues of due process; one can say, in fact, that the question of which specific safeguards of the Constitution are appropriately to be applied in a particular context overseas can be reduced to the issue of what process is "due" a defendant in the particular circumstances of a particular case.

On this basis, I cannot agree with the sweeping proposition that a full Article III trial, with indictment and trial by jury, is required in every case for the trial of a civilian dependent of a serviceman overseas. The Government, it seems to me, has made an impressive showing that at least for the run-of-the-mill offenses committed by dependents overseas, such a requirement would be as impractical and as anomalous as it would have been to require jury trial for Balzac in Porto Rico.[7] Again, I need not go into details, beyond

[7] The practical circumstances requiring some sort of disciplinary jurisdiction have already been adverted to. These circumstances take on weight when viewed in light of the alternatives available to Congress—certainly a crucial question in weighing the need for dispensing with particular constitutional guarantees abroad. What are these alternatives? (1) One is to try all offenses committed by civilian dependents abroad in the United States. But the practical problems in the way of such a choice are obvious and overwhelming. To require the transportation home for trial of every petty black marketeer or violator of security regulations would be a ridiculous burden on the Government, quite aside from the problems of persuading foreign witnesses to make the trip and of preserving evidence. It can further be deemed doubtful in the extreme whether foreign governments would permit crimes punishable under local law to be tried thousands of miles away in the United States. (2) Civilian trial overseas by the United States also presents considerable difficulties. If juries are required, the problem

stating that except for capital offenses, such as we have here, to which, in my opinion, special considerations apply, I am by no means ready to say that Congress' power to provide for trial by court-martial of civilian dependents overseas is limited by Article III and the Fifth and Sixth Amendments. Where, if at all, the dividing line should be drawn among cases not capital, need not now be decided. We are confronted here with capital offenses alone; and it seems to me particularly unwise now to decide more than we have to. Our far-flung foreign military establishments are a new phenomenon in our national life, and I think it would be unfortunate were we unnecessarily to foreclose, as my four brothers would do, our future consideration of the broad questions involved in maintaining the effectiveness of these national outposts, in the light of continuing experience with these problems.

So far as capital cases are concerned, I think they stand on quite a different footing from other offenses. In such cases the law is especially sensitive to demands for that procedural fairness which inheres in a civilian trial where the judge and trier of fact are not responsive to the command of the convening authority . . . [Moreover, the] number of such cases would appear to be so negligible that the practical problems of affording the defendant a civilian trial would not present insuperable problems.

On this narrow ground I concur in the result in these cases.[8]

---

of jury recruitment would be difficult. Furthermore, it is indeed doubtful whether some foreign governments would accede to the creation of extraterritorial United States civil courts within their territories—courts which by implication would reflect on the fairness of their own tribunals and which would smack unpleasantly of consular courts set up under colonial "capitulations." (3) The alternative of trial in foreign courts, in at least some instances, is no more palatable. Quite aside from the fact that in some countries where we station troops the protections granted to criminal defendants compare unfavorably with our own minimum standards, the fact would remain that many of the crimes involved—particularly breaches of security—are not offenses under foreign law at all, and thus would go completely unpunished. Add to this the undesirability of foreign police carrying out investigations in our military installations abroad, and it seems to me clear that this alternative does not commend itself.

[8] In Kinsella v. United States ex rel. Singleton, 361 U.S. 234, decided three terms after *Covert*, the Court, over Justice Harlan's dissent, held Article 2(11) unconstitutional as applied to civilian dependents charged with *noncapital* offenses. (Companion cases, Grisham v. Hagan, 361 U.S. 278, and McElroy v. United States ex rel. Guagliardo, 361 U.S. 281, applied the holdings of *Covert* and *Singleton* to civilian employees.) The opinion was written by Justice Clark, who had dissented in *Covert*. [Ed.]

Katzenbach v. Morgan

384 U.S. 641, 659 (1966)

Section 4(e) of the Voting Rights Act of 1965 provides, among other things, that no person who has successfully completed the sixth grade in a public or accredited private school in Puerto Rico shall be denied the right to vote in any election because of his inability to read or write English, if the "predominant classroom language" in that school was other than English.[1] The statute, if valid, pro tanto superseded the election laws of New York, which required an ability to read and write English as a condition of voting. Registered voters in New York City brought a federal court action challenging the constitutionality of section 4(e) insofar as it prohibited enforcement of the New York law. A three judge panel held, 2–1, that the federal statute exceeded the power delegated to Congress and thus violated the Tenth Amendment.

On direct appeal, the Supreme Court reversed, 7–2. It held the federal statute valid under section 5 of the Fourteenth Amendment,[2] rejecting the argument that Congress could not act under that section to supersede state legislation unless the state law in question was held by the judiciary to be in violation of the Fourteenth Amendment. Rather, in the Court's view, the power of Congress under section 5 extended to the enactment of all legislation "appropriate" to the enforcement of the substantive provisions of the amendment. Since the effect of the Voting Rights Act was to enhance the political power of the Puerto Rican community in New York, the statute might rationally have been designed by Congress to enable that community "better to obtain 'perfect equality of civil rights and the equal protection of the laws.'" Moreover, Congress might have concluded that the New York eligibility statute invidiously discriminated against Puerto Rican residents, and such a judgment was not plainly irrational. Thus, the majority reasoned, the Voting Rights Act must be sustained under accepted standards of judicial review of acts of Congress.

Justice Harlan saw the majority's approach in this case as an abdication of judicial responsibility to determine whether state action was consistent with the Fourteenth Amendment.

---

[1] 42 U.S.C. § 1973 b(e).

[2] "The Congress shall have power to enforce, by appropriate legislation, the provisions of this article."

260

Mr. Justice Harlan, whom Mr. Justice Stewart joins, dissenting.

Worthy as its purposes may be thought by many, I do not see how § 4(e) of the Voting Rights Act of 1965, 79 Stat. 439, 42 U.S.C. § 1973b(e) (1964 ed. Supp. I), can be sustained except at the sacrifice of fundamentals in the American constitutional system—the separation between the legislative and judicial function and the boundaries between federal and state political authority . . .

The Court declares that since § 5 of the Fourteenth Amendment gives to the Congress power to "enforce" the prohibitions of the Amendment by "appropriate" legislation, the test for judicial review of any congressional determination in this area is simply one of rationality; that is, in effect, was Congress acting rationally in declaring that the New York statute is irrational? Although § 5 most certainly does give to the Congress wide powers in the field of devising remedial legislation to effectuate the Amendment's prohibition on arbitrary state action, I believe the Court has confused the issue of how much enforcement power Congress possesses under § 5 with the distinct issue of what questions are appropriate for congressional determination and what questions are essentially judicial in nature.

When recognized state violations of federal constitutional standards have occurred, Congress is of course empowered by § 5 to take appropriate remedial measures to redress and prevent the wrongs. But it is a judicial question whether the condition with which Congress has thus sought to deal is in truth an infringement of the Constitution, something that is the necessary prerequisite to bringing the § 5 power into play at all. Thus, in *Ex Parte Virginia* [100 U.S. 339], involving a federal statute making it a federal crime to disqualify anyone from jury service because of race, the Court first held as a matter of constitutional law that "the Fourteenth Amendment secures, among other civil rights, to colored men, when charged with criminal offenses against a State, an impartial jury trial, by jurors indifferently selected or chosen without discrimination against such jurors because of their color." 100 U.S. at 345. Only then did the Court hold that to enforce this prohibition upon state discrimination, Congress could enact a criminal statute of the type under consideration.

A more recent Fifteenth Amendment case also serves to illustrate this distinction. In *South Carolina* v. *Katzenbach,* 383 U.S. 301, decided earlier this Term, we held certain remedial sections of this Voting Rights Act of 1965 constitutional under the Fifteenth Amendment, which is directed against deprivations of the right to vote on account of race. In enacting those sections of the Voting Rights Act the Congress made a detailed investigation of various state practices that had been used to deprive Negroes of the franchise. In passing upon the remedial provisions, we reviewed first the "voluminous legislative history" as well as judicial precedents supporting the basic congressional finding that the clear commands of the Fifteenth Amendment had been infringed by various state subterfuges. See 383 U.S. at 309, 329–330, 333–334. Given the existence of the evil, we held the remedial steps taken by the legislature under the Enforcement Clause of the Fifteenth Amendment to be a justifiable exercise of congressional initiative.

Section 4(e), however, presents a significantly different type of congressional enactment. The question here is not whether the statute is appropriate remedial legislation to cure an established violation of a constitutional command, but whether there has in fact been an infringement of that constitutional command, that is, whether a particular state practice or, as here, a statute is so arbitrary or irrational as to offend the command of the Equal Protection Clause of the Fourteenth Amendment. That question is one for the judicial branch ultimately to determine. Were the rule otherwise, Congress would be able to qualify this court's constitutional decisions under the Fourteenth and Fifteenth Amendments, let alone those under other provisions of the Constitution, by resorting to congressional power under the Necessary and Proper Clause. In view of this Court's holding in *Lassiter, supra,* that an English literacy test is a permissible exercise of state supervision over its franchise, I do not think it is open to Congress to limit the effect of that decision as it has undertaken to do by § 4(e).[3] In effect the Court reads § 5 of the Fourteenth Amendment as giving Congress the power to define the *substantive* scope of the Amendment. If

[3] In a portion of the opinion that has been omitted, the Justice argued at greater length that New York's requirement of an English literacy test as a qualification for voting did not violate the Fourteenth Amendment. He relied on Lassiter v. Northampton Election Bd., 360 U.S. 45. [Ed.]

that indeed be the true reach of § 5, then I do not see why Congress should not be able as well to exercise its § 5 "discretion" by enacting statutes so as in effect to dilute equal protection and due process decisions of this Court.[4] In all such cases there is room for reasonable men to differ as to whether or not a denial of equal protection or due process has occurred, and the final decision is one of judgment. Until today this judgment has always been one for the judiciary to resolve.

I do not mean to suggest in what has been said that a legislative judgment of the type incorporated in § 4(e) is without any force whatsoever. Decisions on questions of equal protection and due process are based not on abstract logic, but on empirical foundations. To the extent "legislative facts" are relevant to a judicial determination, Congress is well equipped to investigate them, and such determinations are of course entitled to due respect. In *South Carolina* v. *Katzenbach, supra,* such legislative findings were made to show that racial discrimination in voting was actually occurring . . .

But no such factual data provide a legislative record supporting § 4(e) by way of showing that Spanish-speaking citizens are fully as capable of making informed decisions in a New York election as are English-speaking citizens. Nor was there any showing whatever to support the Court's alternative argument that § 4(e) should be viewed as but a remedial measure designed to cure or assure against unconstitutional discrimination of other varieties, e.g., in "public schools, public housing and law enforcement," to which Puerto Rican minorities might be subject in such communities as New York. There is simply no legislative record supporting such hypothesized discrimination of the sort we have hitherto insisted upon when congressional power is brought to bear on constitutionally reserved state concerns.

Thus, we have here not a matter of giving deference to a congressional estimate, based on its determination of legislative facts, bearing upon the validity *vel non* of a statute, but rather what can at most be called a legislative announcement that Congress believes a state law to entail an unconstitutional deprivation of equal protection. Although this kind of declaration is of course entitled to the

---

[4] The majority denied that this inference could be drawn from its decision. [Ed.]

most respectful consideration, coming as it does from a concurrent branch and one that is knowledgeable in matters of popular political participation, I do not believe it lessens our responsibility to decide the fundamental issue of whether in fact the state enactment violates federal constitutional rights.

In assessing the deference we should give to this kind of congressional expression of policy, it is relevant that the judiciary has always given to congressional enactments a presumption of validity. However, it is also a canon of judicial review that state statutes are given a similar presumption. Whichever way this case is decided, one statute will be rendered inoperative in whole or in part, and although it has been suggested that this Court should give somewhat more deference to Congress than to a state legislature, such a simple weighing of presumptions is hardly a satisfying way of resolving a matter that touches the distribution of state and federal power in an area so sensitive as that of the regulation of the franchise. Rather it should be recognized that while the Fourteenth Amendment is a "brooding omnipresence" over all state legislation, the substantive matters which it touches are all within the primary legislative competence of the States. Federal authority, legislative no less than judicial, does not intrude unless there has been a denial by state action of Fourteenth Amendment limitations, in this instance a denial of equal protection. At least in the area of primary state concern a state statute that passes constitutional muster under the judicial standard of rationality should not be permitted to be set at naught by a mere contrary congressional pronouncement unsupported by a legislative record justifying that conclusion.

To deny the effectiveness of this congressional enactment is not of course to disparage Congress' exertion of authority in the field of civil rights; it is simply to recognize that the Legislative Branch like the other branches of federal authority is subject to the governmental boundaries set by the Constitution. To hold, on this record, that § 4(e) overrides the New York literacy requirement seems to me tantamount to allowing the Fourteenth Amendment to swallow the State's constitutionally ordained primary authority in this field. For if Congress by what, as here, amounts to mere *ipse dixit* can set that otherwise permissible requirement partially at naught I see no reason why it could not also substitute its judgment for that of the States in other fields of their exclusive primary competence as well.

I would affirm the judgments in each of these cases.

Wesberry v. *Sanders*

376 U.S. 1, 20 (1964)

Both the *Reid* v. *Covert* and *Katzenbach* v. *Morgan* opinions (see above) make clear the Justice's unwillingness to yield judicial control to Congress. *Wesberry* v. *Sanders* is perhaps the Justice's sharpest statement of opposition to what he regarded as an unwarranted and dangerous invasion by the judiciary of the sphere of legislative responsibility.

Wesberry, an apportionment case decided before the "one man, one vote" pronouncement of *Reynolds* v. *Sims* (see above) involved an attack by registered voters on the Georgia statute creating that state's congressional districts. The plaintiffs' claim of malapportionment was dismissed by a three-judge federal court for nonjusticiability, but on appeal the Supreme Court reversed. After holding the controversy justiciable, six members of the Court, speaking through Justice Black, found the Georgia statute invalid. They chose to rely not on the equal protection clause—which was to serve as the keystone in *Reynolds* v. *Sims*—but rather on Article 1, § 2 of the Constitution. This article's mandate that members of the House of Representatives be chosen "by the People" was held by the majority to require that "as nearly as is practicable one man's vote in a congressional election is to be worth as much as another's."

Justice Harlan's dissent may well be the most strongly worded he has ever written; it surely does not disguise his anger at what he views as unsound history, poor reasoning, and a dangerous departure from the Court's proper role in our constitutional system. Demands of space have necessitated omission from the present excerpt of the bulk of the historical materials relied on by the Justice in his dissent, but it may be of interest to note the accusation leveled by one historian at the arguments made by the majority:

> To put the matter bluntly, Mr. Justice Black, in order to prove his point, mangled constitutional history. The quotations from the debates of the Convention on which he builds . . . have nothing at all to do with the question of representation within the states . . . Perhaps a constitutional historian may be forgiven if he views the entire performance with some astonishment, not unmixed with admiration for the Court's creative historical imagination.[1]

[1] Alfred H. Kelly, "Clio and the Court: An Illicit Love Affair," in 1965 *Supreme Court Review* 119, 135–136 (1965).

Mr. Justice Harlan, dissenting.

I had not expected to witness the day when the Supreme Court of the United States would render a decision which casts grave doubt on the constitutionality of the composition of the House of Representatives. It is not an exaggeration to say that such is the effect of today's decision. The Court's holding that the Constitution requires States to select Representatives either by elections at large or by elections in districts composed "as nearly as is practicable" of equal population places in jeopardy the seats of almost all the members of the present House of Representatives . . .

Only a demonstration which could not be avoided would justify this Court in rendering a decision the effect of which, inescapably as I see it, is to declare constitutionally defective the very composition of a coordinate branch of the Federal Government. The Court's opinion not only fails to make such a demonstration, it is unsound logically on its face and demonstrably unsound historically . . .

Disclaiming all reliance on other provisions of the Constitution, in particular those of the Fourteenth Amendment on which the appellants relied below and in this Court, the Court holds that the provision in Art. I, § 2, for election of Representatives "by the People" *means* that congressional districts are to be "as nearly as is practicable" equal in population. Stripped of rhetoric and a "historical context," which bears little resemblance to the evidence found in the pages of history, the Court's opinion supports its holding only with the bland assertion that "the principle of a House of Representatives elected 'by the People'" would be "cast aside" if "a vote is worth more in one district than in another," i.e., if congressional districts within a State, each electing a single Representative, are not equal in population. The fact is, however, that Georgia's 10 Representatives *are* elected "by the People" of Georgia, just as Representatives from other States are elected "by the People of the several States." This is all that the Constitution requires.[2]

[2] Since I believe that the Constitution expressly provides that state legislatures and the Congress shall have exclusive jurisdiction over problems of congressional apportionment of the kind involved in this case, there is no occasion for me to consider whether, in the absence of such provision, other provisions of the Constitution, relied on by appellants, would confer on them the rights which they assert.

Although the Court finds necessity for its artificial construction of Article I in the undoubted importance of the right to vote, that right is not involved in this case. All of the appellants do vote. The Court's talk about "debasement" and "dilution" of the vote is a model of circular reasoning, in which the premises of the argument feed on the conclusion. Moreover, by focusing exclusively on numbers in disregard of the area and shape of a congressional district as well as party affiliations within the district, the Court deals in abstractions which will be recognized even by the politically unsophisticated to have little relevance to the realities of political life.

In any event, the very sentence of Art. I, § 2, on which the Court exclusively relies confers the right to vote for Representatives only on those whom *the State* has found qualified to vote for members of "the most numerous Branch of the State Legislature." So far as Article I is concerned, it is within the State's power to confer that right only on persons of wealth or of a particular sex or, if the State chose, living in specified areas of the State. Were Georgia to find the residents of the Fifth District unqualified to vote for Representatives to the State House of Representatives, they could not vote for Representatives to Congress, according to the express words of Art. I, § 2. Other provisions of the Constitution would, of course, be relevant, *but, so far as Art. I, § 2, is concerned,* the disqualification would be within Georgia's power. How can it be, then, that this very same sentence prevents Georgia from apportioning its Representatives as it chooses? The truth is that it does not.

The Court purports to find support for its position in the third paragraph of Art. I, § 2, which provides for the apportionment of Representatives among the States. The appearance of support in that section derives from the Court's confusion of two issues: direct election of Representatives within the States and the apportionment of Representatives among the States. Those issues are distinct, and were separately treated in the Constitution. The fallacy of the Court's reasoning in this regard is illustrated by its slide, obscured by intervening discussion from the intention of the delegates at the Philadelphia Convention "that in allocating Congressmen the number assigned to each State should be determined solely by the number of the State's inhabitants," to a "principle solemnly embodied in the Great Compromise—equal representation in the

267

House for equal numbers of people." The delegates did have the former intention and made clear provision for it. Although many, perhaps most, of them also believed generally—but assuredly not in the precise, formalistic way of the majority of the Court—that within the States representation should be based on population, they did not surreptitiously slip their belief into the Constitution in the phrase "by the People," to be discovered 175 years later like a Shakespearian anagram.

Far from supporting the Court, the apportionment of Representatives among the States shows how blindly the Court has marched to its decision. Representatives were to be apportioned among the States on the basis of free population plus three-fifths of the slave population. Since no slave voted, the inclusion of three-fifths of their number in the basis of apportionment gave the favored States representation far in excess of their voting population. If, then, slaves were intended to be without representation, Article I did exactly what the Court now says it prohibited: it "weighted" the vote of voters in the slave States. Alternatively, it might have been thought that Representatives elected by free men of a State would speak also for the slaves. But since the Slaves added to the representation only of their own State, Representatives from the slave States could have been thought to speak only for the slaves of their own States, indicating both that the Convention believed it possible for a Representative elected by one group to speak for another nonvoting group and that Representatives were in large degree still thought of as speaking for the whole population *of a State*.[3]

There is a further basis for demonstrating the hollowness of the Court's assertion that Article I requires "one man's vote in a congressional election . . . to be worth as much as another's." Nothing that the Court does today will disturb the fact that although in 1960 the population of an average congressional district was 410,481, the States of Alaska, Nevada, and Wyoming each have a Representative in Congress, although their respective populations are 226,167, 285,278, and 330,066. In entire disregard of population, Art. I, § 2, guarantees each of these States and every other State "at Least

---

[3] It is surely beyond debate that the Constitution did not require the slave States to apportion their Representatives according to the dispersion of slaves within their borders. The above implications of the three-fifths compromise were recognized by Madison. See *The Federalist*, No. 54 . . .

one Representative." It is whimsical to assert in the face of this guarantee that an absolute principle of "equal representation in the House for equal numbers of people" is "solemnly embodied" in Article I. All that there is is a provision which bases representation in the House, generally but not entirely, on the population of the States. The provision for representation of *each State* in the House of Representatives is not a mere exception to the principle framed by the majority; it shows that no such principle is to be found.

Finally in this array of hurdles to its decision which the Court surmounts only by knocking them down is § 4 of Art. I which states simply:

> The Times, Places and *Manner* of holding Elections for Senators and Representatives, shall be prescribed in each State by the Legislature thereof; but the Congress may at any time by Law make or alter such Regulations, except as to the Places of chusing Senators. (Emphasis added.)

The delegates were well aware of the problem of "rotten boroughs," as material cited by the Court makes plain. It cannot be supposed that delegates to the Convention would have labored to establish a principle of equal representation only to bury it, one would have thought beyond discovery, in § 2, and omit all mention of it from § 4, which deals explicitly with the conduct of elections. Section 4 states without qualification that the state legislatures shall prescribe regulations for the conduct of elections for Representatives and, equally without qualification, that Congress may make or alter such regulations. There is nothing to indicate any limitation whatsoever on this grant of plenary initial and supervisory power. The Court's holding is, of course, derogatory not only of the power of the state legislatures but also of the power of Congress, both theoretically and as they have actually exercised their power. It freezes upon both, for no reason other than that it seems wise to the majority of the present Court, a particular political theory for the selection of Representatives . . .

The unstated premise of the Court's conclusion quite obviously is that the Congress has not dealt, and the Court believes it will not deal, with the problem of congressional apportionment in accordance with what the Court believes to be sound political principles. Laying aside for the moment the validity of such a consideration as a factor in constitutional interpretation, it becomes relevant to examine the history of congressional action under Art. I, § 4. This history reveals that the Court is not simply undertaking to exercise a power which the Constitution reserves to the Congress; it is also overruling congressional judgment.

Congress exercised its power to regulate elections for the House of Representatives for the first time in 1842 . . . In 1872, Congress required that Representatives "be elected by districts composed of contiguous territory, and containing as nearly as practicable an equal number of inhabitants, . . . no one district electing more than one Representative."[4] This provision for equal districts which the Court exactly duplicates in effect, was carried forward in each subsequent apportionment statute through 1911. There was no reapportionment following the 1920 census. The provision for equally populated districts was dropped in 1929, and has not been revived, although the 1929 provisions for apportionment have twice been amended and, in 1941, were made generally applicable to subsequent censuses and apportionments . . .

[*After concluding that the omission in the 1929 statute was deliberate, the opinion continued:*] For a period of about 50 years, therefore, Congress, by repeated legislative act, imposed on the States the requirement that congressional districts be equal in population. (This, of course, is the very requirement which the Court now declares to have been constitutionally required of the States all along without implementing legislation.) Subsequently, after giving express attention to the problem, Congress eliminated that requirement, with the intention of permitting the States to find their own solutions. Since then, despite repeated efforts to obtain congressional action again, Congress has continued to leave the problem and its solution to the States. It cannot be contended, therefore, that the Court's decision today fills a gap left by the Congress. On the contrary, the Court substitutes its own judgment for that of the Congress.

The extent to which the Court departs from accepted principles of adjudication is further evidenced by the irrelevance to today's

---

[4] Act of Feb. 2, 1872, § 2, 17 Stat. 28.

issue of the cases on which the Court relies . . . [*Discussion of these cases is omitted.*]

The Court [on the other hand] gives scant attention, and that not on the merits, to *Colegrove* v. *Green*, 328 U.S. 549, which is directly in point; the Court there affirmed dismissal of a complaint alleging that "by reason of subsequent changes in population the Congressional districts for the election of Representatives in the Congress created by the Illinois Laws of 1901 . . . lacked compactness of territory and approximate equality of population." *Id.* at 550–551. Leaving to another day the question of what *Baker* v. *Carr*, 369 U.S. 186, did actually decide, it can hardly be maintained on the authority of *Baker* or anything else, that the Court does not today invalidate Mr. Justice Frankfurter's eminently correct statement in *Colegrove* that "the Constitution has conferred upon Congress exclusive authority to secure fair representation by the States in the popular House . . . If Congress failed in exercising its powers, whereby standards of fairness are offended, the remedy ultimately lies with the people." 328 U.S. at 554. The problem was described by Mr. Justice Frankfurter as "an aspect of government from which the judiciary, in view of what is involved, has been excluded by the clear intention of the Constitution . . ." *Ibid.* Mr. Justice Frankfurter did not, of course, speak for a majority of the Court in *Colegrove;* but refusal for that reason to give the opinion precedential effect does not justify refusal to give appropriate attention to the views there expressed.[5]

Today's decision has portents for our society and the Court itself which should be recognized. This is not a case in which the Court vindicates the kind of individual rights that are assured by the Due Process Clause of the Fourteenth Amendment, whose "vague contours," *Rochin* v. *California*, 342 U.S. 165, 170, of course leave much room for constitutional developments necessitated by changing conditions in a dynamic society. Nor is this a case in which an emergent set of facts requires the Court to frame new principles to protect recognized constitutional rights. The claim for judicial

[5] The Court relies in part on Baker v. Carr [369 U.S. 186] to immunize its present decision from the force of *Colegrove*. But nothing in *Baker* is contradictory to the view that, political question and other objections to "justiciability" aside, the Constitution vests exclusive authority to deal with the problem of this case in the state legislatures and the Congress.

relief in this case strikes at one of the fundamental doctrines of our system of government, the separation of powers. In upholding that claim, the Court attempts to effect reforms in a field which the Constitution, as plainly as can be, has committed exclusively to the political process.

This Court, no less than all other branches of the Government, is bound by the Constitution. The Constitution does not confer on the Court blanket authority to step into every situation where the political branch may be thought to have fallen short. The stability of this institution ultimately depends not only upon its being alert to keep the other branches of government within constitutional bounds but equally upon recognition of the limitations on the Court's own functions in the constitutional system.

What is done today saps the political process. The promise of judicial intervention in matters of this sort cannot but encourage popular inertia in efforts for political reform through the political process, with the inevitable result that the process is itself weakened. By yielding to the demand for a judicial remedy in this instance, the Court in my view does a disservice both to itself and to the broader values of our system of government.

Banco Nacional de Cuba v. Sabbatino

376 U.S. 398 (1964)

Farr, Whitlock & Co., an American commodity broker, entered a contract in 1960 to purchase sugar from a Cuban corporation (C.A.V.) whose stock was owned principally by residents of the United States. The Cuban government shortly thereafter expropriated the property of C.A.V. and allowed the ship carrying the sugar to leave Cuban waters only after Farr, Whitlock had entered contracts of purchase with a Cuban bank identical to those it had entered with C.A.V. The bank's assignee, another Cuban bank, then demanded payment by Farr, Whitlock in New York. After receiving a promise from C.A.V. to indemnify it against any loss, Farr, Whitlock accepted the shipping documents, including the bills of lading, but refused to pay the Cuban bank and ultimately transferred the funds constituting the proceeds of sale to Sabbatino (court-appointed receiver of C.A.V.'s New York assets) to abide a judicial determination as to their ownership.

The Cuban bank then brought this action in a federal court, seeking recovery of the funds deposited with Sabbatino. The complaint alleged that Farr, Whitlock had converted the bills of lading covering the sugar and rested this allegation on a claim of title to the sugar in the Cuban government. Proceeding on the basis that a taking in violation of international law does not convey good title, the district court granted summary judgment against the bank, holding that the expropriation of C.A.V.'s assets was invalid because (1) its purpose was retaliation against the United States, (2) it discriminated against American nationals, and (3) it failed to provide adequate compensation. The Court of Appeals affirmed, relying in part on letters from the State Department which it took as evidence that the executive branch had no objection to judicial determination of the validity of the expropriation decree.

On certiorari, the Supreme Court reversed the judgment below in an 8–1 decision, with Justice Harlan writing for the majority. After disposing of preliminary questions, including the ability of an agency of the Cuban government to bring suit in an American court,[1] the opinion turned to a detailed analysis and application of the "act of state" doctrine—the principle that the judiciary will not examine the validity of acts by a recognized foreign sovereign within its own territory. The care with which the opinion was written, its sensitivity to problems confronting other branches of the federal government, and its insistence that judicial power not be used to intrude upon the conduct of our foreign affairs all make this decision a leading example of the Justice's craftsmanship and philosophy.

Mr. Justice Harlan delivered the opinion of the Court.

The question which brought this case here, and is now found to be the dispositive issue, is whether the so-called act of state doctrine serves to sustain petitioner's claims in this litigation. Such claims are ultimately founded on a decree of the Government of Cuba expropriating certain property, the right to the proceeds of which is here in controversy. The act of state doctrine in its traditional formulation precludes the courts of this country from inquiring into the validity of the public acts a recognized foreign sovereign power committed within its own territory . . .

---

[1] The opinion distinguished between a government not recognized and one, like that of Cuba, which was recognized but with which diplomatic relations had been severed. The opinion also concluded that any ambiguity in the State Department letters referred to by the Court of Appeals had been removed by the position taken by the United States in the Supreme Court: that the decision below should be reversed.

The classic American statement of the act of state doctrine, which appears to have taken root in England as early as 1674, and began to emerge in the jurisprudence of this country in the late eighteenth and early nineteenth centuries, is found in *Underhill v. Hernandez*, 168 U.S. 250, where Chief Justice Fuller said for a unanimous Court (p. 252):

> Every sovereign State is bound to respect the independence of every other sovereign State, and the courts of one country will not sit in judgment on the acts of the government of another done within its own territory. Redress of grievances by reason of such acts must be obtained through the means open to be availed of by sovereign powers as between themselves.

Following this precept the Court in that case refused to inquire into acts of Hernandez, a revolutionary Venezuelan military commander whose government had been later recognized by the United States, which were made the basis of a damage action in this country by Underhill, an American citizen, who claimed that he had been unlawfully assaulted, coerced, and detained in Venezuela by Hernandez.

None of this Court's subsequent cases in which the act of state doctrine was directly or peripherally involved manifest any retreat from *Underhill* . . .

The outcome of this case, therefore, turns upon whether any of the contentions urged by respondents against the application of the act of state doctrine in the premises is acceptable: (1) that the doctrine does not apply to acts of state which violate international law, as is claimed to be the case here; (2) that the doctrine is inapplicable unless the Executive specifically interposes it in a particular case; and (3) that, in any event, the doctrine may not be invoked by a foreign government plaintiff in our courts.

Preliminarily, we discuss the foundations on which we deem the act of state doctrine to rest, and more particularly the question of whether state or federal law governs its application in a federal diversity case.[2]

We do not believe that this doctrine is compelled either by the

---

[2] Although the complaint in this case alleged both diversity and federal question jurisdiction, the Court of Appeals reached jurisdiction only on the former ground. We need not decide, for reasons appearing hereafter, whether federal question jurisdiction also existed.

inherent nature of sovereign authority, as some of the earlier decisions seem to imply, see *Underhill, supra,* or by some principle of international law . . .

Despite the broad statement in [*Oetjen* v. *Central Leather Co.,* 246 U.S. 297] that "The conduct of the foreign relations of our Government is committed by the Constitution to the Executive and Legislative . . . Departments," 246 U.S. at 302, it cannot of course be thought that "every case or controversy which touches foreign relations lies beyond judicial cognizance." *Baker* v. *Carr,* 369 U.S. 186, 211. The text of the Constitution does not require the act of state doctrine; it does not irrevocably remove from the judiciary the capacity to review the validity of foreign acts of state.

The act of state doctrine does, however, have "constitutional" underpinnings. It arises out of the basic relationships between branches of government in a system of separation of powers. It concerns the competency of dissimilar institutions to make and implement particular kinds of decisions in the area of international relations. The doctrine as formulated in past decisions expresses the strong sense of the Judicial Branch that its engagement in the task of passing on the validity of foreign acts of state may hinder rather than further this country's pursuit of goals both for itself and for the community of nations as a whole in the international sphere. Many commentators disagree with this view; they have striven by means of distinguishing and limiting past decisions and by advancing various considerations of policy to stimulate a narrowing of the apparent scope of the rule. Whatever considerations are thought to predominate, it is plain that the problems involved are uniquely federal in nature. If federal authority, in this instance this Court, orders the field of judicial competence in this area for the federal courts, and the state courts are left free to formulate their own rules, the purposes behind the doctrine could be as effectively undermined as if there had been no federal pronouncement on the subject . . .

If [as we hold] the act of state doctrine is a principle of decision binding on federal and state courts alike but compelled by neither international law nor the Constitution, its continuing vitality depends on its capacity to reflect the proper distribution of functions between the judicial and political branches of the Government on matters bearing upon foreign affairs. It should be apparent that the greater the degree of codification or consensus concerning a particular area of international law, the more appropriate it is for the judiciary to render decisions regarding it, since the courts can then focus on the application of an agreed principle to circumstances of fact rather than on the sensitive task of establishing a principle not inconsistent with the national interest or with international justice. It is also evident that some aspects of international law touch much more sharply on national nerves than do others; the less important the implications of an issue are for our foreign relations, the weaker the justification for exclusivity in the political branches. The balance of relevant considerations may also be shifted if the government which perpetrated the challenged act of state is no longer in existence, for the political interest of this country may, as a result, be measurably altered. Therefore, rather than laying down or reaffirming an inflexible and all-encompassing rule in this case, we decide only that the Judicial Branch will not examine the validity of a taking of property within its own territory by a foreign sovereign government, extant and recognized by this country at the time of suit, in the absence of a treaty or other unambiguous agreement regarding controlling legal principles, even if the complaint alleges that the taking violates customary international law.

There are few if any issues in international law today on which opinion seems to be so divided as the limitations on a state's power to expropriate the property of aliens. There is, of course, authority, in international judicial and arbitral decisions, in the expressions of national governments, and among commentators for the view that a taking is improper under international law if it is not for a public purpose, is discriminatory, or is without provision for prompt, adequate, and effective compensation. However, Communist countries, although they have in fact provided a degree of compensation after diplomatic efforts, commonly recognize no obligation on the part of the taking country. Certain representatives of the newly independent and underdeveloped countries have questioned whether rules of state responsibility toward aliens can bind nations that have not consented to them and it is argued that the traditionally articulated standards governing expropriation of property reflect "imperialist" interests and are inappropriate to the circumstances of emergent states.

The disagreement as to relevant international law standards reflects an even more basic divergence between the national interests of capital importing and capital exporting nations and between the social ideologies of those countries that favor state control of a considerable portion of the means of production and those that adhere to a free enterprise system. It is difficult to imagine the courts of this country embarking on adjudication in an area which touches more sensitively the practical and ideological goals of the various members of the community of nations.

When we consider the prospect of the courts characterizing foreign expropriations, however justifiably, as invalid under international law and ineffective to pass title, the wisdom of the precedents is confirmed. While each of the leading cases in this Court may be argued to be distinguishable on its facts from this one . . . the plain implication of all these opinions, and the import of express statements in *Oetjen*, 246 U.S. at 304, and *Shapleigh* [v. *Mier*, 299 U.S. 468] at 471 is that the act of state doctrine is applicable even if international law has been violated . . .

The possible adverse consequences of a conclusion to the contrary of that implicit in these cases is highlighted by contrasting the practices of the political branch with the limitations of the judicial process in matters of this kind. Following an expropriation of any significance, the Executive engages in diplomacy aimed to assure that United States citizens who are harmed are compensated fairly. Representing all claimants of this country, it will often be able, either by bilateral or multilateral talks, by submission to the United Nations, or by the employment of economic and political sanctions, to achieve some degree of general redress. Judicial determinations of invalidity of title can, on the other hand, have only an occasional impact, since they depend on the fortuitous circumstance of the property in question being brought into this country. Such decisions would, if the acts involved were declared invalid, often be likely to give offense to the expropriating country; since the concept of territorial sovereignty is so deep seated, any state may resent the refusal of the courts of another sovereign to accord validity to acts within its territorial borders. Piecemeal dispositions of this sort involving the probability of affront to another state could seriously interfere with negotiations being carried on by the Executive Branch and might prevent or render less favorable the terms of an agreement that could otherwise be reached. Relations with third countries which have engaged in similar expropriations would not be immune from effect.

The dangers of such adjudication are present regardless of

whether the State Department has, as it did in this case, asserted that the relevant act violated international law. If the Executive Branch has undertaken negotiations with an expropriating country, but has refrained from claims of violation of the law of nations, a determination to that effect by a court might be regarded as a serious insult, while a finding of compliance with international law would greatly strengthen the bargaining hand of the other state with consequent detriment to American interests.

Even if the State Department has proclaimed the impropriety of the expropriation, the stamp of approval of its view by a judicial tribunal, however impartial, might increase any affront and the judicial decision might occur at a time, almost always well after the taking, when such an impact would be contrary to our national interest. Considerably more serious and far-reaching consequences would flow from a judicial finding that international law standards had been met if that determination flew in the face of a State Department proclamation to the contrary. When articulating principles of international law in its relations with other states, the Executive Branch speaks not only as an interpreter of generally accepted and traditional rules, as would the courts, but also as an advocate of standards it believes desirable for the community of nations and protective of national concerns. In short, whatever way the matter is cut, the possibility of conflict between the Judicial and Executive Branches could hardly be avoided.

Respondents contend that, even if there is not agreement regarding general standards for determining the validity of expropriations, the alleged combination of retaliation, discrimination, and inadequate compensation makes it patently clear that this particular expropriation was in violation of international law. If this view is accurate, it would still be unwise for the courts so to determine. Such a decision now would require the drawing of more difficult lines in subsequent cases and these would involve the possibility of conflict with the Executive view. Even if the courts avoided this course, either by presuming the validity of an act of state whenever the international law standard was thought unclear or by following the State Department declaration in such a situation, the very expression of judicial uncertainty might provide embarrassment to the Executive Branch.

Another serious consequence of the exception pressed by respondents would be to render uncertain titles in foreign commerce, with the possible consequence of altering the flow of international trade. If the attitude of the United States courts were unclear, one buying expropriated goods would not know if he could safely import them into this country. Even were takings known to be invalid, one would have difficulty determining after goods had changed hands several times whether the particular articles in question were the product of an ineffective state act.

Against the force of such considerations, we find respondents' countervailing arguments quite unpersuasive. Their basic contention is that United States courts could make a significant contribution to the growth of international law, a contribution whose importance, it is said, would be magnified by the relative paucity of decisional law by international bodies. But given the fluidity of present world conditions, the effectiveness of such a patchwork approach toward the formulation of an acceptable body of law concerning state responsibility for expropriations is, to say the least, highly conjectural. Moreover, it rests upon the sanguine presupposition that the decisions of the courts of the world's major capital exporting country and principal exponent of the free enterprise system would be accepted as disinterested expressions of sound legal principle by those adhering to widely different ideologies.

It is contended that regardless of the fortuitous circumstances necessary for United States jurisdiction over a case involving a foreign act of state and the resultant isolated application to any expropriation program taken as a whole, it is the function of the courts to justly decide individual disputes before them. Perhaps the most typical act of state case involves the original owner or his assignee suing one not in association with the expropriating state who has had "title" transferred to him. But it is difficult to regard the claim of the original owner, who otherwise may be recompensed through diplomatic channels, as more demanding of judicial cognizance than the claim of title by the innocent third party purchaser, who, if the property is taken from him, is without any remedy.

Respondents claim that the economic pressure resulting from the proposed exception to the act of state doctrine will materially add to the protection of United States investors. We are not convinced, even assuming the relevance of this contention. Expropriations take place for a variety of reasons, political and ideological as well as economic. When one considers the variety of means possessed by this country to make secure foreign investment, the persuasive or coercive effect of judicial invalidation of acts of expropriation dwindles in comparison. The newly independent states are in need of continuing foreign investment; the creation of a climate unfavorable to such investment by wholesale confiscations may well work to their long-run economic disadvantage. Foreign aid given to many of these countries provides a powerful lever in the hands of the political branches to ensure fair treatment of United States nationals. Ultimately the sanctions of economic embargo and the freezing of assets in this country may be employed. Any country willing to brave any or all of these consequences is unlikely to be deterred by sporadic judicial decisions directly affecting only property brought to our shores. If the political branches are unwilling to exercise their ample powers to effect compensation, this reflects a judgment of the national interest which the judiciary would be ill-advised to undermine indirectly.

It is suggested that if the act of state doctrine is applicable to violations of international law, it should only be so when the Executive Branch expressly stipulates that it does not wish the courts to pass on the question of validity. We should be slow to reject the representations of the Government that such . . . [an approach] would work serious inroads on the maximum effectiveness of United States diplomacy. Often the State Department will wish to refrain from taking an official position, particularly at a moment that would be dictated by the development of private litigation but might be inopportune diplomatically. Adverse domestic consequences might flow from an official stand which could be assuaged, if at all, only by revealing matters best kept secret. Of course, a relevant consideration for the State Department would be the position contemplated in the court to hear the case. It is highly questionable whether the examination of validity by the judiciary should depend on an educated guess by the Executive as to probable result and, at any rate, should a prediction be wrong, the Executive might be embarrassed in its dealings with other countries. We do not now pass on the *Bernstein* exception[3] but even if it were deemed valid, its suggested extension is unwarranted.

---

[3] This exception to the act of state doctrine, as applied in Bernstein v. N.V., etc., 210 F.2d 375 (2d Cir.), arises when the Executive indicates to the parties or the court that it wishes to relieve the court of any constraint on the exercise of its jurisdiction in the particular case. [Ed.]

However offensive to the public policy of this country and its constituent States an expropriation of this kind may be, we conclude that both the national interest and progress toward the goal of establishing the rule of law among nations are best served by maintaining intact the act of state doctrine in this realm of its application . . .

The judgment of the Court of Appeals is reversed and the case is remanded to the District Court for proceedings consistent with this opinion.

It is so ordered.[4]

[4] In his dissent Justice White argued that unless the State Department, on further reflection, specifically objected to examination of the validity of the Cuban decree, the act of state doctrine should not preclude the courts from passing on that issue in light of the principles of international law. Objecting to the Court's conclusion, he said: "No other civilized country has found such a rigid rule necessary for the survival of the executive branch of its government."

In subsequent legislation, Congress opted for an approach in expropriation cases similar to that urged by Justice White. See 22 U.S.C. § 2370(e) (2), enacted as part of the Foreign Assistance Act of 1965. [Ed.]

VI

Coda

In an unpublished address at Villanova Law School in 1962, Justice Harlan observed how hard it was for someone sitting on the Supreme Court to select an appropriate topic for a speech. Either he may find his vote on a case later coming before the Court already committed or embarrassed by his previous abstract discussion, or his utterances may invite suspicion that he is trying to gain a constituency for views he has failed to espouse successfully with his colleagues in the conference room. He also noted that one who has any concern for the staying power of his audience must be sensitive to the fact that the donning of a judicial robe often seems to lead otherwise normal human beings to believe that they must, and do, speak with the voice of deity.

It is therefore not surprising that the Justice's extrajudicial writings and addresses have steered clear of the specific controversies that have occupied the Court during his years on the bench. But these materials do add depth to the picture presented by his judicial work. In particular, three themes have recurred in the Justice's speeches and papers, and all three are represented in the selection included here. First, there is an abiding faith in the ability of our people and our institutions to survive the crises of the moment—a faith that has led the Justice to demur from the widely held view that the judiciary should be looked to as a principal recourse for the remedying of social ills. Second is a continuing concern that the value of the federal system and of the principle of separation of powers as basic safeguards of a free society will be overlooked or depreciated in the effort to achieve quick solutions. And finally, there is the Justice's own profound interest in improving the standards of the practicing bar and in increasing the awareness of lawyers of their responsibility to the institutions they serve.

Another significant aspect of the Justice's extrajudicial work consists of the tributes he has paid to those men he most respects. The simplicity and eloquence of those tributes are evident in the selection included here. As others have remarked, such tributes often have much to tell about the qualities the author himself prizes most highly.

Thoughts on America—Its People, Its Traditions, and Its Courts

Live and Let Live

No thoughtful observer of the American scene since the fighting of World War II ended can fail to be concerned about some of the excesses of thought, utterance, and action that have too frequently characterized our outlooks in this perplexing period of history. Such excesses are usually sought to be justified in the name of preserving our freedoms, even though when squarely faced their un-American character cannot be obscured. We have lived long enough in this period of tensions so that we should now be able both to see in better focus the factors in our national life which have brought about such excesses, and also to re-examine the premises on which we should base our future course in order to maintain our cherished way of life.

I daresay many of you have had the experience of some of your friends in other countries telling you that they cannot understand the emotional extremes that have sometimes manifested themselves over here in dealing with the communist problem. And you have undoubtedly met pessimistic persons in this Country who seem to

Excerpt from an address delivered at Brandeis University, October 30, 1955.

think that the American people have somehow changed their character and are, at least in this area of our affairs, willing to see the light of individual freedoms dimmed. Those who feel this way either do not understand us or have become victims of the era through which we are passing. They will do well to remind themselves of other periods of our history when some of our traditional ways of life seemed to hang in the balance under the stress of emotion. More immediately, their confidence in the enduring capacity of our way of life will be restored simply by observing how the people in any of our great cities or small towns are continuing to lead their individual and community lives.

On reflection such pessimists will come to see, I think, that the excesses of the times do not represent a change in the true character of our people, but are rather the product of some of the traits in our national temperament. We have a passion for getting things done. We have a weakness for panaceas, and we are loath to let time take a hand in the solution of our problems. We are easy prey to overstatement. We like to see things in black or white. All this leads us as a society to move in extremes, and we are apt to meet particular situations in terms of absolutes rather than with the immediate sense of proportion that some other free societies seem to have been able to achieve. Yet in a different way we too in the end emerge with things in sensible balance. The excesses we have been experiencing in this Country in recent years represent nothing more serious than the play of these forces in our national temperament. We would like to drive communism from our shores with one fell stroke. No one who has faith in our Country can doubt that we shall succeed in putting behind us the excesses of the present period, as we have the excesses of other times in the past.

Let those who are discouraged also consider that these traits are sources of great strength and ultimate stability in our national life. They have enabled us to adapt ourselves quickly to unprecedented conditions. We should not forget what our peace-loving and un-soldiered people were able to do in two world wars. And we should recognize that these same qualities have enabled us, almost overnight, to cast aside our historic aloofness from world affairs and to assume the position of free-world leadership which has been thrust upon us. Again, we are learning fast in this new role, and as we go forward it is not hard to discern that our initial yearnings for absolute and final solutions in the international field are yielding to the sober recognition that we must gird ourselves for the long pull. The same thing will be true in the solution of our internal problems, and I submit that those who doubt that we shall remain true to our traditions are as shortsighted as those false prophets who would have us believe that we cannot survive what may be ahead within the framework of the traditional notions of our way of life.

What are some of the premises with which we should face the future? We must abandon the idea that there are any quick and easy solutions to these problems, any more than there are any quick ways for ending the ideological assaults which are being made upon our way of life from without. The ultimate issue between the free world and the communist world is which way of life holds the greatest promise for the individual. Indeed, communism itself recognizes as much, for we are constantly being told by its leaders that the suppression of individual freedoms in communist countries is but a temporary phenomenon, which will disappear when communist ideology has become firmly established in the world. But unless it is to be assumed that at some point the innate instinct for individual freedom can be overcome among a people, communism, as hitherto practiced, is inevitably doomed to self-destruction sooner or later. This will come either as the result of communist governments liberating their own people or through the people themselves casting off the yoke upon their individual liberties.

The only hope for the ultimate survival of communist society lies in its continued ability to maintain the police state. Such a supposition not only runs counter to all the teachings of history, but ignores the powers of the rays of freedom that are ultimately bound to penetrate from the free world into the communist countries. This is why the exponents of communism have set their sights on nothing short of world communism, and this, not the mere safeguarding of military secrets, is the basic reason for their iron curtains.

What of our own society and outlook? Surely our heritage of freedoms—vital, progressive, and enduring as it has shown itself to be—is in no real danger from the appeal of an alien ideology which was the product of an era which had never envisioned, much less tasted, a way of life such as ours. And we shall certainly be able to cope with foreign agents and those who actually do advocate the violent overthrow of our Government. Nor so long as we con-

287

tinue to remain morally and materially strong, as we shall if we stand true on all scores to our way of life, need we fear physical danger if the leaders of the communist world should run amuck. The history of the English-speaking peoples gives every assurance of that.

The dangers of which we must really beware are, I think, of a quite different character. They are that we shall fall prey to the idea that in order to preserve our free society some of the liberties of the individual must be curtailed, at least temporarily. How wrong that kind of a program would be is surely evident from the mere statement of the proposition. I have no doubt that the apostles of communism would like nothing better than to see us follow such shallow and unwise counsel, for just as surely as the relaxation of curbs on individual freedoms would be fatal to communism, so the imposition of such curbs in this Country would divide and frustrate us, leading inevitably to the impairment of the strength of our society. Curbs on freedom are not always easy to discern. And we must be careful that measures designed for legitimate ends are not made instruments of oppression. For example, "security risk," originally a military term applied to persons who could not be entrusted with information that might be useful to the enemy, has now been taken over into our political vocabulary. We must take care that it is not used as a disguise for the ugly trait of condemning mere unorthodoxy, non-conformity, or the free expression of ideas.

We hear much talk these days about the Constitution being our guarantee that what has happened in other countries will not happen here. But the Constitution is not a self-executing document. Its vitality is no greater than the purpose of those who are sworn to uphold it—not merely the purpose of those at the top of the executive, legislative, and judicial branches of the federal and state governments, but equally that of all those down the line whose actions more closely touch the daily lives of people.

We also frequently hear it said that if others fail, the courts, which are withdrawn from political and partisan strife, will step into the breach. But the courts are not the full answer to all the problems that are bound to arise in assuring that our free ways of life will remain undiminished. The role of the courts is by no means as wide as many seem to assume. It must be remembered that the courts do not enact the laws, and that the function of constitutional and statutory interpretation which is theirs operates within narrow limits, which should exclude all considerations of legislative wisdom or policy. For example, since the founding of the Republic less than 80 Acts of Congress have been held unconstitutional by the Supreme Court of the United States. We should remind ourselves also that except in those states—Massachusetts being one—whose courts have power to render advisory opinions, it is only those questions which are presented by actual litigations that ever reach the courts—obviously but a small fraction of those involved in the multitude of executive, legislative, and administrative actions which have daily impact on people.

The point I make is that in the last analysis it is the independence, alertness, and common sense of our people that are the final bulwark of our way of life, whether it be in protecting civil liberties, economic freedoms, and property rights, or in preventing erosion of our institutions. I am not talking theoretically, but with the utmost realism, when I say that the responsibility which rests on the individual citizen for keeping the American system intact in the difficult times ahead is a very real and great one.

Thoughts at a Dedication: Keeping the Judicial Function in Balance

One of the current notions that holds subtle capacity for serious mischief is a view of the judicial function that seems increasingly coming into vogue. This is that all deficiencies in our society which have failed of correction by other means should find a cure in the courts. The principal theme of these remarks will be to challenge the validity of that thesis from the three principal standpoints that are most frequently heard in its support. These are: doubt whether the federal system is any longer adequate to meet the needs of modern American society; impatience with the slowness of political solutions generally; and an urge for quick and uncompromising panaceas for things that call for reform. I venture to say at the outset that this cosmic view of the place of the judiciary is not only

Excerpts from an address delivered at the American Bar Center, Chicago, Illinois, August 13, 1963, published in 49 *A.B.A.J.* 943 (1963), reprinted with permission.

inconsistent with the principles of American democratic society but ultimately threatens the integrity of the judicial system itself.

Our federal system, though born of the necessity of achieving union, has proved to be a bulwark of freedom as well. We are accustomed to speak of the Bill of Rights and the Fourteenth Amendment as the principal guarantees of personal liberty. Yet it would surely be shallow not to recognize that the structure of our political system accounts no less for the free society we have. Indeed, it was upon the structure of government that the Founders primarily focused in writing the Constitution. Out of bitter experience they were suspicious of every form of all-powerful central authority and they sought to assure that such a government would never exist in this country by structuring the federal establishment so as to diffuse power between the Executive, Legislative, and Judicial Branches. The diffusion of power between federal and state authority serves the same ends, and takes on added significance as the size of the federal bureaucracy continues to grow.

Federalism as we know it in this country does not, however, have to find justification only in terms of history or of its significance as an instrument of freedom. What other political system could have afforded so much scope to the varied interests and aspirations of a dynamic people representing such divergencies of ethnic and cultural backgrounds, and at the same time unified them into a nation blessed with material and spiritual resources unparalleled in history?

A federal system is of course difficult to operate, demanding political genius of the highest order. It requires accommodations being made that may often seem irksome or inefficient. But out of that very necessity usually come pragmatic solutions of more lasting value than those emanating from the pens of the best of theoretical planners. Unless we are prepared to consider the diversified development of the United States as having run its course and to envisage the future of the country largely as that of a welfare society we will do well to keep what has been called "the delicate balance of federal-state relations" in good working order . . .

Apart from what they regard as the shortcomings of the federal system some well-meaning people apparently believe that the judicial rather than the political process is more likely to breed better solutions of pressing or thorny problems. This is a compliment to the judiciary but untrue to democratic principle. That point of view is some times difficult for judges to resist for it carries ostensibly authentic judicial hallmarks—the function of statutory construction and the power of judicial review. If the Congress or a state legislature has passed an inadequate statute why should it not be revised by judicial construction? If the statute is one that is manifestly unwise, harsh, or out-of-date, why should it not be abrogated by the exercise of the power of judicial review? It is said that there can be nothing wrong with the courts so acting because whatever they may do can always be undone by legislative enactment or constitutional amendment.

The objections to such alluring but deceptive plausibilities are more deep-seated than might appear at first blush. For in the end what would eventuate would be a substantial transfer of legislative power to the courts. A function more ill-suited to judges can hardly be imagined, situated as they are, and should be, aloof from the political arena and beholden to no one for their conscientious conduct. Such a course would also denigrate the legislative process, since it would tend to relieve legislators from having to account to the electorate. The outcome would inevitably be a lessening, on the one hand, of judicial independence and, on the other, of legislative responsibility, thus polluting the blood stream of our system of government. We should be on guard against any such deliberate or unwitting folly.

The late Speaker of the House Sam Rayburn once observed that "one of the greatest statements that was ever made by anybody was: 'Just a minute.'" He was referring to the catalytic effect of time as a factor in the legislative process. The same factor is important in the judicial process. A judicial decision which is founded simply on the impulse that "something should be done" or which looks no further than to the "justice" or "injustice" of a particular case is not likely to have lasting influence. Surely Mr. Justice Holmes, a man of unsurpassed judicial sensitivity, was not being untrue to that quality when he wrote to a friend: "I have said to my brethren many times that I hate justice, which means that I know if a man begins to talk about that, for one reason or another he is shirking thinking in legal terms." Our scheme of ordered liberty is based, like the common law, on enlightened and uniformly applied legal principle, not on *ad hoc* notions of what is right or wrong in a particular case. The stability and flexibility that our constitutional system at once possesses is largely due to our having carried over into constitutional adjudication the common-law approach to legal development.

Woodrow Wilson in an academic address dealing with the function of colleges in the training of men for the "Nation's Service" epitomized that approach in these eloquent words:

> But not all change is progress, not all growth is the manifestation of life. Let one part of the body be in haste to outgrow the rest and you have malignant disease, the threat of death. The growth that is a manifestation of life is equable, draws its springs gently out of the old fountains of strength, builds upon old tissue, covets the old airs that have blown upon it time out of mind in the past. Colleges ought surely to be the best nurseries of such life, the best schools of the progress which conserves. Unschooled men have only their habits to remind them of the past, only their desires and their instinctive judgments of what is right to guide them into the future; the college should serve the State as its organ of recollection, its seat of vital memory. It should give the country men who know the probabilities of failure and success, who can separate the tendencies which are permanent from the tendencies which are of the moment merely, who can distinguish promises from threats, knowing the life men have lived, the hopes they have tested and the principles they have proved.

What Part Does the Oral Argument Play in the Conduct of an Appeal?

The art of advocacy—and it is an art—is a purely personal effort, and as such, any oral argument is an individualistic performance. Each lawyer must proceed according to his own lights, and if he tries to cast himself in the image of another, he is likely to become uneasy, artificial, and unpersuasive. But after you make allowance for the special talents of individuals, their different methods of

Excerpt from an address delivered at the Judicial Conference of the Fourth Circuit, Asheville, North Carolina, June 24, 1955, published in 41 *Cornell L. Q.* 6 (1955), © Copyright 1955 by Cornell University, reprinted with permission.

handling arguments, their different techniques, it seems to me that there are four characteristics which will be found in every effective oral argument, and they are these: *first*, what I would call "selectivity"; *second*, what I would designate as "simplicity"; *third*, "candor"; and *fourth*, what I would term "resiliency." Let me address myself briefly to each.

By "selectivity," I mean a lawyer's selection of the issues to be argued. There is rarely a case which lends itself to argument of all of the issues within the normal time limitations upon oral argument. On the other hand, there is hardly a case, however complicated, where, by some selection of the issues to be argued, one hour is not enough. I am not talking about the unusual type of case, which we have from time to time in all courts, where in the nature of things extra time is essential. But in most cases, I think, the skillful advocate would not want more time for oral argument than the ordinary rules of court permit. However, it often happens that lawyers who attempt to cover *all* of the issues in the case find themselves left with the uncomfortable feeling that they have failed to deal with any of the issues adequately. You will find that thoughtful selection of the issues to be argued orally is a basic technique of every good appellate advocate.

Most cases have one or only a few master issues. In planning his oral argument the wise lawyer will ferret out and limit himself to the issues which are really controlling, and will leave the less important or subordinate issues to the court's own study of the briefs. Otherwise, one is apt to get tanglefoot, and the court is left pretty much where it began.

The next thing I refer to is "simplicity." Simplicity of presentation and expression, you will find, is a characteristic of every effective oral argument. In the instances where that quality is lacking, it is usually attributable to one of two reasons—lack of preparation or poor selection of the issues to be argued. There are some issues that do not lend themselves to oral argument as well as they do to written presentation. The preparation of an oral argument is a good deal more than merely making a short form summary of the briefs. An oral argument which is no more than that really adds nothing to a lawyer's cause.

The process of preparation that the appellate advocate undergoes involves, *first*, the selection of the issues he will argue; *second*, a marshaling of the premises on which those issues depend; *third,* planning the structure of his argument; and, *fourth,* deciding how he shall express his argument. It is sometimes forgotten by a lawyer who is full of his case, that the court comes to it without the background that he has. And it is important to bear this in mind in carrying out the preparation for argument in each of its phases. Otherwise the force of some point which may seem so clear to the lawyer may be lost upon the court.

The third thing which is of the essence of good advocacy is "candor." There is rarely a case, however strong, that does not have its weak points. And I do not know any way of meeting a weak point except to face up to it. It is extraordinary the number of instances one sees where through a question from the court or the argument of one's adversary a vulnerable point is laid bare, and the wounded lawyer ducks, dodges, and twists, instead of facing up to the point four square. Attempted evasion in an oral argument is a cardinal sin. No answer to an embarrassing point is better than an evasive one. With a court, lack of candor in meeting a difficult issue of fact or of law goes far to destroying the effectiveness of a lawyer's argument, not merely as to the point of embarrassment, but often as to other points on which he should have the better of it. For if a lawyer loses the confidence of the court, he is apt to end up almost anywhere.

The fourth and final thing which I have suggested goes to the root of a good oral argument is "resiliency." For some reason that I have never been able to understand, many lawyers regard questioning by the court as a kind of subversive intrusion. And yet, when one comes to sit on the other side of the bar, he finds very quickly that the answer made to a vital question may be more persuasive in leading the court to the right result than the most eloquent of oral arguments. I think that a lawyer, instead of shunning questions by the court, should welcome them. If a court sits through an oral argument without asking any questions, it is often a pretty fair indication that the argument has been either dull or unconvincing.

I am mindful, of course, that the court's privilege of asking questions is sometimes abused, and that often the price a lawyer has to pay is some interruption in the continuity of his argument, and perhaps some discomforture—and in extreme instances perhaps never getting through with what he had planned to say. And yet,

I think that the price is well worth what the lawyer may have to pay in the loss of the smooth-flowing quality he would like his argument to have. A lawyer can make no greater mistake, I can assure you, in answering questions by the court than to attempt to preserve the continuity of his argument by saying: "Judge, I have dealt with that in my brief" or by telling the judge who asks the question that he will come to it "later"—usually he never does. Even if the lawyer does come back to the question later on, the force of his answer, if it is a good one, and often also of his argument in other aspects where he perhaps is in a stronger position, is usually lost—at least upon the judge who has asked the question.

No doubt some judges ask too many questions, and I hasten to say, again as one freshly from the trial bar, that I am one of those who believe that competent lawyers ought to be allowed to try their cases and argue their appeals in their own fashion. Where an over-enthusiastic judge exceeds the bounds of what the lawyer might consider fair interruption, the lawyer will have to handle that problem for himself. I can tell you, however, how two lawyers, one a freshman and the other a seasoned barrister, dealt with such a situation. The freshman lawyer was trying his first case, a negligence case, in which his client, the plaintiff, was a lovely young lady. Of course, he called her as the first witness. After the young man had gotten his client's name, age, and address on the record, the court interrupted and started to ask questions. The young lawyer stood first on one foot and then on the other as the court's questioning continued. He finally sat down, and in due course the court came to the end of his questioning and said: "Counselor, you may now continue with the witness. Proceed." The young man arose and said: "If your Honor please, I have no more questions to ask because I think the court has covered my case very thoroughly. But," he added, "I would like to make a statement. If your Honor please, this is my first case, my first client. I have prepared my case thoroughly. I have gone back to the Year Books on the law; I have questioned all eye witnesses to the accident with the greatest care; but if your Honor wants to try this case, it is all right with me, except, for goodness' sake, don't lose it!"

The examination of the more seasoned barrister was interrupted at a sensitive point by a question which the lawyer did not care for. "Have you an objection, counselor?" said the court as the lawyer put on a remonstrative look. "Perhaps, your Honor," replied the lawyer, "but I would first like to inquire on whose behalf your Honor put that question." "What difference would that make, counselor?" asked the court. "All the difference in the world," said the lawyer, "for if your Honor is asking the question on behalf of my opponent, then of course I must object to it, but if your Honor asks the question on my behalf, then I simply withdraw it."

Now I suppose that most of what I have said is an old story to a group of such experienced trial lawyers as composes this audience. My excuse for saying it is that of the varied sensations that a man going from active practice to the bench experiences, in the short time that I have been on the bench one of the things that has astonished me most is the number of disappointing arguments to which courts have to listen. They seem to be due, in some cases, to lack of preparation; in others to lack of capacity; but more generally, I think, the explanation is to be found in the increasing tendency to regard the oral argument as being of little importance in the decision of appeals. I should like to leave with you, particularly those of you who are among the younger barristers, the thought that your oral argument on an appeal is perhaps the most effective weapon you have got if you will give it the time and attention it deserves. Oral argument is exciting and will return rich dividends if it is done well. And I think it will be a sorry day for the American bar if the place of the oral argument in our appellate courts is depreciated and oral advocacy becomes looked upon as a pro forma exercise which, because of tradition or because of the insistence of his client, a lawyer has to go through.

B

Tributes

To Emory R. Buckner

The New York Bar has given to the country many distinguished lawyers, but few of them, I venture to say, have left so deep an imprint on the next generation of the profession as has Emory R. Buckner. The true source of that imprint is not to be found, however, so much in his abilities as a lawyer, in his skills as an advocate, in his architecture of one of New York's great law firms, in the renown of the cases that he handled, or in his achievements in public office—notable as each of these facets of his career was—as in the remarkable gift he possessed for training and inspiring young lawyers and launching them on their careers. His influence was not of the pedantic sort, but was born of the human and professional stuff that sticks with those who were exposed to it. To vouchsafe that there have been countless instances when lawyers bearing the responsibility for ticklish decisions have first asked themselves, "What would Buck have done?" is not to indulge in hyperbole. This book has

Excerpts from the introduction to Martin Mayer, *Emory Buckner* (1968), reproduced with the permission of Harper & Row Publishers (and of Curtis Brown, Ltd. with respect to the British Commonwealth other than Canada).

its origins in the belief of some of those who held Emory Buckner in high esteem and affection that an account of his life is a legacy which should be left to oncoming generations of lawyers. As one of those, I am grateful to the others, to the author, and to the Cromwell Foundation which has ensured the accomplishment of the project, for allowing me to introduce this book to its readers.

The essence of Buckner's method for indoctrinating young lawyers, which because of his own professional calling lay primarily in the field of trial and appellate practice, was to place real responsibility upon them at the earliest stage and to hold them strictly accountable for their performance. A "first-year man" who was given a memorandum of law to write was made to feel that his legal conclusions upon the point involved would be accepted at face value. The novice examining for the first time a witness in open court under Buckner's eye was largely left to his own devices. And the more mature man who was put in charge of a case as Buckner's first assistant, called by him the *tenant in capite,* was looked to by Buckner as the ringmaster of the entire operation. If soft spots developed in the performance of his associates at any point, Buckner preferred to ride them out with his client or the court rather than to unmask such deficiencies "in public," and to leave retribution, always straightforward but nonetheless considerate and kindly, to another day. More important from the standpoint of his fledglings, Buckner was always at pains, usually at the inception of his retainer, to warn the client that Mr. so-and-so would play an important role in the management of the case. Time and again I have seen him do this even at the risk of forfeiting his retainer to another lawyer not so prone to delegate major responsibilities to juniors.

The cornerstone of the Bucknerian litigation method was objective and relentless preparation. Buckner was never content simply to do the best he could with the case as put to him by his client, but insisted upon making his own investigation of every fact and circumstance before reaching his estimate of the situation. He conceived the duty to his clients to lie quite as much in disentangling them from unwise or improvident litigation as in pressing an unquestionably good claim or defense to a successful conclusion in court. It was not a rare occurrence for a client to find himself astonished by the different aspect which his case assumed under the spotlight of a Buckner-type investigation.

I would describe the type of investigation that was Buckner's *forte* as something akin to what in scientific terms is called pure or experimental research, that is, Buckner turned his young lawyers loose to ferret out the facts and to discover the controlling legal principles untrammeled by any preconceived framework of the case. He was unsparing in his use of manpower, often recruiting from the outside on an *ad hoc* basis when the size of the organization deemed necessary for a particular case would unduly tax the resources of his own office staff. He looked for imagination as well as industry in those who worked for him, and was always receptive even to the most fanciful ideas of the youngest man on the totem pole. He was accustomed to tell his staff that he expected each man to do his segment of the job as if he were solely responsible for it, and that after he was satisfied that he had done his work "one-hundred-percent" he should then put in an "extra ten-percent" effort; only then should he submit his work-product for the consideration of his superior . . .

Preparation of a lawsuit, however thorough, avails little apart from the use that is made of it, and hence it is appropriate that something should be said about Emory Buckner's qualities as a barrister. Epitomizing, I would carve those qualities into four parts: an unerring instinct for getting at the jugular of a case and holding his adversary, the court, and the jury to it; a capacity to simplify and synthesize even the most complicated set of facts into a harmonious, understandable, and satisfying picture; the use of cross-examination to make of his adversary's witnesses affirmative elements for his side of the case—by putting them "under ether" as Buckner used to say—and not merely as an instrument for destroying credibility; and a genuine and disarming sense of fairness to his opponents which never failed to add strength to his own client's cause . . .

A word should be added on one of the intangibles in Emory Buckner's makeup as a trial lawyer. He possessed to a remarkable degree what he used to describe as "courtroom antennae," that is, a capacity to sense and adapt himself to the subtle changes of atmosphere that often occur in a protracted trial, and to summon to his aid the "flash of genius" usually necessary to dissipate or neutralize the impact of an untoward trial event.

Buckner entered the courtroom prepared to do battle, with the precision of a military commander who has skillfully deployed his troops. He considered the mechanics of presentation almost as important as the contents of his case, believing that the orderly and rapid-fire development of the facts and legal points tended to undermine the opposition and to instill confidence in the court and jury for his side of the case. Every witness was on deck when his appearance was called for; every exhibit was snapped into play in accordance with the trial plans; and pre-prepared memoranda of law were always at hand to assist the court with respect to points on which it had been anticipated rulings might have to be made. Nothing annoyed Buckner more than to have an assistant fumble in the courtroom the mechanical handling of the part of the case which he had been assigned to prepare. Yet when trial vicissitudes seemed to indicate the desirability of changes in the grand design Buckner, through overnight or recess conferences with his staff and sometimes even by pure improvisation in the courtroom, always seemed able to contrive a reoriented presentation that proceeded as smoothly as if it had been originally planned that way.

Lamentably, Emory Buckner before he had reached his mid-fifties and at the very peak of his reputation was taken from the active trial bar by a succession of illnesses. His last major jury trial took place in 1932, a case in which he represented one of the principal executives of the Bank of the United States, involving a New York state criminal prosecution arising out of the Bank's failure during the great economic depression of that period. Notwithstanding his infirmities Buckner continued during the last ten years of his life, which ended on March 11, 1941, to draw important litigation to his firm, although to be sure not in the quantity that he had attracted before. While he continued to supervise the office litigation with his accustomed care and imagination, the actual courtroom work passed more and more into the hands of his younger partners and principal associates. For most lesser men this would have been a disheartening, if not devastating, chapter in their careers, but not so with Emory Buckner, who seemed to regard the passing of the torch to his "boys" as the true fulfillment of his own professional philosophy.

To Joseph M. Proskauer

It is my privilege to make the closing remarks at this notable occasion, and I do so by giving you a recipe for use at times when your minds seek refuge from current confusions by dwelling on the lives of remarkable people you have known. Put into the hopper of your reflections the following human ingredients:

1. A cosmic sense of spiritual values, not limited by the tenets of one's own faith.

2. Intellectual endowments of a rare and creative order that have led their possessor to the pinnacle of his own profession, and beyond that caused him to roam widely in the fields of music, art, poetry, and literature.

3. A love of country and an understanding of its institutions that have from time to time brought domestic and foreign leaders in different spheres to seek advice from this person in delicate situations, and have led him into important but often unobtrusive roles in local and national affairs.

4. Shining integrity, undeviating courage, and unremitting energy in confronting every private or public matter into which he has been brought.

5. A strong sense of family responsibility, deep-seated loyalty to his friends, and a wise and resourceful counsellor in time of trouble.

6. Joy in the beauty and solitude of the North Country, which for many years took him over hill and dale on horseback and still takes him in avid but impatient pursuit of the trout and bass which abound in its streams and ponds.

7. A connoisseur of good food and wine, a lover of conviviality, and a relentless opponent at the bridge, canasta, and scrabble tables.

8. Understanding and appreciation of the gentler sex.

9. Externally, an aggressive and sometimes even boastful demeanor; internally, a man of true humility, sensitivity, and tolerance.

10. Finally, a zest for life that overcomes all vicissitudes.

Excerpt from remarks at a dinner in honor of Joseph M. Proskauer, New York City, October 25, 1967.

Add to these ingredients, which are now in the tenth decade of their stirring, a dash of the present, and who could emerge from this recipe but a Joe Proskauer?

To the fine tributes that have been paid our distinguished friend by those who have preceded me, it is appropriate that something should be added about the notable and financially unrewarded public service that Judge Proskauer rendered as Chairman of the New York State Crime Commission from 1951 to 1954. The Commission was established by Governor Dewey to investigate disquieting rumors of corrupt or unsavory relationships between local public officials and organized crime in various communities in the State of New York. Judge Proskauer undertook this arduous task at a time of life—he was then in his 74th year—when a lesser man might well have felt justified in declining the appointment or at least deemed his duties in the undertaking satisfied by acting as its figurehead. Not so with Judge Proskauer. From the beginning he immersed himself in almost every detail of the enterprise, taking a personal part in the recruitment of the Commission's staff, in the interrogation of many of the witnesses examined in the inquiry, in the preparation of briefs for court proceedings that arose during the course of the Commission's activities, and in the writing of the Commission's reports to the Governor. The Commission's recommendations, among other things, bore fruit in the establishment of the New York Waterfront Commission which has done much to improve conditions in this important area of our City.

Two episodes in this memorable piece of Proskauer public service, in which I had the good fortune to play a part for a time as Chief Counsel to the Commission, bear telling, because they illustrate the interaction of some parts of the recipe I ventured to give you at the outset. A part of the duties of Chief Counsel was to brief the Chairman at the beginning of each day of the public hearings conducted by the Commission as to the evidence that would be produced by the staff. I remember well one such occasion when I undertook to do this on the Staten Island ferry en route to a particularly dramatic day of hearings at the Richmond County Courthouse. I had what I thought to be the close attention of the Chairman to my account of things, but suddenly realized that at the same time he was engaged in animated disputation with my wife, seated on his other side, as to whether a poetic quotation which he thought apt to a previous episode in the Staten Island hearings was from Keats or Shelley.

Another revelation of the kaleidoscopic nature of this man was manifested in the succeeding Commission hearings at Ogdensburg, New York, a community located not far distant from the Proskauer Camp Highwall at Lake Placid. This being during the summer months, it had been arranged that I would come to Camp Highwall the day before the hearing opened to brief the Chairman on the proceedings. When I emerged from the Pullman car at Saranac Lake at an early breakfast hour, appropriately garbed, I thought, in city clothes and carrying a heavily laden briefcase, I found our Chairman on the station platform fully adorned in fishing regalia, and armed with fishing clothes and equipment for me. After a hasty breakfast at a local emporium I was whisked off for a day of fishing, during which my briefing session was interlarded between some eight hours of castings for elusive Adirondack bass and then carried into the evening hospitality of the home camp.

Were there time I could support the validity of my recipe for a Joe Proskauer by many other refining examples; but the time has come when our guest should be given an opportunity to make his rebuttal.

At 90, Joe Proskauer stands among us as the acknowledged elder statesman of our City. Time has, of course, diminished some of his activities, but it has not dimmed in the slightest his qualities as a human being. This great gathering, composed of men and women of many different talents and interests, bears witness to the universality of the man we honor and to the esteem and affection in which he is held by all who know him. I ask you, ladies and gentlemen, to rise and lift your glasses to the continued health and happiness of Joe Proskauer.

To Felix Frankfurter

This collection of *Essays in Legal History,* originally conceived as a living tribute to Mr. Justice Frankfurter but now published in

Introduction to *Essays in Legal History in Honor of Felix Frankfurter,* edited by Morris D. Forkosch, Copyright 1966, by The Bobbs-Merrill Company, Inc., all rights reserved.

memoriam, is worthy of this great figure in the law. The range of subjects dealt with in the pages of this volume and the roster of its contributors are symbolic of the cosmic outlook of this remarkable man. As one who came to know Felix Frankfurter through the unforeseen circumstance of a judicial relationship, I venture these few remarks on some aspects of his judicial philosophy as it was given to me to see at close quarters.

Felix Frankfurter's concern for legal history in his judicial work was more than a reflection of pure scholarship. Confronting and reckoning with the past was for him an indispensable point of departure for tackling any major legal problem and more especially for any sure step forward in the law. He was always distrustful of historically unoriented legal opinions. He steadfastly set his face against the developing of new legal principle out of thin air. He did not hesitate to withhold his assent to results which he personally believed to be good when he felt that they could be achieved only at the expense of ignoring or taking impermissible shortcuts through what had gone before. The essays by some of his former law clerks which delineate these generalizations are valuable contributions to this book.

Justice Frankfurter was a profound believer in the American federal system. The fact that it was ordained by the Constitution would of course have been enough to command its full acceptance by him. But his belief in our federalism had deeper roots. He had unbounded admiration for it, not merely as an act of superb political and legal statecraft through which the Union was achieved, but as something which through its diffusion of governmental functions between federal and state authority afforded safeguards to our free society quite as important as those found in the Bill of Rights or in the judge-made protections evolved under the Due Process and Equal Protection Clauses of the Fourteenth Amendment. Few men in our history have had as great perception of the values of American federalism or as sensitive an understanding of the subtleties that make for its healthy working. Over and over again his dedication to it is reflected in his constitutional opinions. I shall be greatly mistaken if history does not place his belief in federalism at the forefront of his constitutional thinking and rank him high among those who have made lasting contributions to its preservation in the context of their times.

The Frankfurter philosophy of judicial self-restraint had its sources in what he conceived to be the demands of federalism and the requirements of the doctrine of separation of powers governing the allocation of authority within the federal structure. He regarded that quality in the exercise of the judicial function as an essential catalyst in the judiciary's role under our scheme of developing constitutionalism. This led him scrupulously to respect state and federal legislative and executive authority, often, as it seemed to some, at the expense of delay in accomplishing needed legal reform. His judicial self-restraint also reflected a basic humility in his make-up, obscured perhaps by the vigor and positiveness with which he customarily asserted his personal views on legal problems, great or small. Some were puzzled by what seemed to them shifts between "liberalism" and "conservatism" in his attitudes within some areas of the law. In truth, such shifts did not represent changes in his basic constitutional outlook, but rather reflected his contemporary estimates of whether the judiciary was moving too slowly or too fast in the particular context of the times. Justice Frankfurter's legal opinions were more than works of unusual professional skill; they were lessons in judicial approach and in the art of government, frequently carrying messages reaching beyond the confines of the legal fraternity.

Pre-eminent among his many talents was the gift of stimulating others. He had an insatiable curiosity for finding out about people and the things with which they were occupied that led him far afield of his own profession. His advice was sought by countless persons in and out of public life, young and old, and on a great variety of subjects. No problem was too small or too remote from his own experiences to command his enthusiastic attention. Those who came to him always felt enriched either by his sustaining encouragement or by his challenging criticisms or merely by his infectious hand-shake. Few men have touched in a personal way the lives of so many. The publication of this book itself attests to the abundant measure in which he possessed this inspirational quality.

Essays in Legal History both in its conception and execution is a peculiarly fitting memorial to Felix Frankfurter.

305

To Hugo Black

No man more richly deserves the distinction of having an issue of the *Harvard Law Review* dedicated to him than Mr. Justice Black. I feel fortunate in being invited to participate in this event.

At eighty-one and with thirty years of service on the Court behind him, Mr. Justice Black continues to "carry on" with his accustomed dedication, vigor, and eloquence. In the entire history of the Court only eight Justices have served as long as Mr. Justice Black,[1] and happily there are no signs that the end of his active tenure is yet anywhere near in sight. During his long service Mr. Justice Black has had the satisfaction of seeing many of the views which he expressed in dissent in earlier years become the currently prevailing doctrine of the Court, and he continues to press forward with unabated enthusiasm and positiveness such of his views as have not yet been accepted by the majority of his Brethren.

Among the many ways in which Mr. Justice Black's judicial service has enriched the Court and the entire federal judicial system are three facets of his outlook about which too little is found in the much that has been written about him, and which in my view are of especial importance in these confused times. The first is his steadfast adherence to the traditional concept of the federal judicial role. He rejects the open-ended notion that the Court sits to do good in every circumstance where good is needed, and insists that we federal judges are contained by the terms of the Constitution, no less than are all other branches of governmental authority. He considers himself to be a judge of cases, not of "causes," and unhesitatingly sets himself against federal judicial intervention whenever he is unable to find in the Constitution or valid legislative authority the basis for such action. Those who have purported to discern in some of Mr. Justice Black's recent opinions a shift from "liberalism" to "conservatism" have, it seems to me, missed the true essence of his judicial philosophy. By the same token, I believe that

---

"Mr. Justice Black—Remarks of a Colleague," 81 *Harvard Law Review* 1, Copyright © 1967 by The Harvard Law Review Association.

[1] John Marshall (34 years); Bushrod Washington (30 years); William Johnson (30 years); Joseph Story (33 years); John McLean (31 years); James Wayne (32 years); Stephen Field (34 years); and the first Mr. Justice Harlan (33 years).

those who undertake to quarrel with any of Mr. Justice Black's constitutional views—and I am one who has not infrequently found myself in disagreement with him—can only fairly do so on the basis of constitutional disputation, and not by attributing to him, in the jargon of the day, an "activistic" approach to the judicial function.

Second, long before racial disturbances broke out in this country, Mr. Justice Black warned that the great social changes taking place in our society could only be properly accomplished through the orderly process of law. Although in the forefront of those who saw the need for change, he has always been insistent that illegal pressures to attain or hasten that end cannot be countenanced, and has unequivocally spoken out against all forms of unlawful tactics when others have been tempted to temporize or condone.

The third aspect of the Black judicial outlook to which I shall refer is the Justice's sensitivity to the image of the Court as an institution completely detached from other branches of government. It can be stated with confidence, I think, that Mr. Justice Black shares the view that members of the Court should not be called on to perform, during their term of active service, official duties outside the realm of the judicial concern. He has invariably stood in opposition to the members of the Court attending as a body any official function or occasion which might subject them to the appearance of partisanship. And for himself he has scrupulously eschewed extra-judicial pronouncements of his own views upon any of the great issues of the times. No Justice, whether coming from the political arena or otherwise, has worn his judicial robes with a keener sense of the limitations that go with them than has Mr. Justice Black.

Mr. Justice Black is a superb colleague in every sense of the term. He is stimulating and challenging in debate. He is forthright and clear in the expression of his own views and in his criticisms of those of others. He is generous when in agreement, and when in disagreement he is understanding and tolerant to a degree perhaps not always apparent in his written opinions. Personal relationships with him never fail to be congenial, mellowing, and rewarding, and the hospitality of his lovely Virginia home, presided over by his charming wife, is an experience in southern graciousness that is always delightful. The esteem and affection in which Mr. Justice Black is held by all of his colleagues and friends was marked in a notable way last Term by an informal reception given him at the White House by President and Mrs. Johnson on the occasion of the Justice's eighty-first birthday, attended by, among others, all of his past law clerks and the members of his household staff.

There can be little doubt that few men who have assumed the responsibilities of this great office have laid them down with their place in history better assured than will be the case with Mr. Justice Black.

Index

INDEX

INDEX